Unconscious communication
in practice

Unconscious communication
in practice

Unconscious communication in practice

Edited by
E. Mary Sullivan

Open University Press
Buckingham · Philadelphia

Open University Press
Celtic Court
22 Ballmoor
Buckingham
MK18 1XW

email: enquiries@openup.co.uk
world wide web: http://www.openup.co.uk

and
325 Chestnut Street
Philadelphia, PA 19106, USA

First Published 1999

A catalogue record of this book is available from the British Library

ISBN   0 335 20198 9 (pb)   0 335 20199 7 (hb)

Library of Congress Cataloging-in-Publication Data
Unconscious communication in practice / E. Mary Sullivan, (ed.).
      p.   cm.
   ISBN 0-335-20199-7 (hbk.). – ISBN 0-335-20198-9 (pbk.)
   1. Communicative psychotherapy.   2. Psychotherapist and patient.   3.
Subconsciousness.   I. Sullivan, E. Mary, 1945–   .
RC489.C65U53   1998   98–16395
616.89'14–dc21   CIP

Copy-edited and typeset by The Running Head Limited, Cambridge
Printed in Great Britain by St Edmundsbury Press Ltd, Bury St Edmunds,
Suffolk

Contents

Acknowledgements

My thanks go first and foremost to the authors of these chapters, for their willingness to set down their observations and reflections on a new and difficult perspective in the field of psychoanalysis and psychotherapy; much of what appears in this volume is the fruit of their very personal engagement in the clinical practice of an approach which demands a considerable degree of self-awareness. I wish to record also the most important contribution to this experience – that of the clients of these practitioners. It is their unconscious wisdom and insight which has been so necessary to the development of this approach, and it is upon their sharing of personal material that all development in the field is based.

The conflict between confidentiality and the requirement to share experience and observation in the service of research is a real difficulty in the field of psychotherapy. Publication of this material is in itself a breach of confidentiality, although measures have been taken to disguise salient features.

I wish to thank my colleagues on the Management Committee of the European Society for Communicative Psychotherapy.

Acknowledgement is made to Routledge for permission to reprint here Kitty Warburton's (1995) paper on 'Student counselling: a consideration of ethical and framework issues', originally published in *Psychodynamic Counselling*, 1(3), July.

All references to Freud are based on James Strachey (ed.) *The Standard Edition of the Complete Psychological Works of Sigmund Freud*, 24 vols, London: Hogarth, 1953–73.

Notes on contributors

Vesna Bonac has a private practice as a communicative psychoanalyst in Vancouver, Canada. She is a former student of Robert Langs and is currently editor of the *International Journal for Communicative Psychoanalysis and Psychotherapy*; she is also founder and co-editor of the Communicative Psychoanalysis on Internet. She has published clinical studies in Canadian and international journals on unconscious processes, secure-frame anxiety, human development and transference phenomena.

Fiorella Gatti-Doyle is a lecturer, clinical supervisor and psychotherapist in private practice. She is a founding member of the European Society for Communicative Psychotherapy and Director of Psychotherapy and Counselling for the Centre for Personal Construct Psychology. Her particular interest and research focuses on self-analysis and self-processing psychotherapy. She is also an author and broadcaster.

Gabrielle Gunton is a psychotherapist working in private practice. She also works with adults in the National Health Service environment, and with young people within schools. She is currently carrying out doctoral research work with people in pain, using a communicative approach.

Carol Holmes is a senior lecturer at the School of Psychotherapy and Counselling at Regent's College; she also works in private practice as a communicative psychotherapist. She is the current Chair of the European Society for Communicative Psychotherapy, and the author of *There's No Such Thing as a Therapist* (Karnac, 1998).

Gae Oaten is a visiting tutor at the School of Psychotherapy and Counselling at Regent's College. She is also a supervisor and communicative psychotherapist in private practice and in a primary care setting.

Marie-Luise Petersen is a lecturer at the Institute for Analytic Child and Adolescent Psychotherapy in Hanover, Germany.

James Raney MD is on the clinical faculty of the University of Washington School of Medicine, and is a training and supervising psychoanalyst with the Seattle Institute for Psychoanalysis. He maintains a private practice in Seattle, Washington.

David Livingston Smith was a founding member and first Chair of the European Society for Communicative Psychotherapy. He is also the author of *Hidden Conversations: An Introduction to Communicative Psychoanalysis* (Routledge, 1991) and numerous papers in professional journals.

E. Mary Sullivan is a lecturer at the School of Psychotherapy and Counselling at Regent's College, and works privately as a communicative psychotherapist and supervisor. She co-edited, with Bernard Burgoyne, *The Klein–Lacan Dialogues* (Rebus Press, 1997).

Ivan Thorpe is a senior lecturer in counselling psychology at Northbrook College, Worthing.

Kitty Warburton is a student counsellor at a new university.

Preface

This book is based on the work of Robert Langs.

Through the 1970s and 1980s Langs developed his ideas about unconscious perception and unconscious communication on which the communicative approach to psychotherapy is based. These ideas are still surprisingly little known and hardly discussed within current psychoanalytic and psychotherapeutic circles, yet they offer a radical hypothesis, not only about psychotherapy, but about the nature of human communication – and, indeed, the human mind – which should be available for wider discussion and debate.

Langs's work presents evidence for a science of human emotional cognition based on a systematic decoding of unconscious mental processes according to the fundamental rules set out by Sigmund Freud so many years ago. The implications of this for psychoanalysis and psychotherapy are perceived, it seems, as disturbing: explanations for this have been offered elsewhere (Raney 1984; Smith 1991), so I will attempt none. But the evidence deserves to be presented, however tentative and imprecise it may be as yet.

There are remarkably few people practising communicative psychotherapy, and they are scattered around the globe: a number in the Americas, a group based in London, some individuals and groups in Germany, Italy, Scandinavia and Australia. These chapters represent efforts to develop and explore communicative ideas in clinical practice and elsewhere, and are offered for the consideration and scrutiny of practitioners and trainees in the field of psychotherapy and psychoanalysis, and for others interested in the field of human emotional cognition.

References

Raney, J.O. (1984) *Listening and Interpreting: The Challenge of the Work of Robert Langs*. New York: Jason Aronson.

Smith, D.L. (1991) *Hidden Conversations: An Introduction to Communicative Psychoanalysis*. London: Routledge.

Part I

INTRODUCTION

Chapter 1

Communicative psychotherapy without tears

David Livingston Smith

Introduction

Communicative psychotherapy is almost entirely the brainchild of one man: Dr Robert Langs. In the following brief essay I will describe in what I hope is an accessible way the essentials of communicative theory and practice. I cannot go into great detail in an introductory essay of this kind, but interested readers can pursue the more technical literature.

Psychologists recognize three kinds of memory. One kind of memory is the memory of how to do things. It is called *procedural* memory. Remembering how to ride a bike is an example of this kind of memory. A second sort of memory is the memory of what things mean, which is called *semantic* memory. Remembering that Augustus was the name of the first Roman emperor is an example of semantic memory. Finally, there is the type of memory that records events. Psychologists call this *episodic* memory. Remembering an excursion to the seaside with your father when you were 11 years old is an example of episodic memory.

Narration

An interesting feature of episodic memories is their tendency sometimes to pop unbidden into your head. At any moment in the day, you may find yourself going over something that has happened to you, or that you have seen or heard about. Often when people chat with one another they recount episodic memories: 'The strangest thing happened to me this morning . . .', 'Do you know what Joe did last week . . .?', and so on. When people recount such episodes they are, in effect, telling one another stories (narratives). We can therefore call this a process of *narration*. Narration includes more than the expression of episodic memory. It can also be creative. For example, a writer of fiction may invent narratives. Every night when we go to bed we create fictional narratives: our dreams. Narration is an extremely important capacity. In fact, we humans may well have invented language itself in order to tell one another stories:

> Narrative skill is the basic driving force behind language use, particularly speech: the ability to describe and define events and objects lies at the heart of language acquisition. Group narrative skills lead to a collective version of reality; the narrative is almost always public.
>
> (Donald 1991: 257)

Donald continues:

> Bruner (1986) classified narrative skill as a form of thinking, rather than an aspect of language. But it might be seen more simply as the natural product of language itself. Language, in a preliterate society lacking the apparatus of the modern information-state, is basically for telling stories. Language is used to exchange information about the daily activities of the members of the group, to recount past events, and to some extent arrive at collective decisions. Narrative is so fundamental that it appears to have been fully developed, at least in its pattern of daily use, in the Upper Palaeolithic. A gathering of modern post-industrial Westerners around the family table, exchanging anecdotes and accounts of recent events, does not look much different from a similar gathering in a Stone Age setting. Talk flows freely almost entirely in the narrative mode. Stories are told and disputed; and a collective version of recent events is gradually hammered out as the meal progresses. The narrative mode is basic, perhaps the basic product of language.
>
> (p. 257)

Before moving on, I will tease out some crucial implications of Donald's remarks:

1 Narrative is the basic form of language, and is considerably more ancient than non-narrative speech.
2 Narration is basically public, taking place in the context of social gatherings.
3 Narration promotes social cohesion.

Many years ago Sigmund Freud attempted to create a science concerned with understanding the stories people tell about their lives. He called this 'psychoanalysis'. Freud believed that many stories carry unconscious information – that is, they express in a hidden or encoded way things of which the speaker is unaware. Freud thought that the stories that spontaneously 'pop into one's head' were especially rich in unconscious meaning. The German language has a special word for this: *Einfall*. An *Einfall* is anything that comes to you 'out of the blue'. Freud's whole approach to psychotherapy was based on getting his patients to let such stories spontaneously occur to them. He called this process *freier Einfall* (misleadingly translated as 'free association'). Freud would ask a patient to 'let himself go' in what he says, 'as you would do in a conversation in which you were rambling on quite disconnectedly and at random' (Freud 1904: 251).

Unfortunately, Freud appeared to have been unaware of the social function of storytelling. Despite his advice to the patient to treat the clinical situation as a kind of 'conversation', Freud understood the stories that he heard as messages *from* the patient *to* the patient. Freud did not consider narration as an act of social interchange.

Decoding narratives

Communicative psychotherapy is all about the study of spontaneous narration. Unlike the Freudians (and most post-Freudians) we understand the therapeutic situation as a social system, and we treat the client's stories as extremely important social events. Clients' stories have an immediate significance. They are about what is going on between therapist and client, right there and then. They are a poetic or metaphoric portrayal of the immediate context.

Communicative psychotherapy is based on the following hypotheses:

1 We spontaneously tell stories in social situations in order to communicate our unconscious thoughts about that very situation.
2 Even if the story is manifestly unrelated to the immediate social context it contains disguised information about that context.
3 Once decoded, these unconscious views are, in the main, subtle and incisive readings of the real implications of the here-and-now situation in which they were expressed.

Langs developed these notions in an effort to understand more deeply the interactions between psychotherapists and their clients.

Clients usually do a lot of narrating during their sessions. Langs found that these stories were usually clearly related to the actions of the therapist: what the therapist has said, done, failed to say or failed to do. So, if I am in therapy with you and I tell you a story, my story will be an encoded account of what is going on between us at that very moment! Unless you know how to 'decode' the story you will be completely unaware of this.

How can we decode stories? Basic decoding is surprisingly simple. We have only to take the theme of a story (what the story is about) and relate this to a trigger (something that is going on, or has just gone on, in the therapeutic situation). Let me provide an example to make this clear.

A client complains to her therapist that her mother never answers the telephone when it rings: 'she just doesn't make an effort'. The theme of this story is 'somebody doesn't make an effort to respond to a communication'. What was the trigger? The therapist had been inappropriately silent during the session. It seems clear that the client unconsciously used her mother as a metaphor for the therapist. Out of all the possible episodes that this person might have remembered, the memory of her mother was 'selected-in' because of its resonance with the here-and-now situation. We can represent this as:

unresponsive mother = unresponsive therapist

In this example, the therapist responded by 'confronting' the client. She says: 'Maybe you get so exasperated with your mother because you see your own passivity in her. You might really be angry with yourself for not getting on with your life.'

To this the client replied:

> Yes, you might be right. But you know, my mother really does those things. When I try to talk with her reasonably about it she snaps at me and blames it on me: 'If you were on top of things you would answer your own telephone!' But this isn't fair. She lives in my house but she doesn't pull her weight. She always wants to avoid responsibility.

Once a therapist has intervened, the intervention becomes a trigger for the next story. Knowing that the therapist's remarks are a trigger for this burst of narrative, we can treat it as an *unconscious commentary* on the intervention. The client begins with manifest assent to the intervention. This tells us only that she consciously agrees with the intervention. The next remarks express her unconscious views. The themes are: 'someone really does behave in a certain way, they respond aggressively to attempts at reasonable discussion, they don't pull their weight, they blame others and take no responsibility themselves'. Bringing this into relation with the therapist, it can be decoded as follows:

> In spite of what you say about me, you, therapist, have really been unresponsive to my attempts to be in touch with you. When I express this (through my story about my mother) you respond aggressively, blaming my feelings on me. The fact is that you are refusing to take responsibility for your own actions, and prefer to blame me. You are not pulling your weight in this relationship.

There is clearly something right and true about what we consider to be this client's unconscious message to her therapist. It is plainly true that the therapist really isn't taking responsibility for her actions, and is unfairly placing responsibility on the shoulders of the client. Whereas traditional forms of psychoanalysis consider the unconscious as a distorting influence, the communicative approach, with its disciplined decoding methodology, regards the unconscious as capable of highly accurate observations of interpersonal reality. Communicative psychotherapy calls this distinctive aspect of unconscious functioning the 'deep unconscious wisdom system' (from this point onwards I will, for brevity's sake, call it the 'wisdom system'). The wisdom system seems to have evolved specifically for monitoring social interactions. This apparently is its evolutionary purpose, just as the evolutionary purpose of the heart is to pump blood.

An evolutionary scenario

The wisdom system may have evolved in the following way. During the course of evolution, our hominid ancestors developed complex social structures. The structures were part of the secret of our success. Social organization allowed us to make coordinated collective decisions, establish settlements, engage in cooperative hunting (and later agriculture), and so on. High levels of social organization are not really conceivable in the absence of spoken language, so the evolution of true language was probably the sine qua non for truly complex levels of hominid social organization.

Society is, basically, a collection of rules which all members claim to buy into. In many traditional cultures this process of buying into the rules is marked by an initiation ritual (such as the Jewish bar mitzvah). I said that members 'claim' to buy into the rules of a society because, of course, these rules are often covertly rejected. We call this 'dishonesty', 'exploitation' or, in more extreme cases, 'crime'. It is clear that human beings have a natural, evolved tendency towards breaking the rules of society: the prevalence of crime of all kinds – dishonesty, adultery and exploitation – testify to this. Our rule-breaking propensities require the existence of a massive legal and policing apparatus on the local, national and even international scale.

Normally, social rule-breaking is a form of 'cheating', that is, the rule breaker must not be seen to be breaking the rules. The burglar breaks into a house under the cover of darkness because he must not get caught. If the cheater is 'found out' some penalty is normally extracted. To 'get away with it' the cheater must seem to be playing by the rules. Language helps us cheat, because it enables us to misrepresent our actions, to say one thing while doing another. Language enables us to lie. Because complex social organization is built upon a complex network of rules, there are many opportunities for cheating in human relations. Because there is no advantage to being a 'sucker', natural selection favours the development of cheating detectors, systems within the mind devoted to 'tracking' the behaviour of the people around in order to determine whether or not we are being taken for a ride. It seems likely that the wisdom system is one such cheating detector.

It may be that narration was an ancient method of keeping track of one another. Perhaps Stone Age humans told stories around the camp-fire not as a form of recreation, but rather as a refined form of social regulation. In telling stories, our ancestors sent unconscious signals to one another about everyday social interactions. In telling a story – or selecting a dream, a myth or an episode from their life – archaic humans could express their subliminal awareness that a member of the clan was defaulting on the social contract. Indeed, Haskell (1987, 1989) has demonstrated that in small groups the members select-in narratives that portray here-and-now social interactions within the group, and argues that this may be a modern vestige of an ancient communicative capacity.

The frame

Any social activity is constituted by its rules. For instance, the game of backgammon is defined by its rules. Without the rules it wouldn't be backgammon. Indeed, it wouldn't be a game at all. It would just be a board and some pieces. A different set of rules would make it into a totally different game. We could, in principle, use a backgammon set to play all sorts of games.

The same is true of psychotherapy. Without the rules that make therapy what it is there would just be two people in a room. What transforms two people in a room into a psychotherapy session are such rules as (for instance) the rule that one person is present in order to help the other with their emotional problems, the helping person mainly listens while the other person mainly talks, the meeting lasts for 50 minutes, and so on.

The psychoanalytic term for the ground rules defining psychotherapy is the 'frame'. The 'frame' is essentially a contract between psychotherapist and client defining what it is that they will be doing together. In light of the comments that I have already made about social rules, it will not surprise you that the wisdom system is especially sensitive to the frame. In therapy, clients' narratives are mainly triggered by frame issues. On the unconscious level, clients' narratives mainly deal with their therapists' success or failure in maintaining an appropriate set of ground rules.

Surprisingly, Langs (for example 1992) found that virtually all of us unconsciously seek a basically similar psychotherapeutic frame. We know this because the narrative themes triggered by frame events are basically similar across the board. The optimal or 'secured' frame – the sort of frame all of us seem unconsciously to want – includes the following fundamental components:

1 The therapy is totally private.
2 The therapy is totally confidential.
3 There is a fixed location for the therapy.
4 There is a time fixed for each session.
5 Each session consists of the same number of minutes.

These ground rules regulate space, time and the involvement of third parties. They are the most fundamental aspects of the frame. In addition to these there are other features of the frame which pertain more to role responsibilities.

6 The client pays the therapist a set fee.
7 The client is responsible for paying for all scheduled sessions.
8 The therapist is responsible for attending all scheduled sessions.
9 The therapist is explicit with the client about the ground rules of therapy.
10 The therapist should not coerce or encourage the client in any way.
11 The therapist should not unilaterally terminate the therapy.
12 The therapist is responsible for starting and finishing each session on time.
13 The therapist should subordinate his or her personality to the task of understanding the client.

14 The therapist should spend most of the time silently listening.
15 The therapist's verbal responses should be interpretative.
16 The therapist should conduct the therapy in a manner that accords with the client's unconscious communications.
17 The therapist should not engage in informal physical contact with the client.
18 The therapist should have no contact with the client outside therapy sessions.
19 The therapist should not accept referrals from the client.
20 The therapist should not accept friends or acquaintances of the client into therapy.
21 Gifts should not be given or received.
22 The therapist should take full responsibility for his or her failure to comply with the ground rules.

Of course, not everyone is able even in principle to enforce these ground rules. For instance, working in the National Health Service in Britain makes it impossible to charge a fee and often imposes a unilaterally determined termination date. This does not mean that good psychotherapeutic work cannot be done in such settings, but it does mean that there are aspects of the therapeutic situation which are not in the client's best interests and will constrain the therapeutic work, undermining trust in the therapist and the process.

Death anxiety

Communicative psychotherapists have found that the secure frame evokes a special form of anxiety: 'death anxiety'. Death anxiety is characterized by the conscious or unconscious conviction that one is trapped and about to be annihilated. The discovery of death anxiety has provided a partial answer to the question of why it is that both therapists and clients are impelled to deviate from the secure frame. Such deviations moderate the intensity of the anxiety generated by the frame itself.

There are some therapists and clients who are so vulnerable to death anxiety that they cannot tolerate a secured frame. These appear often to be deeply traumatized individuals who may have had early and overly intense exposure to death, and they may be prone to deal with distress by acting-out or somatizing. An unmodified form of communicative psychotherapy cannot be used by or for these individuals.

Therapeutic technique

Communicative therapeutic technique involves taking your cues from the client's narratives. Your clients will unconsciously tell you what they require. You simply need to be able to listen and to put their advice to work. The ground rules are set out during an initial consultation. From that point onwards, communicative therapists allow themselves to be guided by their clients' unconscious wisdom. As a communicative psychotherapist you must listen to your clients' stories in relation to the immediate triggers that have evoked them. Communicative psychotherapists intervene in response to the narratives composed unconsciously by their clients.

Communicative psychotherapists believe that many of the commonly used forms of intervention are, in fact, inappropriate. They believe this because only certain forms of intervention – used in special circumstances – are unconsciously 'validated'. A validated intervention is an intervention that triggers a positively-toned narrative. In response to the intervention the client produces a narrative involving such themes as caring people, loving interactions, well-functioning machines, appropriate actions, and so on. Such narratives normally indicate that your client's wisdom system thinks that you've 'got it right'.

The three types of intervention used by communicative therapists are:

1 silence
2 frame management
3 interpretation.

Silence, the basic listening attitude, is appropriate so long as the client has not unconsciously indicated the need for a verbal intervention. Silence is a 'holding' intervention that encourages unconscious communication. Frame management is the handling of the therapeutic environment. It includes both maintaining a secure frame and 'rectifying' deviations: that is altering the frame in accord with clients' unconscious recommendations. Silence and frame management are probably the most therapeutically powerful interventions. A therapist who remains silent within a well-structured therapeutic environment can do immense good.

Communicative interpretations implicitly acknowledge the validity – or at least the plausibility – of clients' unconscious perspectives. Communicative interpretations never make sense of what the client has said in terms of fantasies, unrealistic fears or irrational transferences. Of course, as a therapist this means that you have to 'take it on the chin'. Most of your clients' narratives will unconsciously be all about you, and on the whole they will not be flattering. The basic logical form of communicative interpretations runs like this:

> I (*the therapist*) have done (or failed to do) so-and-so. You (*the client*) unconsciously take this to imply such-and-such about me and our work together. This may be why you are distressed/resistant right now.

Once you learn to decode the communications you will find that your clients have far deeper insight into the dynamics of your personality than your analyst does. Of course it is difficult for any therapist to hear such things, and even more difficult to specify them in an interpretation. Many therapists therefore find it too painful to use the method. However, if we ask our clients to face unpleasant truths about themselves, surely we should be prepared to do the same!

After giving an interpretation we wait for the next narrative. This tells us if our interpretation was correct or not. If the interpretation does not receive encoded validation we regard it as incorrect, irrespective of the clients' conscious opinions. Very often an intervention is consciously accepted, or even extolled, but is unconsciously sharply disapproved of.

Many psychotherapists regard communicative practitioners as rigid, dogmatic or stiff-necked because of their limited interventional repertoire. I hope that I have made it clear that communicative therapists intervene when and how they do because they have come to the conclusion that it is only these interventions that consistently elicit encoded validation from clients.

How does it work?

Communicative psychotherapy does not have a clearly articulated theory of 'cure'. In my view it is far better to remain appropriately agnostic about how 'cure' comes about than to concoct fanciful theories having no scientific basis. We often know that something works without understanding how it works.[1] The history of medicine is largely the history of treatments that worked for reasons other than the imaginative reasons concocted by practitioners.

Conclusion

Although it has much to offer to both researchers and practitioners, communicative psychotherapy is not yet widely researched or practised. I hope that this brief introduction will have sparked your interest and encouraged you to investigate the literature and experiment with the method.

Note

1 Of course, in the absence of rigorous outcome studies we should be cautious about making therapeutic claims which may, in the end, prove to be unwarranted.

References

Bruner, J. (1986) *Actual Minds, Possible Worlds*. Cambridge, MA: Harvard University Press.

Donald, M. (1991) *Origins of the Modern Mind*. Cambridge, MA: Harvard University Press.

Freud, S. (1904) Freud's psycho-analytic procedure, *S. E. 7*.

Haskell, R. (1987) Giambattista Vico and the discovery of metaphor, in R.E. Haskell (ed.) *Cognition and Symbolic Structures*, 67–82. Norwood, NJ: Ablex Publishing.

Haskell, R. (1989) Analogical transforms: a cognitive theory of origin and development of equivalence transformation, part II, *Metaphor and Symbolic Activity*, 4: 257–77.

Langs, R. (1992) *A Clinical Workbook for Psychotherapists*. London: Karnac.

Part **II**

THEORY INTO PRACTICE

THEORY AND PRACTICE

Chapter 2

Understanding patients' countertransferences

David Livingston Smith

Introduction

In this chapter I use some principles of contemporary biological thought to make sense of some features of the 'helping' relationship in counselling, psychotherapy and psychoanalysis. Although I believe that my reflections on the clinical interactions will be of use to practitioners of a variety of theoretical orientations, my particular focus will be the communicative approach to psychotherapy because of its incisive analysis of patient–therapist interchanges.

I want to make it clear at the outset that I am not a biologist, and therefore make no pretence of possessing special knowledge or expertise in this domain beyond that of an educated layperson. I would also like to make it clear that the present chapter is not intended as an advertisement for the communicative approach. Detailed accounts of communicative psychoanalysis can be found elsewhere (for example Smith 1991, 1995; Langs 1995).

Patients' countertransferences

Balint and Balint (1939) described analysts' transferences as 'euphemistically' called 'countertransferences'. They seem to call the term 'countertransference' a euphemism because it is a way of avoiding the acknowledgement that analyst and patient are both in the same boat. The key to this may well lie in the 'counter-' of countertransference. The 'counter-' suggests a reactive process. The one who transfers takes, as it were, the psychopathological initiative. The one who countertransfers responds to this initiative. Psychoanalytic language allows us to speak of the patient initiating a transference, but we rarely hear about analysts initiating countertransferences.

One of the most influential works on countertransference was Paula Heimann's 'On countertransference' (1950). In this short paper – only four pages long – Heimann famously argued that psychoanalysts should use their countertransference reactions (note how easily the notion of *reactivity* creeps in!) as a basis for making inferences about their patients' unconscious concerns.

Heimann's paper provides a clinical vignette which I will quote at length. I believe that it illustrates a self-serving form of thinking about the therapeutic interaction which all of us are inclined to slip into. My primary purpose is not therefore to criticize Heimann, but rather to use her work to exemplify what I believe to be a *universal* tendency.

> A recent experience comes to mind. It concerns a patient whom I had taken over from a colleague. The patient was a man in his forties who had originally sought treatment when his marriage broke down. Among his symptoms promiscuity figured prominently. In the third week of his analysis with me he told me, at the beginning of the session, that he was going to marry a woman whom he had met only a short time before.
>
> It was obvious that his wish to get married at this juncture was determined by his resistance against the analysis and his need to act out his transference conflicts. Within a strongly ambivalent attitude the desire for an intimate relation with me had already clearly appeared. I had thus many reasons for doubting the wisdom of his intention and for suspecting his choice. But such an attempt to short-circuit analysis is not infrequent at the beginning of, or at a critical point in, the treatment and usually does not represent too great an obstacle to the work, so that catastrophic conditions need not arise. I was therefore somewhat puzzled to find that I reacted with a sense of apprehension and worry to the patient's remark. I felt that something more was involved in his situation, something beyond the ordinary acting out which, however, eluded me.
>
> (pp. 75–6)

In his further associations which centred round his friend, the patient, describing her, said she had had a 'rough passage'. This phrase again registered particularly and increased my misgivings. It dawned on me that it was precisely because she had had a rough passage that he was drawn to her. But still I felt that I did not see things clearly enough. Presently he came to tell me his dream. He had acquired from abroad a very good second-hand car which was damaged. He wished to repair it, but another person in the dream objected for reasons of caution. The patient had, as he put it, 'to make him confused' in order that he might go ahead with the repair of the car.

(p. 76)

Heimann then goes on to say that this dream provided a key for understanding her apprehensiveness:

When he gave me the particulars of the car – very good, second-hand, from abroad – the patient spontaneously recognised that it represented myself. The other person in the dream who tried to stop him and whom he confused stood for that part of the patient's ego which aimed at security and happiness and for the analysis as a protective object.

(p. 76)

Now comes her interpretation:

The dream showed me that the patient wished me to be damaged (he insisted on my being the refugee to whom applies the expression 'rough passage' which he had used for his new friend). Out of guilt for his sadistic impulses he was compelled to make reparation, but this reparation was of a masochistic nature, since it necessitated blotting out the voice of reason or caution. The element of confusing the protective figure was in itself double-barrelled, expressing both his sadistic and masochistic impulses: insofar as it aimed at annihilating the analysis, it represented the patient's sadistic tendencies in the pattern of his infantile anal attacks on his mother; insofar as it stood for his ruling out his desire for security and happiness, it expressed his self-destructive trends. Reparation turned into a masochistic act again engenders hatred, and, far from resolving the conflict between destructiveness and guilt, leads to a vicious circle.

(pp. 76–7)

Finally, Heimann brings the man's earlier remarks into line with these notions:

The patient's intention of marrying his new friend, the injured woman, was fed from both sources, and the acting-out of his transference conflicts proved to be determined by this specific and powerful sadomasochistic system.

(p. 77)

To my mind, this interpretation gets less and less plausible as it goes on. By this I mean that Heimann's formulations seem less and less constrained by logic and evidence. The patient's interpretation of the good, second-hand car from abroad as standing for Heimann seems plausible enough. She was, after all, from abroad, although strictly speaking it was he who was 'second hand', having come to Heimann from another analyst. None the less, we could understand Heimann as a newly acquired item who had seen a lot of prior use. It is at least understandable why the man who cautions the patient might be seen as the cautious side of the patient, although there are no compelling reasons presented on behalf of this formulation. From this point onwards Heimann seems to lose all scientific restraint. She takes the patient's dream of wanting to *repair* the car as expressing a wish to *destroy* her. She then brings in the notion of anal attacks on the patient's mother, sadism and masochism seemingly out of nowhere. Heimann seems to have been satisfied by her interpretation, but should we?

Consider what Heimann does with the dream icon of the car. The car is described as having four properties: it is very good, from abroad, second-hand and damaged. Rating these four properties I think it reasonable to say that the first is definitely positive, the second two are neutral, while the fourth is rather negative. Consider how Heimann goes about relating these to herself. She takes the first three positive-to-neutral items on board as pertaining to herself, but she rejects the fourth, attributing it to the patient's destructive wishes. It is as if she is saying 'Yes, of course, I'm from abroad, I've had a lot of experience (*second-hand*) and I'm very good, but I'm not damaged. It must be the patient who wants to see me damaged, who wants to damage me!' Why didn't Heimann discuss the image of the car being 'very good' as a mere wish-fulfilment similarly out of accord with reality? The rules of Kleinian technique would have permitted her to treat this as a wishful, defensive idealization, but she gives no indication of having done so.

Of course, the clinical material reported by Heimann might be understood in any number of ways. One of these, in the tradition of Searles and Langs, might be to understand the image of the damaged car as an accurate, rather than a distorted, representation of Heimann. Perhaps Heimann's patient understood some aspect of her psychopathology or emotional vulnerability. Let us assume, for the sake of the argument, that the patient's wish to marry had something to do with his relationship with Heimann (a supposition the truth of which we should not take for granted). Perhaps his wish to marry a traumatized immigrant, which Heimann understood as the acting-out of an essentially sadomasochistic transference (rooted in alleged phantasized anal attacks on his mother), actually expressed his loving concern for her. Within a Langsian frame of reference, one might wonder whether Heimann's departure from her patient's discourse, her thoughts of sadistic anal attacks and so on, stem more from her fear of being exposed than from sober psychoanalytical considerations. This would be an example of countertransference in Freud's original (1910) sense of the term.

The main point developed in Heimann's paper is the idea that analysts' countertransferences can provide valuable information about their patients' unconscious issues. In the example given above, Heimann believed that her sense of alarm derived from her unconscious awareness of her patient's unconscious sadistic impulses towards her. The meaningful relationship between the patients' transferences and analysts' countertransferences could reasonably be taken to be the basis of the informational richness of the latter. Heimann went further though, claiming that analyst's countertransferences are the 'creation' of their patients.

Racker's response

Heinrich Racker, a Kleinian analyst working in Argentina, was occupied with similar problems. Unlike Heimann, Racker (1957) stressed the egalitarian features of the psychoanalytic situation, describing it as

> an interaction between two personalities, in both of which the ego is under pressure from the id, the superego and the external world; each personality has its internal and external dependencies, anxieties and pathological defences, and each of these whole personalities . . . responds to every event of the analytic situation.
>
> (Racker 1957: 132)

Racker believed that the failure to remain aware of this is to maintain the 'social inequality' of analyst and patient and thus contaminate the psychoanalytic situation with the values of the 'patriarchal order'. He therefore objected to the unilateral quality of Heimann's formulation, arguing that 'Just as countertransference is a "creation" of the patient . . . and an integral part of his inner and outer world, so also, in some measure, is transference the analyst's creation and an integral part of his inner and outer world' (Racker 1958: 178).

If patients must accommodate themselves to the unconscious messages and disruptive inputs of their analysts we might, using

Giovanni Trombi's (1987) phrase, speak of 'the patient's counter-transference' – i.e. patients' unconscious responses to their analysts' emotional engagements with them. Unless we come to grips with the issues raised by Racker, we are stuck with a unilateral notion of unconscious communication in the psychoanalytic situation. I think that such a view is clearly absurd.

Racker's position was later extended by Baranger and Baranger (1966), who described the psychoanalytic situation as a 'bipersonal field', a concept derived from the French philosopher Maurice Merleau-Ponty. (R.D. Laing (1959) appears to have derived his very similar notion of a 'behavioural field' from the same source.) According to this view, every event occurring within the bipersonal field is a result of three vectors: the mind of the patient, the mind of the analyst and the psychoanalytic setting.

Little's contribution

At the same time that Paula Heimann was working on her notion of countertransference, Margaret Little was working on hers. Little's (1951) paper on 'Countertransference and the patient's response to it' presents countertransference as something often initiated by the analyst. Little describes analysts' attitudes towards countertransference as 'paranoid', meaning, presumably, either that they are inclined to project their own psychological difficulties onto their patients and/or that they feel persecuted by countertransference. She remarks that 'Not to refer to countertransference is tantamount to denying its existence or forbidding the patient to know or speak about it' (Little 1951: 37). Little believes that patients are nevertheless consciously or unconsciously aware of their analysts' difficulties:

> So much emphasis is laid on the unconscious phantasies of patients that it is often ignored that they really come to know a great deal of truth about them – both actual and psychic. Such knowledge could not be prevented in any case, even if desirable, but patients do not know they have it, and part of the analyst's task is to bring it into consciousness.
>
> (p. 45)

In what is one of the most memorable passages in the psychoanalytic literature on technique, Little writes that

> We often hear of the mirror which the analyst holds up to the patient, but the patient holds one up to the analyst too, and

there is a whole series of reflections in each, repetitive in kind and subject to continual modification. The mirror in each case should become progressively clearer as the analysis goes on, for patient and analyst respond to each other in a reverberative kind of way, and increasing clearness in one mirror will bring the need for a corresponding clearing in the other.

(p. 43)

Ferenczi's contribution

This approach to the problem is strikingly similar to that proposed by Ferenczi (1933), two decades earlier:

> Gradually I came to the conviction that patients have an extremely refined feeling for the wishes, tendencies, moods and dislikes of the analyst, even should these feelings remain totally unconscious to the analyst himself. Instead of contradicting the analyst, instead of accusing him of certain misdemeanours or blunders, patients identify with him ... Generally they permit themselves no criticism of us; such criticism does not even occur to them unless we expressly give them permission to do so ... Therefore we must, from the associations of patients, discern the existence not only of unpleasant things from their past; we must also, more than we have done until now, look for the existence of repressed or suppressed criticism of us.

(Ferenczi 1933: 293)

It is noteworthy that Ferenczi is concerned with valid unconscious criticism which must be inferred from patients' associations. This is far removed from notions of analysing unconscious negative *transference*.

Ferenczi expressed these views in his infamous paper entitled 'Confusion of tongues between adults and the child' (1933). This paper has been discussed mainly in connection with Ferenczi's revival of Freud's seduction theory. It is well known that the paper earned Ferenczi the diagnosis of paranoia at the hands of his psychoanalytic colleagues. Masson (1982) claims – and many have uncritically repeated this claim – that Ferenczi's pathologization stemmed from his views on the sexual abuse of children. To my mind it seems more likely that Freud and others thought he was paranoid because of his view that patients offer encoded criticisms of their analysts. This might well have been seen as a manifestation of 'ideas of reference' – a sign of paranoia.

Ferenczi concluded his paper with an appeal to the psychoanalytic community which is, to my mind, as fresh and relevant today as it was in 1932 when he offered it to the psychoanalysts assembled at the Wiesbaden congress:

> It would please me if you would take the trouble to examine, in practice and in theory, what I have communicated here, and especially if you would follow my advice to pay closer attention than you have in the past to the strange, much veiled, yet critical manner of thinking and speaking of your children, patients and students, and, so to speak, loosen their tongues. You will hear much that is instructive.
>
> (Ferenczi 1933: 302)[1]

Langs's contribution

Langs is the first (and thus far only) theorist within the tradition beginning with Ferenczi and extending through the work of writers like Little and Racker (as well as others I have not mentioned – for further details see Smith 1991) to develop the analysis of patients' countertransferences in a systematic manner (Smith 1991; Langs 1992a, 1992b, 1995). In order to explain this I must first place it in the context of some notions of human nature that are emerging within the communicative psychoanalytic research programme.

According to many contemporary cognitive scientists mind is organized in a modular fashion. This means that the brain contains a number of cognitive systems dedicated to the execution of specific cognitive tasks. We know, for instance, that specific brain regions are responsible for specific aspects of visual experience. These modules operate unconsciously. Some cognitive scientists hold the view (in common, by the way, with Freud) that consciousness is itself a function of a mental module.

These systems would never have come into being if they were not of vital evolutionary significance – i.e. if they were not related to *fundamental* aspects of our life capable of enhancing our reproductive success. I will call these modules – borrowing a useful term from Slavin and Kriegman (1992) – 'deep psychological structures'. Deep psychological structures are fundamentally *adaptive*, that is, they guide us towards meaningful and life-enhancing engagements with our environments.

Of course, one sort of environment to which we must adapt is the social environment. There is a large neo-Darwinian literature on social adaptation. Much of this fascinating literature is concerned with working out what social strategies are most useful for creatures in the long term.

One of the most important tools for understanding interactions between organisms is derived from a discipline called 'game theory'. Game theory provides a way of mathematically modelling the interactions between cooperating and competing entities. Game theory has a host of applications, from the interactions between micro-organisms to international politics.

Biologists such as Maynard Smith (1982) and Axelrod (1984) have used game theory to study issues of altruism and exploitation. To summarize briefly the results of these investigations, imagine that creatures can be of two sorts: 'givers' and 'takers'. A purely altruistic population – a population composed of pure 'givers' – is a bad evolutionary bet because the emergence of even one mutant 'taker' will decimate the population (the 'givers' help and support one another but the 'taker' takes advantage of them, the 'givers' thereby becoming 'suckers'). A population composed entirely of 'takers' isn't very advantageous either, because there is no possibility for reaping the benefits of cooperation. Computer simulations have demonstrated that the best strategy in a mixed population of 'givers' and 'takers' (as well as all shades in between) is what game theorists call the 'tit-for-tat' strategy: cooperate with the givers and default on the defaulters. Those who use 'tit-for-tat' are resistant to exploitation but are able to reap the benefits of cooperation.

There is a social strategy that may have evolutionary advantages over 'tit-for-tat': the strategy of *cheating*. Cheating means deceiving someone (a 'sucker') into thinking that you are cooperating with him when you are in fact covertly exploiting him. It is prima facie plausible that we human animals are evolved cheaters. Because cheating is such a good bet, we are all inclined to adopt it as a strategy. According to this view, *we are all designed to cheat*.

Trivers (1985), an entomologist, has some very interesting things to say about cheating. First, he claims that there are advantages to cheating happening unconsciously rather than consciously. If you remain ignorant of just how you are exploiting some poor sucker you are far less likely to experience conflict or give the show away. Trivers believes that the acquisition of language greatly increases our facility for cheating:

> With the advent of language in the human lineage, the possibilities for deception and self-deception were greatly enlarged. If language permits the communication of much more detailed and extensive information – concerning, for example, events distant in space and time – then it both permits and encourages

the communication of much more detailed and extensive mis-information. A portion of the brain devoted to verbal functions must become specialized for the manufacture and mainten-ance of falsehoods. This will require biased perceptions, biased memory, and biased logic, and these processes are ideally kept unconscious.

(Trivers 1981: 35, in Badcock 1991)

Second, he claims that the very existence of cheating would favour the selection of cheating detectors, built-in apparatuses (modules) dedicated to monitoring our social interactions for the presence of covert exploitation. Finally, Trivers has suggested that these factors might have led to an evolutionary 'arms race' with cheating detectors matched by more efficient forms of cheat-ing which in turn prompt the development of super-sophisticated cheating detectors.

Trivers (1985) suggests that such an 'arms race' may well have shaped the evolution of human psychology. One would expect such factors to be particularly salient and sophisticated among human beings because of the immensely complex nature of the human social environment. Indeed, it has been suggested that the rapid development of the brain over the course of hominid evolution has been driven by the unbelievable complexity of human social envir-onments. In a recent review of Godfrey-Smith's *Complexity and the Function of Mind in Nature*, Dunbar (1996: xii) remarked that 'It is not an exaggeration to say that the average human mind daily executes calculations in the social domain of an order of complexity not far off that required to understand quantum theory.' I imagine that this is a considerable understatement.

In light of these considerations I will assume the following to be true of human nature:

1 Human beings are inclined to exploit others under the guise of appearing to cooperate with them. We are evolved cheaters.
2 Much of this exploitation goes on unconsciously. When we cheat, we often do not consciously realize what we are doing.
3 Because of these propensities, we human animals have evolved highly sophisticated capacities for detecting exploitation. These cheating detectors also operate outside consciousness.

It is essential to my argument that *we cannot help being this way*. Unpleasant as it may seem,[2] the inclination to exploit others is in itself neither a moral failing nor an expression of psychopathology. It is an expression of our evolved nature and part of the essence of being human.

Ground rules

Human social systems are obviously not genetically given, although they are equally obviously built on evolutionary foundations. Social systems are regulated, and indeed *constituted* by rules. The rules of a social system make it what it is.

It is easiest to appreciate the significance of this idea when thinking about games. The rules of a game are its essence; to break a rule of a game is therefore an assault on the game itself. This is why cheating at a game is such a grave offence.

The more there is at stake in a game, the more we are inclined to cheat, and the more game players maintain an attitude of vigilance to detect cheating. If we are playing for 'fun' then cheating is less likely and of less consequence than if we are playing for 'keeps' – for money, status, sex and so on. It is for this reason that cheating in a game for 'keeps' must be especially subtle.

How do we bring cheating to an end in any given instance? The only thing required is the exposure of the cheater. Once this happens, he or she is no longer cheating: that is, the constitutive element of *deception* has been eliminated.

Within the framework that I have been developing here, the discovered cheater has in effect been recognized as having opted out of the game. Within another superordinate set of rules the discovered cheater who wishes to rejoin a game may be punished for his or her transgression. Being penalized may enable the cheater to be reintegrated into the game at some future date. Alternatively, the cheater may be excluded from the game, banished from the social system. Of course, discovered cheaters have several other options. They may attempt to convince the other players that they were not really cheating; they may attempt to secure their advantage by force; or they may choose to quit the game for another with different players.

According to communicative psychoanalytic theory, human beings have, over the course of their evolution, developed a special mental faculty specifically designed to detect cheating in human social systems. This mental system operates outside of conscious awareness, and thus supplements our conscious efforts to detect cheating. Langs calls this faculty the 'deep unconscious wisdom system'. Langs (1996) suggests that this system may have begun to evolve about 1.5 million years ago when our ancestor, *homo erectus*, began to create complex social structures:

> It seems likely . . . that the conscious system began to be overburdened and to move towards a problem of *information-meaning overload*.

There was a rapidly mounting growth in the complexity of the environment, largely in the form of a changing and widening sociocultural scene, the development of complicated, multiple social and work roles and relationships; and greater risks taken in hunting, migrating and other venturesome endeavours. These selection pressures evidently moved the mind towards the development and enhancement of mechanisms that allowed for rapidly responsive automatic actions for which consciousness was by-passed.

(Langs 1996: 126)

The deep unconscious wisdom system is thus particularly sensitive to those rules which constitute the boundaries of social relations. The deep unconscious wisdom system thus has a very narrow cognitive focus, but it performs its function with breathtaking sensitivity to the nuances of social activity. Once it identifies cheating in a social engagement the deep unconscious wisdom system causes one to *signal* awareness of the cheating, so as to bring the cheating to an end. According to communicative theory, this process of signalling also normally operates outside of conscious awareness. Signalling happens through the medium of what is usually called 'unconscious communication'.

The psychoanalytic situation is a relatively simple, two-person social system. The system is bounded by a set of implicit or explicit rules collectively referred to as the 'psychoanalytic frame'. As Mooij (1982: 28) remarks, the analytic ground rules

are not just supervening attributes of the psychoanalytic process which develops by itself anyway and which above all should not be disturbed, but they actually constitute the psychoanalytic domain and make interpretation of what happens within it, possible, whereas other rules, consequently, implement other fields to explore.

Because of its relatively simple nature, the psychoanalytic situation is an ideal arena in which to study the activity of the deep unconscious wisdom system. Because of the special role requirements set out in the rules of the psychoanalytic game, the operation of these processes are far easier to study in the patient than in the analyst.

Let us consider the structure of a normal psychoanalytic engagement. First, note that from the patient's point of view it is a game in which there can be a good deal at stake: it is usually an example of playing for keeps rather than playing for fun. Second, although analyst and patient are involved in what is defined as a cooperative venture, notice that it involves an intrinsically asymmetrical arrangement. Normally, a patient has considerably more at stake than an analyst. In any given analytic relationship, the analyst normally has less to lose than the patient. Because the analyst has less to lose, he or she can afford to treat the analytic situation more casually than the patient. One would expect this to incline the analyst to cheat – to use the patient for his or her ends (for example to use the patient for the gratification of narcissistic, sexual or aggressive needs). Slavin and Kriegman (1992: 234) remark that

> In many respects, analysts are called on to sustain an exquisite alertness to self-deception and avoidance of deception that, given the realities of normal parent–offspring conflict, actually far exceeds what any healthy, good-enough parent could or should provide.

By the same token, one would expect patients to be particularly vigilant in monitoring the behaviour of their analysts for any signs of cheating.

According to communicative psychoanalytic theory, this is precisely what occurs. Patients monitor the behaviour of their analysts from moment to moment with respect to the defining ground rules of the analytic situation. That is, *they are consistently unconsciously concerned with the way in which their analysts' behaviour coheres with the psychoanalytic frame*. Because of the asymmetry noted earlier, analysts are irresistibly inclined to cheat – to take more than they are entitled to from their patients.

On what basis do I make these claims? This question brings us to a wonderful and neglected aspect of human communication: the propensity for storytelling. Most people have an irrepressible tendency to tell stories to one another that are manifestly unrelated to their immediate circumstances. These can be anything from narrating the plot of a recent film, to giving an account of an argument with one's spouse. Langs's most fundamental discovery is simply that the stories that patients tell in therapy are normally highly meaningful responses to their analysts' management of the ground rules of analysis. Violations of the ground rules normally evoke negatively-toned narratives expressing the specific properties detected in the violation. These are expressed through the *themes* of the narratives, for example seduction, violence, exploitation and dishonesty. According to Langs, this is a lawful process. That is, the violation of a psychoanalytic ground rule will, predictably and reliably, evoke negatively-toned narratives.

Normally in the natural world an evolved signalling function presupposes that organisms of the same type are able to use the signal

(Millikan 1984). The dances performed by honeybees would be use-less and evolutionarily unthinkable if honeybees were unable to interpret the dances. The slap of a beaver's tail as a signal of impend-ing danger would be meaningless if beavers did not respond to tail-slaps as danger signals. Indeed, the human capacity for speech would be meaningless in the absence of the capacity for speech compre-hension. Millikan (1984) refers to this aspect of the relationship between 'producers' and 'consumers' of communications as their 'relational proper function'.

According to the argument presented earlier, the function of unconscious communication is mainly to expose cheating. This view implies that the 'consumers' of these communications are able unconsciously to understand them. For what it is worth, my own experience as a supervisor supports this contention. Even (or perhaps especially) when they do not consciously understand the significance of unconscious communications, psychotherapists normally respond meaningfully to them. However, *psychotherapists do not usually respond to unconscious communications by mastering their 'countertransference', rather, they respond by renewed efforts to overwhelm the patient.*

Anecdotal evidence suggests that in less asymmetrical situ-ations unconscious communication often has a different kind of impact. For example, waiting in the playground to collect my daugh-ter from school I overheard a conversation between two of the mothers. One of these two women aggressively dominated the con-versation, thus violating the social rule of mutuality in conversation between peers. The other mother, who had hitherto been quiet, next began to speak about an acquaintance who obnoxiously dominated everyone in her proximity. The previously dominant woman then fell silent and the two of them drifted apart. From a communicative perspective the quiet woman had signalled to the dominant woman that she was exploiting her. This communication discharged a regu-latory function, causing the dominant woman to stop. Had this been a psychoanalytic situation, this outcome would have been quite unlikely. Imagine a situation in which a psychoanalyst has been overly active and dominant. The patient responds by an account of how her mother never gave her any space. I hold that the most likely response from the analyst would be an *intensification* of her domin-ant activity, probably in the form of questions or elaborate interpret-ations about the patient's relationship with her mother. In fact, I think that this is just the sort of thing that happened when Paula Heimann's patient mentioned the damaged car. Obviously I don't have enough information about either the session or the frame of the analysis to do anything more than speculate, but I suspect that

Heimann had done something indicating to the patient that she (Heimann) was in some sense damaged – as a person or as a professional – and that it might be dangerous to try to repair her. I think that it was probably something like this which impelled Heimann to formulate florid interpretations about his anal sadism.

These considerations may imply that there is something about the psychoanalytical situation itself that works against the psychoanalytic process. The psychoanalytic situation is such that analysts will, inevitably, be inclined to exploit their patients, and patients will, equally inevitably, be deeply suspicious of their analysts. It is a situation in which patients unconsciously signal their awareness of cheating in almost everything they say and in which analysts are driven by their human nature – their inclination to cheat while remaining unaware of their cheating – to attempt to override these signals. Of course, it is possible to try to honour and interpret these signals rather than attempting to override them. This is precisely what communicative psychoanalysts attempt to do.

Perhaps a brief example will make this clear.[3] During a psychotherapy session a trainee asked his mildly agoraphobic patient a number of questions. Experience teaches that questions virtually always elicit unconscious disapproval. That is, in response to this kind of intervention, we almost always react with negatively-toned narratives typically referring to intrusive people (an unconscious representation of the psychotherapist). In this instance the patient responded as follows:

> My mother always wants to go shopping with me because she knows it makes me nervous and wants to help, but she is always talking to me and this just makes it worse. If she really wants to help me she should shut the hell up. When my son cried as a baby I would sometimes get so fed up I would pick him up and shake him, screaming at him to shut up. I know that it's a mother's job to handle a crying baby, but I just couldn't do it. I went into a panic and tried too hard. I guess I was inexperienced. If I have another child I'll try and do it differently. I'm feeling sad.

From a communicative perspective, these remarks are seen as provoked by the therapist's interventions. They are subtle and incisive depictions of the therapist. The therapist, who was just learning the communicative approach, offered a very good communicative interpretation:

> After you started talking to me today I asked you lots of questions. You answered these, and then you went on to other

subjects. You spoke of how your mother fails to help you because she talks to you too much and this gets you nervous. Then you talked about how you couldn't handle your baby crying, how you shook him and screamed 'shut up'. You were inexperienced and don't want to do this again. I think that these things are all linked. Maybe when I asked you all those questions it felt like your mother talking to you, and you felt that I was making you worse rather than helping you. Maybe, deep down, you want me to say less and quietly provide support, just like you wanted her to shut up. I think that you shaking your baby and screaming at him might also be a picture of you and me. I think that maybe when I asked you all those questions it felt like I couldn't handle your emotions and that I was trying to control you. It may have actually felt violent – like shaking a baby – and led you to conclude that I am an inexperienced therapist. From what you have said it seems better for me to give you more space rather than talking so much.

Although therapeutically powerful, this is an unnatural and therefore emotionally costly strategy. As Slavin and Kriegman (1992: 234) state,

> From the therapist's point of view, there are . . . many intrinsic unnatural dimensions to the analytic situation. Although the therapist is paid and generally finds a professional identity in the work, he or she is also expected to tolerate extraordinary violations of very deep, evolved norms of reciprocity and self-expression – norms that generally push us to express our personal identity and exercise interpersonal influence in human relationships

I have been an advocate of the communicative approach to psychotherapy for well over a decade. I have been continually surprised at the difficulty both I and my supervisees consistently experience when attempting to apply what is, to my mind, a simple and lucid psychotherapeutic procedure. After all, all that the communicative approach enjoins one to do is to interpret and heed our clients' encoded accounts of our own behaviour. Why should this be so terribly difficult? Now, I think I know. In doing this work we act in a way that is deeply antagonistic to our evolved propensity for deceptive and self-serving social engagements. In forcing ourselves to become conscious of such engagements we are acting in contradiction to our evolved talent for remaining unaware of our own exploitativeness.

Acknowledgements

I would like to thank Emmy van Deurzen for reading and commenting on an earlier draft of this chapter.

Notes

1 Myers (1996) has made an important contribution to the study of Ferenczi's views on these matters.
2 As Badcock (1994) suggests, the very fact that these thoughts seem unpleasant may be part of the evolved propensity to unconscious cheating. The emotional inclination to reject these ideas may help us to conceal our own exploitativeness from conscious awareness.
3 Although based on a real interaction, this account is heavily disguised. It is included for illustrative purposes only.

References

Axelrod, R. (1984) *The Evolution of Co-operation*. London: Penguin.
Badcock, C. (1991) *Evolution and Individual Behaviour: An Introduction to Human Sociobiology*. Oxford: Basil Blackwell.
Badcock, C. (1994) *PsychoDarwinism: The New Synthesis of Darwin and Freud*. London: HarperCollins.
Balint, M. and Balint, A. (1939) On transference and countertransference, in M. Balint, *Primary Love and Psycho-Analytic Technique*. New York: Liveright.
Baranger, M. and Baranger, W. (1966) Insight and the analytic situation, in R. Litman (ed.) *Psychoanalysis in the Americas*. New York: International Universities Press.
Dunbar, R. (1996) Minds, for the use of, *Times Higher Education Supplement*, 5 April: xii.
Ferenczi, S. (1933) Confusion of tongues between adults and the child, in *Final Contributions to the Problems and Methods of Psycho-Analysis*. London: Hogarth.
Freud, S. (1910) Five lectures on psycho-analysis, *S. E.* 11.
Heimann, P. (1950) On counter-transference, *International Journal of Psycho-Analysis*, 31: 81–4.
Laing, R.D. (1959) *The Divided Self*. Harmondsworth: Penguin.
Langs, R. (1992a) *A Clinical Workbook for Psychotherapists*. London: Karnac.
Langs, R. (1992b) *Science, Systems and Psychoanalysis*. London: Karnac.
Langs, R. (1995) *Clinical Practice and the Architecture of the Mind*. London: Karnac.
Langs, R. (1996) *The Evolution of the Emotion-Processing Mind*. London: Karnac.
Little, M. (1951) Countertransference and the patient's response to it, *International Journal of Psycho-Analysis*, 47: 255–74.

Masson, J.M. (1982) *The Assault on Truth: Freud's Suppression of the Seduction Theory*. Harmondsworth: Penguin.

Maynard Smith, J. (1982) *Evolution and the Theory of Games*. Cambridge: Cambridge University Press.

Millikan, R.G. (1984) *Language, Thought and Other Biological Categories*. Cambridge, MA: Bradford/MIT.

Mooij, A. (1982) *Psychoanalysis and the Concept of a Rule*. Heidelberg: Springer-Verlag.

Myers, P. (1996) Sandor Ferenczi and patients' perceptions of analysis, *British Journal of Psychotherapy*, 13(1): 26–37.

Racker, H. (1957) The meaning and uses of countertransference, *Psychoanalytic Quarterly*, 26: 303–57.

Racker, H. (1958) Countertransference and interpretation, *Journal of the American Psychoanalytic Association*, 6: 215–21.

Slavin, M.O. and Kriegman, D. (1992) *The Adaptive Design of the Human Psyche: Psychoanalysis, Evolutionary Biology and the Therapeutic Process*. London: Guilford.

Smith, D.L. (1991) *Hidden Conversations: An Introduction to Communicative Psychoanalysis*. London: Routledge.

Smith, D.L. (1995) Communicative psychotherapy, in M. Jacobs (ed.) *In Search of Supervision*. Buckingham: Open University Press.

Trivers, R. (1981) Sociobiology and politics, in E. White (ed.) *Sociobiology and Human Politics*. Lexington, MA: Lexington Books.

Trivers, R. (1985) *Social Evolution*. Menlo Park, CA: Benjamin/Cummings.

Trombi, G. (1987) La teoria della tecnica di Robert Langs: l'approcio 'communicative', *Psicotherapia e Scienze Umane*, 21(3): 55–95.

Chapter **3**

Confessions of a communicative psychotherapist

Carol Holmes

Introduction

The link between confession and psychotherapy has been noted by a number of writers in this field. This chapter will discuss the notion of confession and its specific application to communicative psychoanalytic psychotherapy, which stands in direct opposition to both traditional psychoanalysis and the more mainstream forms of psychotherapy.

One of the guiding principles of communicative technique resides in the therapist's acknowledgement of the patient's curative capacities; in this way the issue of power within the therapeutic encounter is consistently addressed. Some psychotherapy research suggests, however, that the need to enter the profession may be related to the practitioner's need to gain power and prestige.

It is further proposed that the therapist's preferred method of working may also be unwittingly motivated by and utilized as a nefarious means for addressing some of the practitioner's own unresolved issues. This text will also consider how some of these inevitable risks may nevertheless be employed by the communicative therapist as a curative and/or defensive tool within the consulting room.

The technique of communicative psychoanalytic psychotherapy is naturally informed by its fundamental philosophy of human nature, which is in many respects in direct contrast to that of traditional psychoanalytic theory and practice. The key elements of the approach focus on the perceptive abilities of the unconscious part of the mind and on the unconscious significance of interpersonal boundary issues for both the patient and the therapist.

The communicative model of psychoanalytic psychotherapy

Robert Langs (1973, 1987, 1992), the founder of the approach, has developed a model of the mind which is based upon and is in keeping with a plethora of consistent clinical observations of the patient–therapist interaction. These empirical impressions suggest that patients are incisively alert and concerned with the immediate conditions of the therapeutic encounter. Furthermore, due to the nature of unconscious communication, the patient will tend to convey these interpersonal concerns in a symbolic, narrative or derivative manner. In communicative terms the patient–therapist interaction constitutes a relatively closed system, with each individual constantly monitoring, responding and reacting to each other both consciously and especially unconsciously, in a continuously circular fashion. Framework or ground rule disturbances are therefore viewed primarily in an interpersonal light rather than regarded as emanating solely from one party or the other.

The relevance of death anxiety as a core human concern is inextricably linked to communicative ideas and practice, and to the limits of the therapeutic environment. Langs (1988, 1997) asserts that the mainspring of psychotherapy and psychoanalysis is the negotiation of this basic existential dread. Bearing this in mind, a disturbance of therapeutic boundaries is viewed as a manic form of defence and denial of death anxiety issues which will appertain to both members of the therapeutic dyad. While a framework modification may provide some relief from existential anxiety it also provokes unconscious persecutory fears, which in turn engender a sense of guilt in both the patient and the therapist (Langs 1988, 1997).

The technique of communicative psychotherapy is therefore clearly demarcated and defined. One of the major criticisms levelled against the approach argues that the method itself is inordinately rigid: by comparison to most – if not all – other approaches, which seem to take pride in the idea that the therapist's responses to the patient should be executed in a manner which is far more liberal, intuitive and ad hoc, this critique is understandable. Nevertheless, the focus on boundaries is of central importance to the approach. The therapist's scrupulous and rigorous concern in this area is therefore an authentic attempt to acknowledge and reduce the defensive and biased components of the therapist's interpersonal interventions. The approach has clear unambiguous guidelines for intervening, as well as distinct criteria for confirming or refuting the validity of the therapist's interventions.

Communicative interventions are primarily concerned with the patient's unconscious communications, which are viewed as perceptive rather than distorted and as an essential guide and aspect of the treatment process. Therefore, while the patient is required to *free associate*, the therapist's task is far more complex and personally exacting. The therapist's attention is diligently focused on the encoded and narrative communications from the patient that are linked to the immediate interpersonal interaction, and especially on those that reveal concerns related to current framework disturbances.

Communicative technique

Langs's (1982) rationale for developing the approach was to address the issue of therapist bias and the formidable inequality of power accorded to the therapist. The communicative therapist makes use of distinct guidelines for predicting, listening, intervening and validating her interventions. In this way, Langs has attempted to place psychotherapy on a more judicious and equitable footing, rather than as the process of merely intervening and interpreting as a result of the therapist's purely subjective formulations and assumptions. The communicative therapist is expected to listen to patients' narratives; before intervening, she waits to hear a number of stories that coalesce around a particular theme. It is also expected that the patient will provide a 'bridge' that will link the theme in some way to the therapeutic situation, as well as some reference to the source or impetus that has prompted the patient's interpersonal concern.

Illustration

Patient A, after complying with the therapist's request to tape-record the session for supervisory purposes, related a story about having hassle at work. He then went on to say,

> Some of the people there really don't know what they are doing. They just try to ingratiate themselves with the bosses. It's hard for me to speak openly and honestly, I'm worried that some of them may even be eavesdropping and putting me in a vulnerable position. They have no integrity, it really annoys me. I wish they would just let me get on with my job.

The patient speaks of people who are incompetent and unprofessional who are trying to curry favour with their supervisors. He then goes on to explain his concern about speaking openly, which under these conditions would leave him exposed. Finally he speaks of their lack of integrity, and his wish to merely get on with the job in hand. His final statement may be viewed as a symbolic request for the therapist to stop impeding the therapeutic process by introducing a third party into the relationship, which would enable the patient to get on with his therapeutic work.

If the patient relates a number of messages with a similar theme then the therapist should be alerted to the particular significance of the ground rules for the patient. However, communications from the patient which allude to unhelpful and damaging behaviour are also likely to give rise to anxious feelings in the therapist and therefore to a natural reluctance to focus on these deprecating messages.

If the therapist is able to discern these interpersonal references, which by and large tend to allude to the therapist's shortcomings, inadequacies or malpractice, then she should be able to formulate a plausible intervention that is based upon the related themes, the bridge and the stimulus that has prompted the patient's material. The therapist is then further required to listen to the patient's response to the intervention in order to ascertain its validity. Validation is also considered in derivative terms rather than conscious agreement. The ensuing stories should contain within them some positively-toned reference, followed by the likelihood of a negative image which will refer to securing the frame in terms of the restrictions and limitations that link to death-related anxieties. The communicative practitioner therefore devotes her professional life to listening for, acknowledging and hopefully heeding the patient's unconscious, perceptive, reflections of the therapist's personal and interpersonal difficulties. In other words the task of the communicative therapist is to scrutinize diligently the patient's unconscious material for themes which relate to her own psychopathology and malpractice in order ultimately to confess them to the patient.

Confession and psychoanalysis

A number of writers have testified to the close connection between the religious confessional and latter-day psychotherapy (for example Ellenberger 1970; Szasz 1978; Brown and Pedder 1979). I apologize to Nietzsche (1882) when he stated that 'God is dead', for it seems that he is very much alive and kicking, and only flimsily disguised in the secular robes of the psychotherapist. Freud's early notion of the cathartic method lends some weight to the beneficial affect of 'getting it all off your chest' in the presence of an authority figure who is in some way directly linked to a higher plane by having transcended the mortal concerns of the mere patient. The religious confessional is used as a method to declare one's sins to God via a priest who is his closest representative, in order that the so-called sinner may obtain absolution. Redemption is therefore acquired through confession, the priest or therapist receiving the sinner's or 'patient's' confession. In their early pioneering work in *Studies on Hysteria* Freud and Breuer wrote about the notion of confession. They explain:

> We meet the same urge as one of the basic factors of a major historical institution – the Roman Catholic Confessional. Telling things is a relief: it discharges tension even when the person to whom they are told is not a priest and even when no absolution follows.
>
> (Breuer and Freud 1893: 211)

Much later on in his career in 'The question of lay analysis', Freud again speaks of confession:

> 'I understand,' says our impartial person. 'You assume that every neurotic has something oppressing him, some secret. And by getting him to tell you about it you relieve his oppression and do him good. That, of course, is the principle of confession, which the Catholic Church has used from time immemorial in order to secure dominance over people's minds'. We must reply: 'Yes and no! Confession no doubt plays a part in analysis – as an introduction to it, we might say. But it is far from constituting the essence of analysis or explaining its effects. In confession the sinner tells what he knows; in analysis the neurotic has to tell more'.
>
> (Freud 1926: 189)

Confession and communicative practice

In the communicative 'confessional', however, these positions are somewhat reversed: it is the therapist's rather than the patient's framework misdemeanours which are considered to be of concern to the patient and which the therapist is required to acknowledge in light of the patient's encoded messages. In this way the patient is felt to gain a sense of interpersonal trust, safety and ego enhancement. Rather than donning the role of some mighty and omnipotent force, it may be said that the communicative psychotherapist aligns herself more with the patient, in contrast to the traditional confessional where two separate individuals of very different status meet with the idea that one of them may receive atonement through the power and presence of the other person.

Nietzsche (1882) somewhat paradoxically refuted the idea of a Supreme Being by proposing that there were no Gods because 'if there were Gods how could I endure it not to be God' (Russell 1961: 719). Although the communicative approach attempts to redress the power imbalance of the therapeutic interaction by its focus on the patient's unconscious supervisory efforts as an aid for the therapist to address her own personal and interpersonal difficulties, it seems that the research that has investigated the motives for entering the so-called 'helping professions' may in itself partly explain the need to harness and maintain a sense of power by either fair means or foul. It may be conjectured that the choice of any particular mode of thera-peutic practice, whatever its theoretical basis, may be utilized by the practitioner as both a therapeutic aid and as a defensive procedure against the therapist's own personal and interpersonal difficulties. The following section will explore this idea in terms of communica-tive practice.

Communicative practice hinges upon the therapist's conscien-tious and scrupulous inspection of their own errors in the consulting room, which are considered to be disclosed to them by the patient in their narratives. The therapist is then duly required to confess these mistakes to the patient and to modify them in light of the patient's unconscious suggestions. It should not be difficult to see how this subversive and radical therapeutic position undermines in one fell swoop the very foundations of mainstream psychotherapy, as one of the major tenets of the approach rests on the assumption that a powerful element of cure is derived from the therapist's – rather than the patient's – admission of their interpersonal difficulties or deficiencies.

Let us be clear what is implied by the use of this term: confes-sion has been defined in a variety of similar as well as contradictory ways. To confess is to be frank, open, to unveil, to 'take the lid off', to 'own up' and to 'come clean'; as well as to unburden oneself. Other descriptions include to confirm, endorse, assure and to be reliable and trustworthy, as well as to acknowledge, feedback, recognize, correspond, support and accept. In contrast confession is also recog-nized as penitence, repentance, contrition, self-reproach and remorse, and, finally, the admission of the existence, truth or reality of something (Carney and Waite 1985: 468–73).

The discerning patient

The concept of transference as a distorted element of the patient's impressions of the analyst is considered from a communicative perspective as a fundamentally flawed, biased and asymmetrical notion. (I think it was Karl Kraus who noted that psychoanalysis is the only business where the customer is always wrong.) The communicative model of human interaction rests upon a very different premise and emphasizes that it is the patient, rather than the therapist who is very aware (albeit unconsciously) and concerned with the inconsistencies, prejudices and distortions that emanate from the therapist's management of the interaction. In this way the therapist is devoted to addressing the implications of the patient's perceptions of the therapist's misconduct. Remaining with the confessional analogy, it seems that the so-called sinner confesses his misdemeanours in order to achieve a position that is more akin to the priest (i.e. nearer to God). It may be said that the patient in mainstream psychotherapy also perceives the inherent split, or difference, between herself and the supposedly healthy therapist and may endeavour in some way to attempt to heal the rift between them.

This idea may in part account for the notion of 'flight into health', or in communicative terms, 'cure by nefarious comparison' (Langs 1982: 298). That is when the patient unconsciously realizes that the therapist is not what they are purporting to be and is therefore experienced as crazier and more needy than the patient. Presumably the need to be more God-like or omnipotent in either the religious or therapeutic sense links to the need to deny the terror of mortality and our inherent vulnerability.

To cure and be cured

When Karl Marx (1970) stated that 'All religion is an opium to which alienated people turn for tranquillisation', he was referring to the population in general, but this statement may also be seen to be especially poignant for those who turn to psychotherapy as a profession. It may be considered as a continuous occupational hazard and pitfall that needs to be consistently addressed as part of the therapeutic process. Anthony Storr, in his discussion on the personality of the psychotherapist, tells of a conversation that he had with the head of a monastery who said that 'everyone that comes to us does so for the wrong reasons', to which Storr added: 'the same is generally true of people who become psychotherapists' (Storr 1979: 165). Guggenbühl-Craig also reiterates this idea and how this particular issue is often ignored. He states:

All people who believe they harbour a desire to help mankind, must also be aware that the preoccupation with misfortune, social maladjustment, ignorance, illness etc, constitutes a very grave psychological problem in itself. In the preparatory training for these professions there is much talk of the difficulties created by 'case' and patients but hardly any mention of one's dark side.

(Guggenbühl-Craig 1971: 153)

Both Storr and Guggenbühl-Craig seem to endorse the idea that our reluctance to address our own difficulties as part of the therapeutic process is a ubiquitous issue which is shameful and therefore needs to be ignored and denied, yet it may well be the pivotal issue which can influence how we function as therapists.

Mother's little helper

Research into factors which may influence the individual to take up psychotherapy as an occupation is relatively thin on the ground. However, Merodoulaki (1994) found that the relationship between and with parents in childhood was an important influential factor in choosing psychotherapy as a career. The psychotherapist as a child was often found to play the role of arbitrator between parental discord; psychotherapists as children were also often a source of emotional support for one or other parent. Therapists also mostly recalled their childhood as difficult mainly due to separation of one sort or another compared to a control group. Other results from research carried out in this area indicate that therapists as children also had a substantial amount of power in relation to their parents. The paper concluded that it would be interesting to investigate whether early experiences have any association with the therapist's theoretical and philosophical approach. Rycroft (1970) proposed that obsessional characters are often attracted to psychology as it seems to hold out the possibility of knowing about and therefore controlling those aspects of themselves and others which are most elusive and unpredictable.

The communicative model of the mind

The communicative model of the mind, unlike its Freudian counterpart, demarcates the operation of the unconscious into two opposing and diverse components. These are classified as the deep unconscious wisdom system and the deep unconscious memory system. The deep unconscious wisdom system, as its name suggests, is considered to experience, process and express insightful and sagacious perceptions of others, expressing these primarily through symbolic and encoded communications. This aspect of the unconscious is felt to be more able to appraise, comprehend and discern interactional disturbances and discrepancies, as it is not subject to the same defences that preoccupy the conscious system and the deep unconscious memory system. Furthermore, derivative communications often allude to interpersonal framework issues, unlike the conscious system and the deep unconscious memory system, both of which tend to deny the significance of appropriate interpersonal limits. The communicative model, while also endorsing the primitive sexual and aggressive aspects of the unconscious system, also emphasizes its paradoxical and superego qualities, especially in terms of anxiety and guilt. Therefore while the deep unconscious wisdom system favours secure frame conditions, the deep unconscious memory system requests and requires a more disturbed framework in order to alleviate anxiety and guilt. Langs (1982) also contends that it is not unusual for patients to seek out a therapist who will provide a pathological mode of relatedness analogous to their early significant interaction. He further suggests that guilt and masochism and an unconscious need for punishment are also influential factors in the patient's selection of a therapist.

Langs (1982) also postulates that while most patients experience an unconscious sense of guilt, therapists in general dread the experience of conscious guilt. Bearing this in mind, the communicative therapist is required to perform her professional duties in many ways that go against the grain. She is expected to and chooses to listen for and respond to the patient's unconscious perceptions about the therapist's shortcomings and interpersonal conflicts.

Anxiety, guilt and psychoanalysis

Melanie Klein (1948), an object relations theorist, revised some of Freud's ideas of the conflictual tension between the life and death instinct by placing the emphasis on aggressive and destructive impulses. From a Kleinian position the newborn baby preserves its fragile sense of self by projecting its aggression externally onto the mother (or breast) in an attempt to deflect the death instinct away from itself during the first three months of extra-uterine life. In the paranoid-schizoid position, anxiety is first and foremost concern for the self and is therefore literally felt as a matter of life and death. The infant's ability to maintain itself is, from this perspective, dependent upon the rejection of its destructiveness.

According to Klein the depressive position begins to arise as the infant is able to gain some sense of itself as an entity, which coincides with its beginning to experience the mother as a whole object. The quality of the infant's anxiety now begins to take on a different tone, and depressive anxiety is initiated to modify the intensity of the paranoid-schizoid position. Klein (1929) considered depressive anxiety, when tolerated, to be the fount of all creativity, and the depressive position a time when the infant can begin to feel depression, remorse, love and concern for another person.

The onset and working through of the depressive position is viewed as a tortuous and poignant struggle that we revisit throughout our lives whenever we experience a loss of any kind, as it entails the acknowledgement of our vulnerability and the awareness of our need and dependence upon others. It is a time when our omnipotent defences give way as we concede our attachment to external objects. Klein (1933) considered that the struggle between love and hate (life and death) was the most compelling of human dilemmas and that the reconciliation of these opposing instinctual impulses is imperative for the achievement of fulfilling and caring interpersonal relationships.

Klein's (1955) concept of reparation was conceived from her observations and analytic work with children at play. She noticed that children consistently tended to display compassionate behaviour after committing aggressive and sadistic acts. Klein also associated the capacity to repair with the experience of guilt. Hanna Segal (1989: 124) explains: 'Guilt appears in the depressive position as a sense of personal responsibility about one's own aggression against the good object.' Later she states: 'Similarly the increasing confidence in one's own reparative capacities lessens the dependence on the external object as well as lessening the need for defensive manoeuvres' (p. 124). Therefore the anxiety and guilt that are activated in the depressive position are considered to be less persecutory and more realistic compared to anxiety that is enacted in the paranoid-schizoid position. Klein (1935) also described the idea of manic defence to explain the way in which the infant or adult may protect themselves from inordinate feelings of anxiety, grief and guilt that inevitably arise in the depressive position. She viewed this primitive defence as a method for the maintenance of omnipotence.

Communicative anxiety

From a communicative perspective (with its reciprocal focus), anxiety needs to be considered in terms of both members of the therapeutic dyad. Langs's thesis is based upon the significance of unconscious communication which is felt to arise as a response to anxiety which the communicator needs to exclude from conscious awareness, precisely because it constitutes a threat. This indirect form of communication therefore serves the individual as a self-protective mechanism, while at the same time revealing (albeit in disguised form) the source of the individual's concern and anxiety.

Guilt and communication

The sine qua non of communicative psychotherapy is the issue of ground rules and the patient's anxieties relating to the therapist's management of the therapeutic frame, which will tend to emerge in encoded form. The therapist's capacity to hear, feed back and manage the therapeutic environment is also related to her ability to contain and tolerate her own anxiety. The Kleinian concept of reparation and its significance for the individual may elucidate its therapeutic influence for both the therapist and especially for the patient. The patient symbolically represents her concern and need for the therapist to be a stable and consistent figure. If the therapist is prepared to heed the patient's advice, it may be said that the patient is able to gain some confidence in their reparative endeavours; which will hopefully mitigate against the need to regress to a more primitive or persecutory mode of relating. At the same time the therapist acknowledges her own aggressive impulses, as expressed through therapeutic errors, which also conveys her recognition and trust in the patient's curative abilities. Furthermore, the therapist displays, by example, her own reparative endeavours, offering a representation of a good object, which may then be introjected by the patient.

Friedman, a communicative psychotherapist, in her paper on the difficulties of learning the approach, suggests that when levels of guilt are not unduly high, then

> guilt is an indication that the therapist is genuinely concerned about providing good treatment, and that he or she has truly heard the patient's complaints about unsound practice. Guilt, however, is often an unbearable feeling so that the therapist may resort to confession or acting out in an attempt to be rid of it.
>
> (Friedman 1987: 173)

Friedman's ideas are also in accord with the Kleinian concept of reparation and guilt in the depressive position.

Searles (1955) also links the therapist's inability to cope with his own guilt and anxiety with a powerful defence for staving off feelings of vulnerability. He explains:

> The therapist experiences guilt in connection with his not meeting the patient's dependency needs fully – even those needs which could not possibly be fully satisfied by anyone. The therapist's need to retain at an unconscious level his own fantasized infantile omnipotence is a potent source of such guilt; he cannot accept his human limitation. He tries unduly much to help the patient by giving advice, and reassurance, by manipulation of his environment in order to shield him from anxiety and frustration, by having extra time with him on an emergency basis and so forth.
>
> (Searles 1955: 135)

Power and psychoanalysis

Goldberg (1993) summarizes Marmor's discussion of Jones's classic paper on 'The God complex' (on the perils of the psychotherapist's authority), stating that

> many who are drawn toward the profession have disavowed their own sense of omnipotence through identification with the supreme being. People with this type of character structure demonstrate intense scopophilia and curiosity about the private lives of others, together with a strong need to be recognised and admired for superior skills in helping others.
>
> (Goldberg 1993: 86)

In this way the analyst and psychotherapist has at hand one of the most readily available and ideal forms of defence and denial to assuage their own anxiety and guilt: one which is, paradoxically, provided by their powerful professional role.

The need to cure others

It seems that the choice of any therapeutic approach may be likened to some extent to the way in which we choose our friends, lovers and therapists. There are of course the overt, conscious motivations, attractions and identifications that influence our choices and that are readily available for us to discern. Nevertheless, the foundation of psychoanalytic ideas is the assumption that it is the more covert, underlying motives which draw and maintain our interest. As Guggenbühl-Craig points out, therapists have little difficulty in applying these principles to their patients, but seem especially reluctant to identify themselves as part of the same species. Fenichel (1945) suggested that sublimation was the only successful defence as it allowed us to express repressed sexual and aggressive drives in creative and socially acceptable ways. Furthermore, the concept of reaction formation, which is defined as a defensive process (defence mechanism) by which 'an unacceptable impulse is mastered by exaggeration (hypertrophy) of the opposing tendency' (Rycroft 1972: 136) might also suggest that a therapeutic approach which focuses on the significance of boundary issues may be likely to attract therapists who are reacting against concerns about personal chaos and interpersonal anxieties and vulnerabilities. In learning the approach it seems that boundary issues per se (getting it right, and personal concerns that focus on stability, control and power) may sometimes take precedence over boundary issues in terms of their meaning and significance for both members of the therapeutic dyad.

Goldberg (1993) elucidates this idea (on the conflict between the need for and the fear of intimacy and closeness in relation to choice of psychotherapy as a profession), stating:

> Numerous reports have suggested that many people who are drawn towards psychotherapy struggle conflictually with issues concerned with relatedness. They are drawn to a service profession in which they identify closely with their clients and yet seem fearful of admitting that their work is a need rather than a vocational choice.
>
> (Goldberg 1993: 101)

It is therefore understandable that many people who do not practise the approach may view it as rigid and over-zealous, since it is not uncommon (especially in the early stages of training) that the technique may be utilized and practised in this defensive way. In so doing, the communicative practitioner attempts to defend herself against guilt regarding damage that she may inflict upon the patient, which relates to issues connected to her own aggressive and destructive impulses. Klein's concept of manic defences that emanate from unbearable feelings of guilt and vulnerability may also throw some light on the practitioner's need: either she wants to hold the therapeutic environment in a rigid way in order to gain a sense of spurious control, or she reflects the anxiety away from herself by blaming the

chaos on the agency or institutional setting. Nevertheless, appropriate acknowledgement by the therapist of the patient's interpersonal
concerns linked to framework disruptions underpins communicative practice; it may be understood in terms of reparation as a creative
and constructive relational endeavour and as a means of expressing
care and concern.

It is therefore the communicative practitioner's professional
responsibility to struggle consistently with issues, both personal
and interpersonal, relating to power and vulnerability, as well
as attempting to be alert to the need and inherent temptation to protect themselves from these existential concerns in the therapeutic
interaction.

I conclude this chapter with a brief vignette from Quentin
Tarantino's film *Pulp Fiction*. This particular scene takes place in a
garage where the two hoodlums Jules and Vincent are endeavouring
to clear up the evidence from their car after Vincent has accidentally
shot and killed their captive.

> *Jules:* I will never forgive you for this.
> *Vincent:* Didn't you ever hear the philosophy that once a man
>   admits his mistakes he is immediately forgiven for all his
>   wrong-doings.

Conclusion

The communicative therapist's prime responsibility is to allow herself to be guided by the patient's unconscious insightful supervisory
and often critical comments on her management of the interaction.
From this perspective the approach may be viewed as a joint, reciprocal venture, as it involves both members of the dyad in both
giving and receiving therapy. In this way the unequal distribution of
power that is generally awarded to the therapist is to some extent
acknowledged and addressed as an integral part of the process.
Although the communicative practitioner willingly engages with
this procedure, it is nevertheless an arduous and sometimes impossible task consistently to listen, heed, and respond to these often
unpalatable interpersonal comments from patients. It is therefore
inevitable, especially in times of stress, that therapists will be unable
either to hear or to focus on the covert messages from the patient and
will instead (as communicative theory suggests) attempt to assuage
their anxieties by disrupting the frame. On the other hand, as proposed in this chapter, when therapists experience heightened levels
of guilt they may attempt to moderate their discomfort by focusing

on the boundaries per se in a rigid manner, or by resorting to confession as a defensive rather than a therapeutic measure.

The communicative approach uncovers the paradoxical qualities of both cure and harm in therapists' activities. Furthermore, as anxiety and guilt play a powerful role in all our lives and intimate personal encounters, it would seem appropriate, vital and ethical that, as a profession, we should attempt to remain open to and aware of the way in which the potential for cure may also be offset by our capacity for its misuse, no matter what therapeutic model we may utilize.

References

Breuer, J.O. and Freud, S. (1893, 1995) Studies on hysteria, *S. E.* 2: 211.

Brown, D. and Pedder, J. (1979) *Introduction to Psychotherapy*. London: Tavistock Publications.

Carney, F. and Waite, M. (eds) (1985) *The Penguin Pocket English Thesaurus*. London: Penguin.

Ellenberger, H.F. (1970) *The Discovery of the Unconscious*. New York: Basic Books.

Fenichel, O. (1945) *The Psychoanalytic Theory of Neurosis*. New York: Norton.

Freud, S. (1926) The question of lay analysis: conversations with an impartial person, *S. E.* 20: 189.

Friedman, P.T. (1987) The making of a communicative psychoanalytic psychotherapist, in *Yearbook of Psychoanalysis and Psychotherapy*, 2: 158–85. New York: Scribner Press.

Goldberg, C. (1993) *On Being a Psychotherapist*. Northvale, NJ: Jason Aronson.

Guggenbühl-Craig A. (1971) *Power in the Helping Professions*. Dallas, TX: Spring Publications.

Klein, M. (1929) Infantile anxiety situations reflected in a work of art and in the creative impulse, in *Love, Guilt and Reparation, The Writings of Melanie Klein*, vol. I. London: Hogarth.

Klein, M. (1933) The early development of conscience in the child, in *Love, Guilt and Reparation, The Writings of Melanie Klein*, vol. I. London: Hogarth.

Klein, M. (1935) A contribution to the psychogenesis of manic depressive states, in *Love, Guilt and Reparation, The Writings of Melanie Klein*, vol. I. London: Hogarth.

Klein, M. (1948) On the theory of anxiety and guilt, in *Envy and Gratitude, The Writings of Melanie Klein*, vol. III. London: Hogarth.

Klein, M. (1955) The psychoanalytic play technique: its history and significance, in *Envy and Gratitude, The Writings of Melanie Klein*, vol. III. London: Hogarth.

Langs, R. (1973) The patient's view of the therapist: reality or fantasy? *International Journal of Psychoanalytic Psychotherapy*, 2: 411–31.

Langs, R. (1982) *The Psychotherapeutic Conspiracy*. New York: Jason Aronson.

Langs, R. (1987) A new model of the mind, in R. Langs (ed.) *The Yearbook of Psychoanalysis and Psychotherapy*, vol. 2. New York: Gardner Press.

Langs, R. (1988) *A Primer of Psychotherapy*. New York: Gardner Press.

Langs, R. (1992) *Science, Systems and Psychoanalysis*. London: Karnac.

Langs, R. (1997) *Death Anxiety and Clinical Practice*. London: Karnac.

Marx, K. (1970) *Critique of Hegel's Philosophy of Right* (trans. A. Jolin and J. O'Malley). London: Cambridge University Press.

Merodoulaki, G.M. (1994) Early experiences as factors influencing occupational choice in counselling and psychotherapy, *Counselling Psychology Review, British Psychological Society*, August: 18–39.

Nietzsche, F. (1882, 1974) *The Gay Science* (trans. W. Kaufman). New York: Random House.

Russell, B. (1961) *History of Western Philosophy*. London: George Allen and Unwin.

Rycroft, C. (1970) *Anxiety and Neurosis*. Harmondsworth: Pelican Books.

Rycroft, C. (1972) *A Critical Dictionary of Psychoanalysis*. Harmondsworth: Penguin.

Searles, H.F. (1955) Dependency process in the psychotherapy of schizophrenia, in *Collected Papers on Schizophrenia and Related Subjects*. London: Maresfield Library.

Segal, H. (1989) *Klein*. London: Karnac.

Storr, A. (1979) *The Art of Psychotherapy*. London: Secker and Warburg.

Szasz, T. (1978) *The Myth of Psychotherapy*. Syracuse, New York: Syracuse University Press.

Chapter 4

The informative value of erroneous questions

James O. Raney

The interrogative mode is one of civilized man's most effective tactics
for putting the other fellow on the defensive.

(George Miller 1967: 125)

Introduction

In this chapter I wish to show how therapists' questions are ineffective and detrimental to the progress of psychoanalysis and psychoanalytic psychotherapy. Derivative listening methods devised by
Robert Langs are applied to brief examples of patient and therapist
interactions. These demonstrate that a technically erroneous question signals a therapist's awareness of unconscious meaning. Questions are powerful interruptions. If supervisors and therapists
examine the communication context in retrospect, especially in
supervision, these errors can provide information that is ultimately
useful to therapeutic progress.

Psychoanalytic psychotherapists, well trained to appreciate the
unconscious and hidden meanings in their patients and their own
communication, still respond unknowingly to the unconscious messages communicated by their patients. These responses are intuitive
and at the moment not recognized as meaningful. The question's
meaning or intent often becomes apparent in retrospect by strong
interruptions and directives to their patients. Questions are one category of strongly directive therapist interventions that are usually
technically incorrect (Olinick 1954, 1957; Dorpat 1984, 1996). Questions signal by their occurrence the therapist's unconscious awareness of some threatening or intolerable meaning in the patient's
communication.

I show that therapists perceive and react to unconscious communications that they do not otherwise apprehend manifestly by way of learned theory or techniques. These unconscious perceptions signal their presence when therapists discard or misapply correct technique. This is the familiar concept of unconscious countertransference that becomes apparent when it becomes problematic and interferes with the progress of therapy. Langs's derivative listening adds an important tool that expands the capacity to recognize and monitor therapists' unconscious countertransference (Langs 1972, 1973, 1978a, 1978c, 1985, 1988).

Derivative listening directs the therapist to the unconscious meaning of the therapist's responses *to the patient*. When a question occurs in a process report of a therapy session, examination of the derivative elements in the patient's narrative before and after the question will often reveal something of the therapist's conflict. When the therapist's question is sufficiently detailed, the question itself will contain derivatives or indicators of the therapist's concern. Therapists may indicate their problem area by omitting the disturbing topic and questioning a more comfortable, often manifest topic. Questions do not address the derivative meaning of patient communication in any useful way. Questions therefore indicate avoidance of the derivatives by the therapist.

Prior work in this area

A few authors have developed good technology to verify or refute specific or individual interventions (Langs 1972, Dorpat 1984, 1996). Robert Langs has developed particular criteria for verification of specific interventions (1978a, 1978b, 1978c, 1985). Despite their utility Langs's criteria, however, tend to be controversial or ignored (Raney 1984). This is unfortunate, because his criteria are useful to study brief line-by-line examples that therapists publish or communicate for other purposes. The specificity of derivative validation with brief examples readily lends itself to open scientific debate.

Human speech is compromise formation (Brenner 1982) and is derivative of unconscious perceptions, emotion and motives. The study of unconscious derivative communication by patients is fairly mature (Smith 1991). Until now researchers and authors working with communicative principles have studied productions of the patient to determine the validity of the therapist's interventions and the progress of the therapy (Langs 1978c; Miller and Dorpat 1996). The interventions of the therapist in the therapy dyad can similarly be studied to determine the intricacy of the patient and therapist

interaction (Langs 1978b). Our patients are already careful unconscious observers of the therapeutic dyad (Ogden 1982; Etchegoyen
1996). I use patient's responses in my examples to demonstrate this
thesis. Each communication from the patient triggers each therapist
intervention, whether the latter are technically derived or intuitive.

Robert Langs proposed a schema with these propositions.
Interpretations are meaningful only when they address *Type 2 derivative* narratives. 'Type 2 derivative' refers to the manifest speech that
is richly symbolic of unconscious meaning. Some recognizable (to
the therapist) allusion to the recent behaviour and management of
the setting by the therapist is included in the definition. This narrative contains symbolic derivative imagery and some direct or thinly
disguised allusion (Type 2 derivatives) to the primary trigger or adaptive context of the therapeutic interaction to that point (Langs
1978b). Such interactions constitute the very important *Type A communicative field*. The Type A field is one in which derivative imagery
is seen as related to the adaptive contexts. The adaptive contexts are
also manifest or very thinly disguised.

Langs has also proposed two other fields. In *Type B communication* words and behaviour are used actively to discharge intolerable
psychological mental contents. Questions, directives, and demands
are hallmarks of the Type B mode and field. *Type C communication* is
dead, non-communicative and aimed at destroying meaning (Langs
1978b). With these modes of communication or relatedness each
party in a relationship attempts to create a communicative field of
the same character.

From the Langsian perspective, *interpretation* of unconscious
meaning into Type B or Type C communicative modes or fields is
fruitless because hypotheses made with declarative statements are
interpreted as action statements (criticisms, directives or questions)
or are responded to as meaningless, irrelevant or annoying. Meaningful interpretations are misinterpreted as action statements in the
Type B action discharge field and are destroyed in the Type C non-
communicative field. They are thereby not available for observation.
Whether technically derived or intuitive, each communication by
the patient triggers each therapist intervention. Validation or refutation usually follows each therapist intervention. Langs's derivative
validation method 'reads' the disguised symbols in both therapist
and patient narratives.

The intervention most likely to affect a non-communicative
mode or field confronts the patient with the evidence of the defensive action or meaningless mode of communication at moments that
the patient might be best receptive to hearing. Such observations are
usually not heard, are strongly resisted and require tactful repetition.

Questions may represent efforts to surmount these difficult resistant responses, and to maintain a non-communicative mode and field, rather than move it to the interpretive Type A communicative field. Questions signal the absence of the important interpretive Type A communicative mode and field. Questions may also be an effort to convert one communicative field into another. Questions might force a Type A mode to a Type B or C mode. Questions might also be an effort to convert a Type C mode when a therapist feels bored or somnolent.

In psychoanalysis or psychodynamic psychotherapy obvious errors in technique are usually attributed to countertransference, therapist defensiveness, incorrect theory and other causes. Such errors are usually forms of inadvertent enactments. As such they are opportunities for recovery, reflection and understanding of the object relations in the transference (Chused 1991). Shifts in communicative modes (for example moving from declarative statements to questions, from speaking to silence, etc.) are indications of signal anxiety and resistance. These are usually 'downshifts' to more action modes or primitive defences. These are also opportunities for intervention when patients initiate such shifts. When therapists initiate such shifts, they signal their own anxiety and resistance to some imminent or obvious meaning.

A therapist may mistakenly consider that his or her interventions are correct, even when not validated. This suggests personal reasons (countertransference) for not listening to the derivative refutation of the intervention. The therapist may rationalize that the patient has, because of transference, not agreed with or heard the interpretation, rather than that it might be incorrect. The proof of validity and precision of the intervention awaits the patient's substantial response.

The narratives of each person in an interaction can be considered associations (Durkin 1965) that are consciously and unconsciously linked. Interventions of the therapist influence the statements of the patient. The interventions of the therapist are in turn stimulated by the response of the patient. The therapist's interventions and the patient's responses link to become a sequence of mutual associations that follow one after the other. Therefore we recognize derivative images of the perceptions and of the unconscious processing in the communication of both the therapist and patient. The net dialogue constitutes the communicative field with discernible ebbs and flows of resistance. Often this resistance appears as shifts of the types of communicative fields.

Many interventions by therapists lack symbolic detail. So do narratives of patients. When patients offer few or no symbols, little or no meaning can be hypothesized. Therapist interventions still can be considered important *indicators*, even when devoid of symbolic derivatives. Indicators signify some neurotic problem or resistance in the communicative field.[1] Any person in the field communicates indicators. Some interventions, as I shall show, do not richly convey unconscious meaning of the problem or the underlying fantasies (Langs 1972: 7; Langs 1987a).[2] The intervention's timing, intensity, repetition or similar non-symbolic aspects will nevertheless still *indicate* the presence of problematic meaning. Questions powerfully[3] indicate meaningful areas. When questions contain symbolic images they become additionally useful derivative sources that suggest the nature of the unconscious meaning.

Questions are not interpretations. They do not interpret unconscious meaning. Questions are grammatically consistent. Questions are directive, ambiguous and powerful *action discharge*, and therefore Type B elements. They tend to create action discharge rather than evoke symbolic and revealing communicative fields (Langs 1978b). They are prima facie evidence of the existence of a Type B communicative field. They are explicit or inferred imperatives rather than observations. Questions do not clarify unconscious meaning (Dorpat 1984), even though that may be their aim in the therapy setting. They are vehicles for projection and especially for projective identification. In psychoanalytic psychotherapy questions create an interrogation state in which it is impossible to provide the right answer. Questions bypass the patient's observing ego or therapeutic alliance that is vital to the therapy (Greenson 1967). Despite these contradictions, therapists generally consider questions to be legitimate interventions.

Questions often signal that the therapist wishes to re-project a disturbing projective identification back 'into' the patient. Rather than identify with the unpleasant role assignment, the therapist, by questioning, attempts to deflect or re-project the role assignment (Ogden 1982). This role can often be identified in the derivatives of therapists' interventions, or in the next derivative story that follows the question. Questioning is one of the most effective diverting interventions in the therapeutic armament.

A therapist's question is a particularly sensitive indicator of unconscious and disturbing meaning. Questions are sometimes subtle. They may appear in an otherwise apparently valid interpretation. The appearance of a question in a case narrative can alert us to some disturbing meaning that is usually 'encoded' in the narrative communications of the patient. Impulses to question, then, are sensitive responses and indicators of perceptions of unconscious meaning. Questions may be incorrectly timed and formulated interventions. Once made, however, they are 'in play' as indicators of some important unconscious meaning in the patient's communication.

Plan of this study

I shall describe several brief examples of psychotherapy dialogues. Each contains a therapist question. By examining the patient's narrative, then the question (or questions) and, finally, the following narrative, I show that the therapist 'heard' the unconscious communication, enough to react with a question. The question either tends to lead to another topic or away from the level of difficult meaning. With the latter, for example, the question may suggest that the therapist is somehow inept in the particular idea or meaning that the patient is trying to project or productively identify 'into' him or her to an important degree.

Typical data in psychoanalytic and psychotherapy reports are edited and selected summaries. These examples are very useful evidence, as my study requires brief sections of conversations. These examples, not originally published for the aims of my study, are therefore 'blind' to my purposes. Questions are embedded in enough narrative to allow illustration and verification possibilities. Each vignette has enough background to hypothesize adaptive contexts (Langs 1973) or triggers (Langs 1988). From my sources[4] I discarded examples that did not meet these criteria. From these data I make conjectures about the *indicator* quality[5] of the therapist's question (Langs 1982: 126 ff.).

Questions have been studied as indicators of the therapist's negation of the patient's meaning (Olinick 1954, 1957, 1980; Dorpat 1984). These papers, however, have not specifically suggested that therapists discern the patient's unconscious meaning before asking the negating question. The therapist may come upon the awareness and meaning of the questioning event only in a post hoc analysis of the motives for the questions (Dorpat 1984; Chused 1991). Dorpat writes that he has 'not found one instance in which the validity and value of questioning can be confirmed in the patient's responses . . .' (Dorpat 1984: 70). The perspective that I take is slightly different. I believe that I have found therapists' questions to be *informative* and therefore valuable, although usually only *in retrospect*.

Case examples

Example 1

The questions in this example (Gabbard *et al.* 1988) demonstrate that this therapist unconsciously perceives the patient's unconscious meaning. Presumably the therapist is moved to speak and to negate meaning by his anxiety (Dorpat 1984) and thereby to relieve his own discomfort.

The patient begins the hour by saying that he is not getting any-where in therapy. He is angry that the therapist refused to grant him a fourth hour per week. After several minutes he describes a dream.

Patient: I had a dream last night – that I think I understand – I want to get some reflection from you – like I had just dozed off at one point – and I was back at my parents' house – and had been running up and down stairs to the front porch – the outside stairs – and just about all I could see were the stairs and that this was *twice the length*[6] that it actually is – *thinking about the length of a regular staircase* – and I would go up until I could see the top step of the porch – the porch is wood – and I am on my mother's porch – this is hers – she spends a lot of time on it – and I immediately turn down, and I run back down the stairs – and when I get to the sidewalk at the bottom of the stairs, I go up and down – I'm doing this over and over – and I'm thinking 'my mother's porch', and then this *other idea flashes through my mind* – 'and your wife is up there now too' which I guess is related to the fact that – within a few weeks our divorce is going to be final – and *I think* – as *I've thought* about this – *what it means, you know*, do I go up the step to the porch and do whatever it is that my mother wants me to do or do I go down the steps and away from the house and live my own life; and then as I go back up, well my wife is up there and – allied with my mother – not only do I have to do what my mother wants, but I've got to do what my wife wants me to do . . . and again this is stuff that I'm putting on her because she's not laying a lot of expectations on me financially; kinds of things which part of me is willing to do and part of me is angry about doing, but I'm going to do them because it – because the healthy part of me knows that that's what I want to do and that's the right thing to do for her and for the kids – but *I think* in a way that's kind of a paradigm of my life – *going up and down the stairs* – or back and forth or whatever analogy you want . . . trying to

figure out what to do to please people who are important to
me . . . and trying to figure out what it is to please myself – I
don't get anywhere, because I don't go far enough onto the
porch to ask my mother or ask my wife 'what is it that you
want me to do?', and I don't get far enough away from the
sidewalk to figure out what it is that I want to do [*pause, five
seconds*] you know – maybe there's another meaning or
symbolism to the dream – I don't know – that's kind of what I
came up with.

The therapist makes an intervention.

Therapist: Did you have any – did any thoughts come to your
mind about – the stairs – these long stairs? The staircases?

The patient has already made five references to thinking about
the dream and thoughts about the dream. He has also revealed some
of his speculations. He refers directly to 'thinking about the length of
a regular staircase' at one point. This therapist's question has been
answered before it was asked. The therapist signals clearly that he is
interested in the stair symbols and wishes to focus on them. At the
same time he suggests that he has not heard or has forgotten that
the patient has referred already to thoughts about the dream. The
patient's dream is rich in possibilities from several theoretical vant-
age points. We can find derivatives of unconscious perception and
ego influences. Frame modifications tend to be important adaptive
contexts and tend to be first-order organizers of derivatives.[7] Using
these perspectives we can find derivative allusions to the struggle
over the request for an added day (the derivative: trying to please
myself vs. trying to figure out the wants of someone else). The
therapist, however, alludes only to the staircase. By doing so he
diverts the focus from the other dream elements, especially away
from the important theme of compliance vs. independence. This
implies a devaluation or rejection of the other ideas (Olinick 1957).

The patient responds to the question by seeming to feel pressure. He notes, for example, that what he is about to say is hard and
that he is aware that he resists it. With a brief pause the patient seems
also to compel the therapist to speak rather than listen to and think
about patient's communicating that he has difficulty in expressing
ideas. The therapist's question implicitly denies (Dorpat 1984) his
own observation.

Has this therapist *perceived* the derivative message of the
patient's response to the dispute about the request for added time?
His question suggests that he, the analyst, has thoughts in his mind
about the stairs, the long stairs, etc. The *dialogue* that continues may

be revealing. The patient may have discerned that the specific of the question suggested something sexual.

> *Patient:* It's hard – I really resist that, because somewhere in the back of my mind is this concept that going up and down stairs – in a dream – has sexual connotations –

The patient, perhaps because of the absence of response by the therapist, repeats his self-observation that something is hard. He then describes a number of sexual allusions. He includes a derivative of incestual feelings in one of his talks with another doctor. He refers to another dream of himself as a little girl, sexual attractions to father, mother, oedipal complex, psychology courses, his penis mutilated or cut off, fear of women and castration fear.

Because *any* intervention perturbs the subsequent patient associations (Arlow 1985: 24–5), these associations or narratives must be studied as *reactive*. Each verbalized idea is responsive to the patient's memories, motivations and needs, as well as to the patient's perception of the therapist's intervention.[8] The net verbalization is a compromise among all of these that the ego determines as acceptable finally to the analyst-listener/transference object (Freud 1923; Brenner 1982).

The patient in this instance produces a flood of sexual ideas in response to the question of whether he had any thoughts. He speaks of another dream that includes a transformed sex, sexual attractions to father and to mother, oedipal complex, genital mutilation, fear of women and castration. The timing of this production is compliant to please the therapist (like a little girl, to please father, to castrate himself). The sexual theme is suspiciously explicit and elaborate. These may reflect his estimate of the *therapist motives* as well. The non-derivative elements of these ideas suggest that the patient unconsciously considers the therapist uninterested in his volunteered thoughts.

At this point the therapist *interrupts him in mid-sentence* with this question:

> *Therapist:* And one of the questions is why is this coming up – and why are these sexual concerns and the reaction to them coming up now?

This sexual focus appears to disturb the therapist. The therapist *interrupts* the patient (who is carrying out his directive) and *by his impatience* notifies the patient that he cannot tolerate some meaning. The therapist's directive, interruption and directive (again) *indicate* the disturbing content. The sexual nature of the disturbance appears in the patient's subsequent derivatives.[9]

The patient then alludes to another patient to whom he is attracted. He raises the possibility that sexual feelings may be a way of masking his anxiety about real treatment issues. He thinks that sexuality is one of his treatment issues and that he is not supposed to talk about it.

The patient here 'interprets' by way of derivatives. He (or someone) is allowing sexual feelings (anxiety) to mask real treatment issues. This is a profound observation. The derivative allusion to another patient to whom he is attracted infers that his therapist may be doing the same thing. This variation on the sexual attraction theme involves another patient (displacing the idea from the immediate therapist–patient dyad). Sexual feelings may be a way of masking his anxiety about real treatment issues! His anxiety here represents identification, at least in part, with the therapist's projected anxiety.[10] He lastly identifies that sexuality may not be talked about, even though it is one of his treatment issues.

The patient confirms that this therapist feels overwhelmed by the transference of his patient and possibly vice versa. Sexual issues may be important, but the central emphasis is on the fear of direct expression hidden by the patient's derivatives and the therapist's manifest bewilderment that he conveys with questions. This hypothesis finds support in the therapist's earlier refusal to add an additional hour and his preference for a single dream. He might better have waited for more associations or addressed the dream's broader thematic possibilities.

Example 2

This patient has engaged in four-times-a-week analysis for about two years. Some time before this vignette the analyst settled a dispute by forgiving a fee for a cancelled hour. Since then and after months of discussion with her supervisor, the analyst and patient agreed that the patient would pay for all scheduled sessions. The analyst has not been comfortable with the new fee arrangement.

> *Patient:* I was in your rest room taking a leak when I thought: What am I going to say? (*pause*) I had a dream: I was on a trip and apparently did not plan to have enough money for the trip. I then thought that I should have enough money. Maybe this dream is related to an interview I had with a company (*pauses*). Now I have hit another brick wall. My thinking is like a maze. Not that that is the thought that goes through my mind (*pauses*).
>
> *Therapist:* Not that that is the thought that goes through your mind. What do you think of that?

The patient has made several brief but evocative allusions. He then refers to a thought but does not speak it. This seems seductive. The analyst takes the bait and mimics the patient's sentence. She then asks the patient what he thinks of 'that'. 'That' seems to refer to the sentence just echoed. The analyst's timing was good, as the patient was both resistant and self-observing at that point. She addresses the withholding resistance, but weakens her intervention with a question.[11] This resembles example 1 where the question *restricts the patient's response*. This question excludes all the content that preceded the patient's final statement. This excluded content includes an explicit reference to activity in her rest room, a reference to insufficient money to complete a trip, an interview followed by a pause, a brick wall, and to thinking that is like a maze. By isolating this content the therapist signifies that she has perceived something that troubles her. Two likely possibilities are bathroom intimacies (sex) and money.

The question creates another difficulty. The patient has just compared his thinking to a maze. The question assigns a difficult thinking task to this maze-compared thinking. Further, the question repeats the patient's sentence that is presumably a product of his maze-like thinking.

The patient's next response seems coy, non-committal or passively resistant. He repeats a version of the analyst's echoed intervention. His repetition of the analyst's intervention may be the best that he can do with a mind that he perceives to be maze-like.

> *Patient:* Well I guess that that 'that' is there. That has to be a thought.

This therapist cannot wait and intervenes again.

> *Therapist:* You have used that before – like going in and not feeling prepared – and you are not prepared for this session either.

This intervention could indicate by derivative the analyst's own state that explains her earlier awkward intervention and question. The derivatives in this observation suggest that the analyst is aware that she was not prepared to deal with all of the patient's communications. She seems to refer to an earlier idea that does not appear in this sequence for material to express the derivative. The patient replies:

> *Patient:* Yes. It must have to do with the money here. But you are also not communicative. It is not nice to be taken off guard by a question – without being prepared. With my parents, I would procrastinate or just not communicate.

> When my father would talk about the facts of life, it was so embarrassing for both of us.

The patient takes the intervention as a criticism and criticizes back about being taken by surprise with the question. He also brings in an allusion to sex (the facts of life) that he displaces to a historical reference. This derivative suggests his unconscious perspective that both he and the analyst have a problem with talking about sex. The analyst keeps up the projective pressure:

> *Therapist:* Your way of surviving unconvertible situations – so you procrastinate or just not talk.

The patient is not daunted. He needs to agree manifestly, and then to dig deep to find a dream that places the onus back with the analyst, disguised in dramatic derivatives.

> *Patient:* It is, isn't it? And that brings back (*hesitates*) a dream. A group of ladies is singing. It is like gospel music. A guy leading the group is dressed up like a band leader in a military-type uniform. But he is prancing around with his fly open and wearing a giant dildo-like penis. It's funny. Like the dream – it came and I felt hesitation to tell it.
>
> It is not what I like to do – free sex – the dildo – I wanted to be freer, but not prance around like that. I had to put a check on my feelings – mother is a model of frustration with her, 'Now look what you have done. You bad boy! You have made me cry'. She might know she is wrong – her idea that adults are the smart ones.

The patient wants to be freer and not limited by the therapist's incorrect directives. The analyst locates the problem 'in' the patient. The patient agrees with apparent relief. Then through the dream symbols the therapist is described as acting like the leader but has inappropriately exposed her sexual concerns and inhibitions at the same time. He hesitates, it is funny, and then the next derivative sequence compares the analyst to his sexually frustrated and frustrating mother.

Example 3

In this example – from weekly private psychotherapy with reduced fee, a single woman in her twenties and a male therapist – the therapist appears to frighten himself. On this date she arrived late and said:

> *Patient:* Look at this. I'm ten minutes late. It probably has to do with you being unwilling to reschedule the last meeting. I knew that some of the scheduling was not going to work out.

(She continued to speak of memories of her father, of emotionally losing him as a child. She noted that she has seen the therapist's face in her mind.)

The therapist interprets that she associated the therapist with her father. She seems to agree and then expresses guilty feelings about criticizing the therapy work as being defined by money. She then says:

> *Patient:* Too bad I'm 29 years old and I still deal with my feelings by acting them out this way and having temper tantrums and being late.
>
> *Therapist:* Oh, I see, when you came into the hour you had mentioned that your being late had to do with my not rescheduling as you had wished. You feel that it is a kind of temper tantrum?
>
> *Patient:* Yes, I can intellectually see it that way. The chain of events is undeniable, even if I don't feel it fully emotionally.

The therapist first notes the link between the patient's father and the therapist. He next links being late with not rescheduling. He questions whether she feels that the being late is a kind of a temper tantrum. The question emphasizes a link between temper tantrum and being late. The more important and likely links are the analyst (she sees his face) and his refusal to reschedule as symbolically and emotionally linked to the emotional loss of her father.[12] This diversion signifies the analyst's unconscious awareness that it is his not rescheduling (holding the frame) that triggers the sense of loss and associated memories of loss of father. He has also thus far ignored the implication of her age reference, that she feels regressed, as a child in relation to the analyst. That the analyst is aware of this may be signified by his weak allusions to being late and temper tantrum.[13]

This emergence of more direct feeling is the likely result of the analyst holding the frame and not responding to her defensive efforts to move him.[14] *Because he has kept the frame secure*, her feelings of connection and yearning are stronger, yet still defended with reversal, avoidance and displacement. The therapist's question then suggests that the therapist *has unconsciously perceived* the immediate threat of the disguised missing/yearning/loving affect about him rather than the manifest temper tantrum. The therapist may fear the potential for dissolution of boundaries from evoked transference and countertransference emotion with this patient (Dorpat 1984). He fails to note that his patient has *lessened the disguise* of her immediate loving affect in response to his *keeping a boundary* (the schedule). The directive value of the question is powerful and her immediate feelings about the therapist remain disguised.

The patient does not provide unconscious confirmation. Her next sentences strongly suggest only manifest compliance. She responds with, 'Yes, I can intellectually see it that way . . .' She unconsciously discerns that the therapist wishes to be obliged. She then *refutes* his interpretation and reconfirms her original statement with the 'intellectually' qualifier. She further disconfirms, '. . . even if I don't feel it fully emotionally'. The therapist's intervention thus supports rather than identifies the defensive structure. *At this moment she and the therapist are aligned in defence against the immediate and most difficult affect.*[15]

Example 4

This woman in her twenties has been concerned about hostile impulses towards her 4-year-old son and about her inability to feel loving with her husband. She talks for several months about attractions to other men. She has just begun a new job that makes finding time to get to her analytic hours difficult.

In this hour the *analyst is five minutes late*. The patient describes not knowing what to talk about, that she had been busy this morning as she is covering for her male co-worker's cases. She notes that her husband seemed especially loving the night before. His feelings have changed; he is more open and emotional. She wonders about how an affair would work. Her husband has been very supportive and thoughtful. She found her husband sitting in her office when she returned after yesterday's analytic session.

The analyst then asked: 'Who is supporting whom?'

This question clearly directs the focus to the relationship of the patient and her husband. The analyst ignores the similarity with her husband sitting in her office when she arrived and the likelihood that she was sitting in her analyst's office when he arrived. His question nevertheless applies to the patient–therapist relationship as if he does not note his tardiness. At some point the patient must 'cover' for him as with her male co-workers. She has already answered – and his question informs her that he has unconsciously heard it, but he cannot acknowledge that he has. In several ways she has already, through derivatives, informed him that she is supporting (covering for) the analyst. She offers another version that neatly condenses her perception of and hopeful revision of the question and answers him again. She adds, however, that a fight might be brewing and that he is disingenuous in his question.

> *Patient:* Oh maybe he is being supportive by letting me be supportive to him. My mother called. She and my father

have had a big fight. Now (*ironic*) I am her big friend. I asked her when my father was going to pick up (*she names her son*). That stopped me. It seemed possessive – well – (*She pauses.*)

She runs out of derivatives and the analyst maintains the projective pressure (Langs 1978b).

Therapist: What stopped you?

This is notably ambiguous as she describes stopping and then stops her narrative. This could refer to either or both. The patient is similarly ambiguous in her response.

Patient: I'm not sure. The words 'my father'. Maybe because mother also said, 'He sure is your father'. It is odd. I never would say 'my mother'. Father once said, 'You have never done anything for anyone' and an aunt told him off. It felt good to tell mother that I had problems with my marriage, but that I would not be coming home. (*silence*) You seem particularly restless today. (*silence*) I thought a while ago that you were going to say something but I kept talking. Maybe I wanted you to talk.

Therapist: Why, then, did you keep talking?

Something is interrupting this patient's narrative. She struggles with trying to bring the trouble into the therapy itself, where it probably belongs. The therapist again demands that she, rather than he, explain the problem. She gamely struggles to speak, and says, very likely, all that she knows consciously. She cannot speak of the lateness and the directive questions except to say that she feels interrupted.

Patient: I guess I have trouble when you say things – it interrupts my train of thought, I disagree, and it bothers me.

Something disturbs this therapist. He is late. He does not mention his lateness. The first stories by the patient suggest a changing, more affectionate spouse. A hint of an inappropriate relationship (an affair) appears as if unrelated to the thread of the narrative. She describes her husband sitting in her office when she arrived; a counterpart of her waiting in the therapist's office when he arrived. She had also mentioned covering for her co-workers that morning. She does not seem ruffled until later. That the husband has appeared affectionate and supportive of her may refer derivatively to earlier progress in the therapy. The odd appearance of an affair may indicate some inappropriate element, however, such as the therapist acting on his feelings by being elsewhere during the first five minutes of her time. The affair reference might be too close to the therapist's unconscious or conscious countertransference feelings, for example guilt over being late, or some of his own fantasies. This prompts his first *interruption* that directs her (back) to her relationship with her husband.

The therapist's first question (Who is supporting whom?) connotes, by way of a telling derivative, that to this point it is *she who supports* the observation and all the meanings of his lateness! The question directs her away from this event. The respective roles of therapist and patient are confused and reversed.

That she can be so frank and direct, however, suggests some trust in the therapist. This may make this an aberrant moment in the therapy. Perhaps because of prior effective work and trust, the patient has shifts in her capacity to express her feelings. This shift catches the therapist by surprise and prompts him manifestly to misinterpret, interrupt and interfere with the progress.

Conclusion

These examples are typical of many similar examples that occur in psychoanalytic therapy supervision and appear in the professional literature. This contribution supports several previous papers (Olinick 1954, 1957, 1980 and Dorpat 1984, 1996) that argue against questions as a component of valid psychoanalytic therapy technique. Supervisors and therapists alike might test the validity of my hypotheses in their own work.

The perspective on questions that is described in this chapter can be used by supervisors to identify specific areas of countertransference interference in the work of their supervisees. Therapists themselves might note the impulse to ask questions as indicators of unconscious transferences or unacceptable projections and identifications.

Notes

1 This may be the case whether the intervention is considered well timed or not, or well formulated or not.
2 I do not specify that the problem or resistance is in either patient or therapist, but in the field. 'Resistance' (to progress or discovery) in psychoanalytic therapy is the product of both parties. When the interaction itself is utilized as informative, as I shall show, the term 'resistance' or 'problem' does not exactly apply.

3 The reader may supervise, consult or listen to case reports from a similar perspective to confirm or refute this assertion.

4 I have disguised the examples without removing the essential features. Disguise for confidentiality has dictated that I do not credit or cite some of the authors of the examples. I express my thanks and great appreciation for their anonymous contributions. I assume the authors suitably disguised the cited case examples.

5 For convenience these questions may be termed therapist-indicators (Langs 1985: 30).

6 The italics are mine. I have used italics in this vignette to highlight the elements that I discuss in the next paragraphs.

7 For example, frame security or modification usually impacts the patient more than spoken interventions (Langs 1985: 92 ff.)

8 I use 'perception' in the broad sense here. I mean 'perception' as an active process that attributes meaning from both the transference and non-transference impingements at that moment.

9 The patient may perceive the interruption itself as a sexual/rape act by the therapist?

10 This is not to say that the patient is not anxious. His own anxiety and prohibitions make for ready reception and resonance for introjection of the therapist's projections and projective identifications.

11 If this were a 'close following' interpretation (Davison *et al.* 1990; Gray 1994) the timing is correct because the patient has alluded to an unspoken thought and then paused, presumably defensively. According to the Langs communicative schema, the pauses and hesitations constitute indicators, and the money theme is symbolically represented. A direct reference to the analysis that would give a better clue to the indicator has not yet appeared in this example. The analyst might wait for a better elaboration of the derivative complex and a more clear representation of the adaptive context before intervening. The question, however, directs neither the defence nor motive that prompts the withholding of the thought and pausing. The analyst in this case was aware of the defence manifested in these two components, but may have felt unprepared to make the more specific correct interpretation or to deal with the prospect of the unknown that might follow the lifting of the defence.

12 While this emotional tie could be the anger or temper, it is not likely she would emotionally miss anger and temper.

13 In the previous example the analyst also unconsciously avoided the regression and intensification of the transference that follows a good interpretation or frame-securing intervention (not granting a request to alter the frame). In example 2 the analyst makes a timely intervention but then interrupts the regression (perhaps signalled by the 'echolalia'). He supplies the derivative explanation that she is not prepared for this. In this case, example 3, the analyst has held the frame, which encourages regression. The analyst notes the transference link in the father allusion, but deflects from the crucial meaning, that she feels loss, and has regressed to angry child state with the analyst.

14 We could imagine here that her effort to influence the analyst to change

the frame is an effort to enlist him to help avoid the pain of loss. If she pleases him she may perpetuate a magical idea that she can keep the therapist/father and avoid the loss.

15 The analyst might offer evidence here that anger and lateness is defensive in itself, and indicates still another category of feeling. Her defensive inhibition or resistance to feel and speak directly of her emotional feelings about the therapist continue, but has weakened. This has frightened the therapist. This example illustrates how such resistance has become a shared enterprise.

References

Arlow, J.T. (1985) The structural hypothesis, in Arnold Rothstein (ed.) *Models of the Mind: Their Relationships to Clinical Work*. New York: International Universities Press.

Brenner, C. (1982) *The Mind in Conflict*. New York: International Universities Press.

Chused, J. (1991) The evocative power of enactment, *Journal of the American Psychoanalytic Association*, 39: 289–308.

Davison, W.T., Pray, M. and Bristol, C. (1990) Mutative interpretation and close process monitoring in a study of psychoanalytic process, *Psychoanalytic Quarterly*, 9: 599–628.

Dorpat, T.L. (1984) The technique of questioning, in James Raney (ed.) *Listening and Interpreting: The Challenge of the Work of Robert Langs*, 55–73. New York: Jason Aronson.

Dorpat, T.L. (1996) *Gaslighting, The Double Whammy, Interrogation, and Other Methods of Covert Control in Psychotherapy and Analysis*. Northvale, NJ: Jason Aronson.

Durkin, Helen. (1965) Personal communication.

Etchegoyen, R.H. (1996) Some views on psychic reality, *International Journal of Psycho-Analysis*, 77: 1–14.

Freud, S. (1923) The ego and the id, *S. E.* 19.

Gabbard, G.O., Horwitz, L., Frieswyk, S., Allen, J.G., Colson, D.B., Newsom, G. and Coyne, L. (1988) The effect of therapist interventions on the therapeutic alliance with borderline patients, *Journal of the American Psychoanalytic Association*, 36: 697–727.

Gray, P. (1994) *The Ego and Analysis of Defense*. Northvale, NJ: Jason Aronson.

Greenson, R. (1967) *The Technique and Practice of Psychoanalysis*, vol. 1. New York: International Universities Press.

Langs, R. (1972) A psychoanalytic study of material from patients, *International Journal of Psychoanalytic Psychotherapy*, 1: 4–45.

Langs, R. (1973) *The Technique of Psychoanalytic Psychotherapy*, vol. I. New York: Jason Aronson.

Langs, R. (1978a) *Technique in Transition*. New York: Jason Aronson.

Langs, R. (1978b) Some communicative properties of the bipersonal field, in R. Langs, *Technique in Transition*, 413–72. New York: Jason Aronson.

Langs, R. (1978c) Validation and the framework of the therapeutic situation, in R. Langs, *Technique in Transition*, 381–411. New York: Jason Aronson.

Langs, R. (1982) *Psychotherapy: A Basic Text*. New York: Jason Aronson.

Langs, R. (1985) Workbooks for therapists, *Listening and Formulating*, vol. II. Emerson, NJ: Newconcept Press.

Langs, R. (1988) *A Primer of Psychotherapy*. New York: Gardner.

Miller, G.T. (1967) *The Psychology of Communication*. New York: Basic Books.

Miller, M.L. and Dorpat, T.L. (1996) Meaning analysis: an interactional approach to psychoanalytic theory and practice, *Psychoanalytic Review*, 83: 219–45.

Ogden, T.H. (1982) *Projective Identification and Psychotherapeutic Technique*. Northvale, NJ: Jason Aronson.

Olinick, S.L. (1954) Some considerations on the use of questioning as a psychoanalytic technique, *Journal of the American Psychoanalytic Association*, 2: 57–66.

Olinick, S.L. (1957) Questioning and pain, truth and negation, *Journal of the American Psychoanalytic Association*, 5: 302–4.

Olinick, S.L. (1980) *The Psychotherapeutic Instrument*. New York: Jason Aronson.

Raney, J. (1984) Narcissistic defensiveness and the communicative approach, in J. Raney (ed.) *Listening and Interpreting: The Challenge of the Work of Robert Langs*. New York: Jason Aronson.

Smith, D.L. (1991) *Hidden Conversations: An Introduction to Communicative Psychoanalysis*. New York: Routledge.

Chapter 5

Moments of mystery and confusion: transference interpretation of acting-out

Vesna A. Bonac

... and so he has no fear, because the source of fear is in the future, and a person freed of the future has nothing to fear.

(Milan Kundera 1996, *Slowness*)

Introduction

Psychotherapy can be a rewarding struggle towards enlightenment. However, before we reach a satisfactory completion, before we shake hands with our patient in a last farewell, we have been through patches of dense fog and we have faced dark mysteries. I would like to address such moments in therapy when the therapist might suddenly feel confused, when things no longer seem to make sense, when our professional expectations are met with their very opposites. I believe that without a communicative resolution of such puzzling and alarming moments in therapy our last handshake might very well mean a premature termination of our patient's treatment.

Communicative psychoanalytic psychotherapy prides itself on clarity of understanding through systematic and disciplined analysis of the patients' communications (for example Smith 1991). Applying the communicative method of listening to the patient's verbal material, the therapist is rewarded by gaining access to the most vital meaning of the patient's inner struggles – even when the patients themselves are amazingly unaware of what they are conveying. Training in communicative psychoanalysis provides the therapist with skills fundamental to the scientific approach (Bion 1961). One learns to pay attention to the minute details of each moment in a session, to identify patients' unconscious perceptions, to translate

narratives into the language of the present of a session and to monitor continuously the state of the analytic frame. A communicative
therapist is alert to the common but striking dissonance between
what patients would sincerely like us to believe that they need from
us on the one hand, and what their unconsciously communicated
verbal material conveys. These complex, albeit essential, therapeutic
skills and knowledge have been provided to a new generation of psychotherapists by the American psychoanalyst Robert Langs through
his teaching and numerous written works (for example 1975, 1976a,
1978a, 1978b, 1979a, 1979b, 1981, 1982). The views presented in
this chapter are based on my private practice of communicative psychoanalysis and my research of the therapeutic process. The communicative way I listen to patients and the way I intervene has
brought considerable clarity and efficiency to my clinical work. I can
say that my patients leave most sessions with a greater sense of
understanding in a specific, albeit limited, area of their functioning.
My communicative interpretations explain to the patient how a specific event, related to the analytic frame, has a profound impact on
the patient's functioning and symptoms. When I hear unconscious
compliments, like 'my aunt was so good at teaching music that she
could take a tone-deaf child and make them play well', or 'my father
was an expert at identifying wild mushrooms – he taught me to distinguish the edible from the poisonous' – I know I have done well. I
leave such sessions tired but refreshed and with a new sense of trust
in the communicative technique.

    None the less, there is a vital area of clinical experience, the
understanding of which has eluded communicative technique for
some time and which has caused, I believe, occasional but significant
misunderstanding of our patients (see also Quinn 1992). I am referring to the relatively rare but none the less quintessential moments
in therapy when our patients create a salutary situation in their therapy, when 'all seems right with the world', yet the patients suddenly,
unexpectedly and alarmingly turn against the therapist and against
themselves. Such a sudden shift in the patient comes as a total surprise to the therapist who struggles to regain the balance, attempting to understand the sudden attack on the analytic frame by
anxiously searching for the triggering event for this change. The confusion and the sense of persecution the therapist is experiencing is
real: nothing at all happened that could constitute a trigger for the
sudden change in the patient. The sudden turn of events pulls the
rug from under the therapist's feet – the therapist is thrown into the
eye of a storm. Such moments in therapy can quickly become very
dramatic and accelerate into chaos: the patient might act-out or
leave therapy in a huff.

Occasionally, such confusing moments are less turbulent. They might pass almost unnoticed by the therapist and leave barely a ripple in the surface of the therapeutic interaction. None the less, all such events seem to leave a silent residue of festering mistrust between the patient and the therapist: unconscious, thus ever-present.

A historical overview

Acting-out by patients has been widely discussed in psychoanalytic literature, in particular by those analysts treating borderline and schizophrenic patients. I shall mention only the pioneers in the field. Freud (1914, 1920) introduced the term and established a basic definition of acting-out as the enactment of unconscious fantasies in the relationship with the analyst in analysis, or in the outside life of the patient. Freud stressed the function of acting-out as a resistance against remembering. Later observations of Fenichel (1945) and Greenacre (1950) were similar: they found that the analyst's failure to interpret the transference at the earliest appropriate time is an especially important source of acting-out that becomes difficult to manage. Johnson and Szurek (1952) reported that they observed children who acted-out their parents' unconscious antisocial impulses. Barchilon (1958) discussed clinical cases where the therapist influenced the patient to act-out the therapist's unconscious solutions, with little relevance to the patient's therapeutic needs.

In his 1958 paper on schizophrenic vulnerability, Searles subtitled one chapter 'Acting-out as a response to, or vicarious expression of, the therapist's unconscious processes', where he explored an important aspect of acting-out not previously discussed in psychoanalytic literature, namely the patient's pathological and visually grotesque behaviour during sessions which was found to be a direct 'acted-out behavioral response to, or expression of, unconscious elements in the therapist' (Searles 1965: 209). Searles termed such behaviour 'introjective acting-out'.

In his unique presentation in 1966, Jose Bleger (1990) discussed the psychotic patient's extreme sensitivity to the changes in the fixed aspects of the analytic frame. He concluded that the impingement on the frame by the actions of the patient represents the most 'perfect' expression of repetition compulsion since it is 'the most complete, the least known, and the least noticeable' to the analyst (Bleger 1990: 422). For Bleger, such psychotic transference involves an even more primitive phenomenon than what Klein observed as the repetition of primitive object relationships.

In his paper on transference, Szasz (1963) discussed the analyst's evaluation of the patient's behaviours. His position on acting-out is similar to that of Klauber (1968). They both consider the possibility that the analyst's personal bias, his or her inner state, as well as the nature of the analytic relationship, may all influence the analyst's evaluation of the patient's behaviour as transference-based or as acting-out, to the extent that their evaluation becomes essentially a subjective judgement.

At the 1968 symposium on acting-out, Anna Freud (1968) proposed that the term 'acting-out' be confined to those behaviours of the patient which are related to the analytic situation and the transference. She emphasized that, although acting-out may be the only way in which aspects of the forgotten past become available for analysis, it remains difficult for the analyst to determine the limits within which acting-out behaviours can be 'accepted' without endangering the analytic work. At the same symposium, Grinberg (1968) focused on the destructive and the communicative aspects of acting-out. He related acting-out to the process of projective identification, that is, the patient is in search of a container. Earlier, Grinberg discussed acting-out as massive projection of the patient's internal objects into the analyst: the patient's gestures and words were observed to be used as instruments of actions. Mitscherlich-Nielson (1968) related acting-out behaviours to the feelings of guilt and the wishes for revenge. Rangel (1968) focused on the resistant and communicative functions of acting-out. Greenacre (1968) discussed the adaptive and maladaptive functions of acting-out. She noted that actions can also function as efforts at reality testing, and thus be part of the therapeutic progress. Earlier, Greenacre (1950, 1963) studied acting-out as resistance in the transference relationship with the analyst, which has important pathogenetical factors. In 1969, Brenner defined acting-out as an unconscious expression, in behavioural terms, of some aspects of transference, and found that the acting-out of transference feelings and fantasies is universal.

Joseph Sandler (1976) extended the concept of transference firmly into the realm of object relations with his novel observation of 'role responsiveness'. He found that the therapist may not become aware of such role pressures by the patient until they have been carried over into action. In a discussion of Sandler's concept of role responsiveness, Troise and Quinn (1991) point out that Sandler's seminal contribution to the understanding of the therapeutic process 'does not adequately address the patient's attempt to impose a role on the therapist by having him agree to a modification in the framework of treatment' (p. 174). This observation concerning the frame is in agreement with the findings of Robert Langs (for example 1973, 1975, 1976a), who found that it is the changes of the analytic framework which have the greatest impact on the therapeutic interaction, and that patients (and their therapists) express their pathology through modifications of the therapeutic frame (Langs 1984/5). Both of Langs's findings constitute the fundamental principles of communicative psychoanalysis.

In 1976, Robert Langs (1976b) termed efforts at re-enactment 'living out', and observed that authors, writing from the traditional psychoanalytic point of view, saw factors which underlie efforts at living out 'primarily as intra-psychic'. Langs developed an original method of clinical observation which makes it possible for the therapist to identify the non-transference aspects of behaviours. He emphasized that it was important to 'offer criteria for identifying the behaviors with important unconscious transference implications, and for separating those behaviors from those lacking in such pathological genetic components – thereby distinguishing pathogenic forms of living out from primarily adaptive actions' (Langs 1976b: 85). In the same publication, Langs comments that 'little attention has been paid to the analyst's own unconscious need to involve the patient in his own re-enactments, or to prompt the patient towards living out' (p. 86). In his classic *Psychotherapy: A Basic Text*, Langs (1982) defines all changes in the analytic frame as acting-out.

Critique of much of psychoanalytic writing on acting-out by communicative authors has been, in my view, a fair assessment of the common errors in the prevalent psychoanalytic technique which allows the analyst indiscriminately to blame the patient for acting-out by way of the analyst's routine interpretations of transference. In spite of the recent increase in the interest in countertransference and in the interactional nature of the therapeutic process in psychoanalytic literature, actual clinical practice seems to be still heavily weighted in favour of unrestrained transference interpretations.

A Canadian psychoanalyst Hassan Azim and colleagues conducted extensive clinical research on the 'accuracy' and 'dosage' of transference interpretations (Azim *et al.* 1992). They found that there is an inverse association between the high concentration of transference interpretations on the one hand, and the quality of the therapeutic alliance and the outcome of therapy for neurotic patients. The finding, that there might be something harmful in the way this most vital of psychoanalytical 'tools' – the interpretation of transference – is clinically applied, is noteworthy.

In the present chapter I shall attempt to show what needs to be done by the therapist in order to make a correct interpretation of acting-out. I shall outline a clinical technique that enables the therapist to determine when the source of acting-out lies within the patient, thus calling for an interpretation of transference. I shall also put forward a thesis that such acting-out, of which the source lies solely within the patient, albeit within the context of an offered secure frame by the therapist, constitutes the patient's clinically observable expression of transference proper. The chapter will end with a new definition of transference, first proposed in a previous paper (Bonac 1996b).

Clinical example

A middle-aged woman had been in once-weekly private treatment on the couch with a woman communicative therapist for almost a year. The patient's initial complaints – of recurring paralysing depression, serious inhibitions at work and difficulties with sustaining relationships with men – had shown considerable improvement. At the beginning of her treatment the patient was informed about the dates of the therapist's yearly summer holiday. The patient had been reminded of the therapist's approaching summer holiday several times during the previous two months prior to the holiday, as themes of 'people going away' appeared regularly in her associations. The patient's material included motifs of 'people coming back from trips in a refreshed state of mind' and of those 'left behind who were able to use the time alone profitably and creatively'. The therapist's approaching summer holiday was clearly the event, related to the therapeutic frame, which was triggering the current mild disturbance in the patient and which gave meaning to her derivative communications.

The patient's concurrent, consciously experienced affect was that of optimism and competence. Her newly gained awareness of the link between the therapist's impending holiday and her own current efforts at adaptation also evoked memories of 'important people who had died of old age' as well as the consciously experienced affect of normal grief. In the few months preceding the summer holiday, the therapist felt that the patient was working-through the pending temporary separation gradually, yet thoroughly and successfully, and that the patient was coping with the approaching interruption of her therapy sessions remarkably well. The patient appeared equipped with a new understanding of the previously unconscious meaning of temporary separation and loss. There were no breaks in the fixed frame, initiated by either the patient or the therapist, during this time.

A startling turn of events occurred in the two sessions before the therapist was scheduled to leave on holiday. During the penultimate session, the patient announced, in an uncharacteristically nonchalant manner, her 'impromptu' decision to 'take a trip' starting on the very day her therapist was due back from holiday. The decision 'felt so right' to the patient, its 'spontaneity had the promise of adventure'. Yet she 'still wanted to know' what the therapist 'thought' about her decision. The therapist was able to show, using the clear derivative meaning of the patient's verbal material, that her planned trip had the unconscious function of magically negating the effects of the approaching loss (of sessions) and of the nearing summer separation (of patient and therapist), and that it was an attempt to punish the therapist ('an eye for an eye') for having caused the patient distress by planning to go away. The patient's displaced and symbolized narratives revealed a 'failed attempt to reach an important goal' through a 'fateful short-cut', with a narcissistic 'display of extravagance' and through 'false impressions' of well-being 'instead of through understanding gained by hard work', leading to 'bitter disappointment in the end and missing out on life'. The unconscious affective experience of the patient's intention to introduce an unnecessary further interruption of her treatment was conveyed by images of suicidal depression.

There was little doubt that her consciously experienced elation at the prospect of travel was a precarious manic attempt not to experience the unbearable suicidal depression caused by the patient's own decision to go away. The patient showed evidence that, by two sessions preceding the therapist's holiday, she was able to cope with some aspects of the triggering event (i.e. the approaching holiday), but not with some other aspects (i.e. the return to treatment after the holiday).

By the time of the penultimate session, however, it became evident that the patient was not yet ready to deal with some other aspects of the approaching holiday. The presence of the patient's active, dynamic-in-session, mostly unconscious anxiety was revealed by the sudden announcement of her rash plan to travel. Her abrupt decision – that is, the intention to act-out – represented the patient's failed attempt at containing the prospect of resuming therapy after the holiday: 'failed', because the patient's announced travel actually increased the length of her absence from therapy and thus aggravated her already distressed affective state. In addition, her rash decision (which was characterized as a 'failed attempt to reach an important goal' through a 'fateful short-cut' instead of 'through understanding gained by hard work' and ending in 'bitter disappointment' and 'missing out on life') gratified her pathological narcissistic, rather than healthy, needs.

At the end of the session, the patient announced that she would take her holiday at the same time as her therapist. This positive development left the therapist with a conveniently smug conviction that the patient had successfully mastered all the issues related to this holiday and that she was fully prepared for the scheduled interruption in her treatment. The analytic frame was thus resecured by the patient herself before the beginning of the last session.

The last session before the holiday

When entering the office, about 15 minutes before the beginning of this patient's session, the therapist saw the patient at a distance in the public corridor: the patient was unusually early. It was apparent to the therapist that the patient made an effort to make eye contact. The therapist chose not to give any immediate sign of acknowledgement of the patient in the corridor. In the past several months prior to this session, the patient had been entering her therapist's waiting room on time, a few minutes before the beginning of her session.

The last session before the holiday started on time, with the patient talking about her successful handling of changes at her new job, how well she was adjusting to the new environment and to new people. She had had a good week away from home and was looking forward to coming home at weekends to her boyfriend. She was looking forward to coming to this session, although she was somewhat anxious about what to talk about. Then she remembered her chronic loneliness as a child and believed it was the main reason for her frequent dramatic acts in adolescence. There were times when she suddenly left her family and dashed off to be alone somewhere. After feeling 'unbearably submerged and limited' by her family, she would 'escape' its confines by 'disappearing' for a while to be alone. What still puzzled her was the way she handled this being alone. Soon she began to feel frantic, even suicidal. To handle this new anxiety, she would plunge into some creative work: she would join a group of singers, or a fitness group and become totally absorbed in what others were doing. Or she would start a new business with others and 'devote her life' to that project for a while. She would be very creative.

In all such dramatic and intense endeavours, the patient would always do things for others. She would bend over backwards to suit others – or, rather, what she imagined others would need or want. She would not wait for others to express their needs or to tell her of their expectations. She would volunteer to do things for people. She remembered how, as a very young child, she was desperately hungry to be noticed. It bothered her that she so needed to be needed. She so craved the attention of others that she would bend and twist her own person to fit others: she was considered a 'good and helpful' girl. She realized this was not good for her: what she was doing limited her greatly.

The patient said she could now see a definite pattern to her life, from very early on: she would be in a relationship which would, for some reason, become unbearable for her, then she would suddenly break away and escape to some other place, alone. Soon her sense of loneliness would become intolerable and she would become desperate for company. Then she would look for, and find, people who were doing something, whatever, and the patient would offer to work for them. She would then proceed silently to mould herself to fit others. She was perceived as an altruistic and cooperative sort of person, when in fact she 'sacrificed her own soul to alleviate unbearable feelings of loneliness'. She would give in to what she thought others expected. Her very creative acts were really not free. She was overcome by anxiety in the end and she ended such 'helpful endeavours' as abruptly as she had begun them. There was no continuity in her life and she was not successful even though she had a good mind. 'What a shame!'

Incredibly, particularly in the light of the past several sessions in which intense working-through of the approaching holiday took place, the patient's dramatic material in this last session totally lacked any direct reference to the most important current event: the therapist's imminent holiday. The patient also did not refer manifestly to her coming to the session early or to her seeing the therapist in the corridor. The patient was therefore unaware that there was any deep connection between the meaning of her free associations on the one hand and the frame-related events: the therapist's holiday, the patient's decision in the previous session to come back to sessions on the same day as her therapist, the patient's coming early to this session, the patient's seeing her therapist outside the office, as well as the therapist's not greeting the patient in the corridor.

Securing the analytic frame

At this point I would like to call attention to the frame-securing function of the patient's change of mind, from a rash, frame-breaking decision to go away and to miss several more sessions, to the patient's own frame-securing decision to resume therapy as scheduled. I shall argue that the therapist's interventions in the previous sessions created an offer of an increasingly secured analytic space for this patient, which in turn generated in the patient the unconscious experience of secure-frame anxiety (see also Langs 1981). The origin of this secure-frame anxiety was separate and distinct from the patient's realistic anxiety due to the imminent interruption of treatment by the scheduled holiday. Although announced by the patient, the decision not to stay away longer than her therapist was not reached spontaneously by the patient. On the contrary, the decision represented the opposite of what the patient had intended to do at the beginning of that session. The patient's frame-securing decision was the result of the therapist's efforts towards a securing of the frame by way of communicative interpretations of (a) the damage to the patient by her own intent to stay away longer, and (b) the patient's own deeply unconscious model of rectification which explained how to correct the situation.

Nevertheless, the most critical trigger for the patient's unconscious experience appeared to be the therapist's announcement that she will be present in her office for all of the patient's sessions after the holiday. Although, in the session before the last, the therapist did not introduce any changes in the frame, the therapist's interpretation and announcement represented an attempt at securing the frame by offering to keep the planned time for the resumption of sessions regardless of what the patient would do. The therapist thus offered the patient an opportunity to 'regain' her therapist right after the summer holiday. The patient's previous 'decision to go away' had, before the decision was reversed, destroyed the scheduled resumption of therapy for certain, and had left the continuation of therapy uncertain.

This is a typical example of every correct communicative interpretation being also a frame securing intervention, affecting both participants in the bipersonal field of the therapeutic interaction (Langs, personal communication 1991). I have discussed in more detail in three previous publications (Bonac 1993a, 1993b, 1996a) the interactional and the experiential aspects of the securing of the frame and repercussions of the manner of such securing for the therapeutic process.

There was another aspect of the frame, first broken (by the patient) and then secured (by the therapist), immediately preceding the beginning of this last session before the holiday: the therapist did not join the patient in establishing a contact between them outside the analytic space.

Let us now focus on the ramifications of the two important events of the securing of the frame before the beginning of the last session: (a) the planned resumption of therapy on the scheduled date and (b) the keeping to a minimum of the extra-therapeutic contact between the patient and her therapist.

Intervention 1: playing-back of derivatives

About 20 minutes into the session, the therapist first intervened with the playing-back of derivatives. The therapist said that there seemed to be something in the patient's therapy which was making her anxious. In some way she seemed to be reminded of the way she felt and acted throughout her life. The therapist then gave a summary of the most compelling themes in the patient's material, bringing into focus the motifs of the verbal material. The therapist concluded her intervention by saying that the patient had described a lifelong struggle to alleviate feelings of unbearable loneliness by sudden frantic escapes and by offering to serve the real or imagined needs of others while sacrificing her own spiritual growth. Since both the therapist and the patient witnessed their brief eye contact in the corridor, the therapist included in her intervention the statement that what the patient was talking about may also have something to do with what happened in the corridor before the session.

Thus the therapist centred her intervention on two dominant motifs: first, the patient's derivatives coalesced around repetitive themes of 'struggling to alleviate feelings of unbearable loneliness of suicidal proportions with frantic plunges into new relationships or new work'. Second, the therapist pointed out the theme of the unbearable confines of intimate relationships, like families, which ended in the patient's ultimate search for other people to serve in self-destructive ways.

Immediately after the therapist's intervention, it 'suddenly occurred' to the patient that this was her last session before the holiday! The patient still did not consciously refer to her own previous decision to come back to therapy as scheduled, to her coming to the session early, or to seeing the therapist in the corridor. Thus the patient became aware of the relevance to her inner struggle of the summer holiday. However, she remained unconscious of the dynamic relevance of her own frame-securing intent (to come back to therapy as scheduled) and of her consequent frame-breaking acting-out (coming to session early and seeking out the therapist in the corridor).

The patient continued to free associate and remembered what it was like growing up in her family. She was chronically lonely as a child as far back as she can remember. Her parents would go off to work and leave her alone, feeling abandoned. The most terrifying thing was that she could not play. She became anxious to the point of paralysis, waiting in terror for her parents to return. So often they returned late and did not let her know that they were back. They barely noticed her existence! When her parents did not come into her room at night, she remained awake through the night, not knowing that they had come back, terrified that they were gone for ever, afraid that she would die. On the rare occasion when they did come in to kiss her goodnight she did feel safe and she slept well.

The patient went on and remembered the neighbourhood children. With them, she pretended to be dull and stupid because she believed they would not accept her as a bright girl. She desperately wanted to blend in with the others. Teachers at school were convinced that she was 'slow': she had played dumb and became dull. Yet underneath she always knew that she was clever and capable. What a waste! Still, sometimes she was brave.

She remembered one time when she offered to walk to the shop to buy milk and bread in a heavy snowstorm. Her mother did not permit her to go because it was 'too dangerous' but her father seemed proud of her offer and let her go. Carrying groceries, she felt strong and worthy of respect. She arrived home tired, wet and cold, but proud of her achievement. Her mother never gave her the chance grow strong. Her mother was herself so afraid of the world that she did not allow the patient to join the neighbourhood children at play for fear that 'she might be injured'. Her father was right to have left her alone to handle her own young life. A few bruises with children were better than being confined to her flat by her mother, alone, watching other children play and grow strong. What she did to herself in later life was just as damaging. She constantly needed to find someone to serve.

Intervention 2: interpretation of acting-out as transference

At this point the therapist offered an interpretation. As this was the last session before the holiday, the therapist decided to mention all of the frame-related events even though the patient did not. A second reason for this inclusion was the patient's theme of 'playing dull and becoming dumb': the therapist did not want to sanction the patient's defensive and self-destructive pretence of ignorance by not talking about the events that they both witnessed before the session.

The therapist said that it seemed that the patient's unusually early arrival to her session and her seeing her therapist in the corridor was perhaps somewhat related to what she was saying. The therapist pointed out that the patient's painful memories of loneliness and the terror she felt as a child (when she thought that her parents had not returned home and had forgotten her very existence) were perhaps related to what the patient was experiencing before this last session. Perhaps the patient found it difficult to trust the therapist's promise to come back on time and to be present for all of her sessions as scheduled. Perhaps the patient was in terror that she would be forgotten and abandoned by her therapist the same way that she had been afraid as a child.

The therapist continued that it seemed that the way her parents handled their coming home might still exert a profound effect on the patient in the present: she is about to wait for the therapist to come back. The therapist also said that there was something paradoxical about the patient's anxiety because it became unbearable at the very moment the patient herself promised to come back at the same time as her therapist. Anxiety appeared at the very moment when the patient secured the scheduled resumption of her therapy. Perhaps, the therapist continued, the patient had little solid ground to stand on when she was faced with a future reunion with someone important. Perhaps her parents had betrayed her trust so many times in such a terrifying way that she no longer had the faith to wait for someone who promised to return. It seems that she dreaded the possibility of betrayal by her therapist to the extent that she was unable to wait and find out.

To prevent yet another experience of the terrible loneliness, the patient did what she had done so many times before in her life: she offered to serve the imagined needs of others and to mould herself to what she thought others expected: perhaps her coming to meet her therapist in the social milieu of the public corridor was such an offer to serve the therapist. The therapist also said that it seems that her (the therapist's) refusal to make social contact in the corridor resembled her father's allowing the patient as a child to be independent and to do something brave. Perhaps the therapist did what the patient believed her mother should have done with the neighbourhood children, that is, to let the patient handle other people in the corridor on her own, without the crippling protection of the mother – or of her therapist.

The patient nodded several times while the therapist spoke. Then, after a short pause, the patient said that there must have been something sadistic about her parents to have let her lay awake at night. There must have been something sick in their minds if they did not to need to come and embrace their small child before bed-time and to make sure that she was all right. She had pleaded with them so many times not to forget to come in and kiss her goodnight. More often than not they did not come.

The patient then remembered her grandfather who had died in her teens. Now, this was a man of his word! He always kept his promises, no matter how difficult. He was a real 'mensch' and was respected in their community. Unlike so many adults, when her grandfather made a promise, even to a small child, he kept it! He took everyone seriously and people relied on him.

When the session came to an end, the therapist stood up announcing the time. As the patient was leaving, there was yet another surprise: the patient said that she had in her purse a cheque to pay for the two sessions. She realized it was the middle of the month. She did not know why she brought this cheque. Actually she knew that she was supposed to bring it to the first session of the next month. There was a pause, and then she said she would bring it again after the holiday. Then the patient left.

Discussion

The session ended with the discovery of yet another acting-out by the patient based on her unconscious belief that the therapist was in need of money. This premature cheque very likely represented yet another attempt by the patient to alleviate unbearable feelings by moulding herself to the imagined needs of others. The important point here is that the cheque had been written before this last session and was therefore a reflection of the anxiety in the patient generated by her own previous re-securing of the frame, namely her decision to come back to sessions on time after the holiday. The fact that the patient did not present the cheque at the beginning of the session (as usual) can be understood as the consequence of the therapist's behaviour in the corridor when the therapist did not show signs of needing the patient.

The dramatic ending of this session testifies to the gravity of the patient's unconscious anxiety and to her propensity for acting-out to alleviate anxiety. The patient's associations, after the inter-pretation, came in two parts, as predicted by the communicative theory of unconscious validation (Langs 1982). First, the patient remembered something about her parents which explained more deeply their harmful behaviour. The second part of the patient's verbal response contains a positive, solid figure from her childhood who was reliable because he kept his promises.

The memory of her parents' sadism represents the 'cognitive' part of the patient's validation of the therapist's interpretation, while the second memory of her grandfather indicates that the patient had introjected the therapist's promise of coming back to sessions on time. The positive figure is also a derivative representation of the patient herself: she decided to keep her promise and come back to therapy on time. The patient's memory of her parents' sadism is also a derivative representation of the patient's unconscious understanding of her own sadism towards her therapist when she was considering leaving her therapist waiting alone for her to come back to sessions.

Unconscious cognitive validation, discovered by Langs (see Langs 1982), is a complex concept and a difficult phenomenon to identify in the material. It is important to remember that it was manifested only after the frame had been secured, after this patient had changed her mind and decided to come back to sessions on time and after the correct interpretation had been offered to the patient. The most confusing and mystical moment thus comes after the interpretation, when the therapist has achieved, and conveyed to the patient, a new level of clarity. What most confuses the therapist is the fact that the negative theme (of the terror caused in the patient by her late-returning parents) emerges precisely at a time when everything is all right and secured in therapy and when the patient has been offered an explanation for her paralysing fears. The therapist who does not expect the emergence of this paradoxical moment might feel quite disoriented and might momentarily doubt her understanding. The therapist's loss of balance and the patient's propensity for disorienting behaviour following a correct interpretation is a common communicative observation.

The mystery and confusion of the therapist can be explained by the logic of the temporal sequence of events. Only after the patient has worked through all the aspects of a change in the frame – that is, only after she feels completely secure about her situation (she is coming back to therapy because she is able to believe in the therapist's promise to be back) – only then is the patient capable of enduring the devastating truth about the sadism of her own parents. Only after the patient understands the extent of her own resulting inability to trust others is she able to face her own sadism, introjected from her parents as a child. This sadism was observable in the session before last, when the patient announced her decision to let the therapist wait for her return. Thus the patient effectively forced the role of a 'terrified child, waiting for her parents' return' on her therapist. The patient also turned this same sadism against herself: the delay would keep her apart from being reunited with her therapist, the very thing that she so longed for.

For the patient, the confusing and disturbing part of this situation is obvious: as long as she remains unconscious of the inner terrifying meaning of her waiting for the resumption of therapy, her only conscious awareness is that of expecting an 'adventure', albeit with powerful unconscious anxiety which drives her rash and frantic acting-out. The patient broke the frame by acting-out as a last attempt to break free of the state of her unconscious and intolerable anxiety in a frantic, manic and automatic attempt to change her situation. We are reminded here of Bleger's (1990) words describing the patient's impingements of frame as least 'visible' to the therapist in terms of meaning; of Sandler's (1976) observation of the therapist's propensity for 'role responsiveness' to the patient's unconscious pressures; and of Langs's (1984/5) finding that patients express their pathology through 'breaks in the frame'.

The immediate problem facing the therapist is thus the lack of 'visible' meaning, hidden in the acting-out, and the difficulty of handling the acting-out without being pulled into joining the patient in action, while the therapist waits for the patient to reveal the meaning via verbal derivatives. The patient's unconscious need to act-out before this session was the result of her inner struggle between her unconscious mistrust of the therapist, based not on any history with this therapist, but on the pathogenic introjection of her parents' behaviour, long ago – and in spite of the trust that her therapist had gained in other respects in the course of her therapy.

This material shows, as do all sessions with similar frame situations, that the expectation of a future event (for example the return from the holiday) is wide open to the destructive effects of traumata from the patient's past. Since there are no perceptions possible about something that has not yet happened, every event that lies in the future is thus open to the influence of our expectations of this event. Our expectations are, in turn, heavily and mostly unconsciously influenced by our past experiences whenever when we are faced with the same situation. This power of past events to influence our expectations of the future lies in our veridical unconscious perceptions, as recorded in our memory, of actual and specific past events. This is how our past silently determines our future. As in the case of this patient, it looks like we are all open to the ravages of our damage from the past at times when we find ourselves in a situation that resembles this past: that is, when we find ourselves in an interpersonal frame which is of the same kind as the one that led to the past traumata.

In this precarious and unstable situation of expecting the future, there is only one straw that can hold us afloat: the other person must be as solid as the patient's grandfather. In therapy, the patients need to be able to rely on their therapist or else therapy ceases to be therapeutic. If the therapist is not solidly grounded in the reality of his or her own role as therapist and does not keep proper boundaries, there is chaos and blind acting-out. At best there is *folie à deux* (for example the therapist accepting the social contact in the corridor would begin, for a limited time, a new role). At worst, the traumatic past is repeated for the patient and the patient's neurotic or psychotic difficulties are reinforced (for example the therapist is not in her office for the scheduled resumption of sessions and thus enacts the patient's defensive demand for an extension of the holiday).

To prevent repeating past traumata of our patients it is important for the therapist to maintain a constant and firm offer of the psychoanalytic frame. With the 'offer' I mean just that: we cannot expect the patients to mould themselves into 'our' frame. They need their own space to express their pathology in any way they can, including breaks in the frame. When the patients are forced into the therapist's frame by the actions of the therapist, when the therapist secures the frame instead of waiting for the patients to work through all their difficulties with the frame, the therapists are acting out of their own deep anxieties. The therapists reveal that they are not capable of waiting for the patient to do their part of the therapeutic work.

The reasons are many: a typical reason is that some therapists cannot bear to allow someone else to do the work on their own, at their own pace, independently. Some therapists make prisoners of their patients by self-righteously securing the frame every time it is broken by the patient, while their sadism gets reinforced by watching their patients struggle with claustrophobic anxiety and with the sense of powerlessness and guilt for not being 'ideal'. Such therapists are themselves a victim of their pathological expectations of the tragedy of failure in their patients.

We must not try to fit the patients into our Procrustean bed of the ideal frame. Ideally, we observe their behaviour and we listen to their derivatives while all the time we tell them explicitly of our offered frame. For example the therapist told the patient that she would be present for the patient's sessions at the scheduled time after the holiday. The patient would be expected to pay for all the sessions for which the therapist was present, whether the patient was there or not – as had been stated at the very beginning of her treatment. In this case, the combination of the therapist's actual presence and her expecting of payment for the sessions is what constitutes her offer of an ideal frame. The context of this firm offer – and this is the critical point – is what makes it possible for the patient's response (verbal, symptomatic and behavioural) to be independent of any pathological influence from the therapist and thus to be a manifestation of transference proper.

Such a moment in therapy is experienced as uncanny and mysterious by both the therapist and the patient. The situation is maddeningly illogical: the therapist knows what is good for the patient, the patient knows what is good for her, the patient decides on her own to do what is good for her. And yet, there appears out of the blue this intolerable anxiety and such destructive derivative representations of dread, paralysis, fear of death, abandonment and dangerous neglect. The danger is that the therapist might feel accused of having perpetrated these destructive deeds. How can the patient talk about abandonment and fear of death when the therapist will be waiting for her, at the very moment when the patient herself had decided to come back to therapy? Things do not make sense. The patient's derivatives are experienced as accusations and lie heavily on the therapist's heart. A well-grounded therapist, who is not susceptible to accepting blame masochistically, might begin to suspect that something irrational might be happening within the patient.

The interpretation of transference is thus effective even though the claustrophobic anxiety, generated by the securing of the frame by the patient, is present but not overwhelming, because it is explained at the very moment transference is manifested. The absence of any therapist's contribution to the patient's acting-out ensures also that the realistic hurt and resulting anger will not be inflicted on the patient since there is no 'blaming of the innocent' by the therapist (see for example Searles 1965). As a result, no unnecessary realistic anxiety is generated in the patient.

In this session, there was no reality base for the patient to feel anxious about the therapist's return. The yearly holiday was not a trauma for the patient – it was in fact an event to which she was adjusting well, as the material in the very beginning of the session demonstrates. What was traumatic to the patient was her own expectation, with no basis in the past or present relationship with this therapist, that her therapist might not return to resume therapy. As has been shown, this expectation was based on the patient's own early life experiences with her parents. The expectation was the patient's unconscious, dynamic-in-session fantasy about a future event and could be identified as a clear transference response to the 'coming back' aspect of the holiday. Transference response involved the patient's effort to re-create in therapy the same traumatic frame conditions as her parents had enacted with her and which was at the root of her terror, her chronic and unbearable loneliness and mistrust.

The patient's mother used the safe and confined space of the home, not for protection, caring and the cultivation of independence, but as a space where broken promises, abandonment, terror and unnecessary confinement took place. Often enough, her mother had changed a space designed for safety and growth into a space of dread and mistrust that stifled the spiritual growth for this patient.

Conclusion

In actual clinical practice, therapists might have less opportunity to give interpretations of transference than to interpret their own breaks in the frame. I hope that the above clinical example and discussion help explain why transference manifestation requires very particular and unique circumstances, as defined by the state of the analytic frame. I also hope that the discussion made it clear why the interpretation of transference demands both sophisticated clinical skill and the solid personal stability of the therapist.

None the less, therapists must not miss any opportunity to interpret transference and thus explain to the patients the sources of their inner difficulties which put obstacles in the path of their personal progress and which bring them, and those around them, pain and suffering.

My clinical work and my observations of unobstructed child–mother interactions (Bonac 1994), as well as the skill and wisdom I have received from the teaching and writing of Robert Langs – all within a larger context of the deep well of knowledge comprising the psychoanalytic literature on transference – led me to formulate the following three propositions as building blocks of my theory of transference (see also Bonac, in press).

Proposition 1

A general definition of transference proper in terms of the bipersonal analytic frame:

Transference proper is defined as patients' paranoid response to their own intended securing of the analytic frame, as offered by the therapist, when the frame-breaking triggers by the parents in the patients' past drive the patients' own frame-breaking indicators in the present therapeutic relationship.

Proposition 2

Motivation for acting-out: The patients' primary unconscious motivation for acting-out and for breaking the analytic frame is their effort to evoke urgently-needed therapeutic response in the therapist in the form of containment and interpretation of the acting-out.

Proposition 3

Psychogenesis of the transference response: The parents' pathological changes in one aspect of the child–parent frame in the past
are responsible for the child's inability to tolerate the same aspect of
the secured frame (termed 'secure-frame anxiety') in later life, which
results in the adult's pathological breaking of that same aspect of the
secured frame in any interpersonal relationship, including psychotherapy or psychoanalysis.

References

Azim, H.F.A. *et al.* (1992) 'Dosage' and 'accuracy' of transference interpretations in short-term psychoanalytic psychotherapy. Conference paper,
Second Annual Research Conference of the International Psychoanalytical Association, 'The Transference', March 1992, London.

Barchilon, J. (1958) On countertransference 'cures', *Journal of the American
Psychoanalytic Association*, 6: 222–36.

Bion, W.R. (1961) *Experiences in Groups and Other Papers*. London: Tavistock.

Bleger, J. (1990) Psycho-analysis of the psycho-analytic frame, in R. Langs
(ed.) *Classics in Psychoanalytic Technique*, 419–27. New York: Aronson.
Reprinted from *International Journal of Psycho-Analysis*, 48: 511–19.

Bonac, V.A. (1993a) Clinical issues in communicative psychoanalysis: interactional aspects of requests for premature termination as reflections of
secured-frame anxiety in adult and child psychotherapy, *International
Journal of Communicative Psychoanalysis and Psychotherapy*, 8: 67–78.

Bonac, V.A. (1993b) Clinical issues in communicative psychoanalysis: premature securing of patient's breaks in psychotherapy frame as expression of therapist's countertransference difficulty with containing
patient's projective identifications, *International Journal of Communicative Psychoanalysis and Psychotherapy*, 8(4): 115–21.

Bonac, V.A. (1994) A communicative psychoanalytic theory of human development: part one – introduction, methodology and theorems, *International Journal of Communicative Psychoanalysis and Psychotherapy*,
9(4): 99–105.

Bonac, V.A. (1996a) The bountiful mother and the fate of transference in
times of managed care, *International Journal of Communicative Psychoanalysis and Psychotherapy*, 10(3): 59–72.

Bonac, V.A. (1996b) Perception or fantasy: a new clinical theory of transference, *International Journal of Communicative Psychoanalysis and Psychotherapy*, 11(2/3).

Brenner, C. (1969) Some comments on technical precepts in psychoanalysis,
Journal of the American Psychoanalytic Association, 17: 333–52.

Fenichel, O. (1945) Neurotic acting out, *Psychoanalytic Review*, 32: 197–206.

Freud, A. (1968) Symposium: Acting-out, *International Journal of Psychoanalysis*, 49: 165–70.

Freud, S. (1914) Remembering, repeating, and working-through (Further recommendations on the technique of psycho-analysis, II) *S. E.* 12: 45–156.

Freud, S. (1920) Beyond the pleasure principle, *S. E.* 18: 3–64.

Greenacre, P. (1950) General problems of acting out, *Psychoanalytic Quarterly*, 19: 455–67.

Greenacre, P. (1963) Problems of acting-out in the transference relationship, *Journal of American Academy of Child Psychiatry*, 2: 144–75.

Greenacre, P. (1968) Symposium. The analytic process, transference, and acting-out, *International Journal of Psycho-Analysis*, 49: 211–18.

Grinberg, L. (1968) Symposium. On acting out and its role in the psychoanalytic process, *International Journal of Psycho-Analysis*, 49: 171–8.

Johnson, A.M. and Szurek, S.A. (1952) The genesis of antisocial acting out in children and adults, *Psychoanalytic Quarterly*, 21: 323–43.

Klauber, J. (1968) The psychoanalyst as a person, *British Journal of Medical Psychology*, 41: 315–22.

Langs, R. (1973) The patient's view of the therapist: reality or fantasy? *International Journal of Psychoanalytic Psychotherapy*, 2: 411–31.

Langs, R. (1975) The therapeutic relationship and deviations in technique, *International Journal of Psychoanalytic Psychotherapy*, 4: 106–41.

Langs, R. (1976a) *The Bipersonal Field.* New York: Aronson.

Langs, R. (1976b) *The Therapeutic Interaction*, vol. II. New York: Aronson.

Langs, R. (1978a) *The Listening Process.* New York: Aronson.

Langs, R. (1978b) *Technique in Transition.* New York: Aronson.

Langs, R. (1979a) *Supervisory Experience.* New York: Aronson.

Langs, R. (1979b) *The Therapeutic Environment.* New York: Aronson.

Langs, R. (1981) *Resistances and Interventions, The Nature of Therapeutic Work.* New York: Aronson.

Langs, R. (1982) *Psychotherapy, A Basic Text.* New York: Aronson.

Langs, R. (1984/5) Making interpretations and securing the frame, *International Journal of Psychoanalytic Psychotherapy*, 10: 3–23.

Mitscherlich-Nielson, M. (1968) Symposium. Contribution to symposium on acting-out, *International Journal of Psycho-Analysis*, 47: 188–92.

Quinn, B.P. (1992) Interpreting patient's unconscious needs for seeking modification of the psychotherapy frame, *International Journal of Communicative Psychoanalysis and Psychotherapy*, 7: 35–8.

Rangel, L. (1968) Symposium. A point of view on acting-out, *International Journal of Psycho-Analysis*, 49: 195–201.

Sandler, J. (1976) Countertransference and role-responsiveness, *International Review of Psycho-Analysis*, 3: 43–7.

Searles, H.F. (1965) *Collected Papers on Schizophrenia and Related Subjects.* Madison, CT: International Universities Press.

Smith, D.L. (1991) *Hidden Conversations: An Introduction to Communicative Psychoanalysis.* London: Tavistock/Routledge.

Szasz, T. (1963) The concept of transference, *International Journal of Psycho-Analysis*, 44: 432–97.

Troise, F. and Quinn, B.P. (1991) Sandler's concept of role-responsiveness and the relationship to the psychoanalytic frame, *Journal of Contemporary Psychotherapy*, 21: 173–84.

Part **III**

ALTERED FRAMES

Chapter **6**

Brief communicative psychotherapy and the fixed altered frame

Gae Oaten

Introduction

The aim of this chapter is to describe and illustrate the fixed altered frame of brief communicative psychotherapy practised within a general practice surgery. The impossibility of achieving an ideal secure therapeutic frame within a medical setting will be examined and the idea of securing an altered frame will be explored. The focus will be on my theoretical attempts to provide secure-frame moments within a fixed altered frame. This will be done through illustrations of my own efforts to establish a relatively stable psychotherapeutic frame and my attempt to practise communicative psychotherapy as a brief therapy approach.

I suggest that it is the attention given to the moment-to-moment details of human communication, and the provision of a technique for listening to the unconscious meaning of that moment which makes communicative technique available to brief psychotherapy. Langs states (1993: 15), 'that the deep unconscious system is at all times primarily focused on and engaged in processing the implications of the immediate (and most recent) communicative exchanges within the therapeutic interaction'. Because of this concentration on the immediate transaction between client and therapist, and because the communicative approach uses a 'model of entering each session without desire, memory or understanding' (Langs 1980: 3), I suggest that communicative psychotherapy is an appropriate psychoanalytic approach for psychotherapy practised briefly, as brief as one therapeutic session.

The clinical material illustrated in this chapter is from my own clinical practice, and the material presented is real. However, the client's name will not be used and other identifying features have been disguised so as to preserve confidentiality.

In the writing of this chapter, putting forward my hypothesis of the fixed altered frame in brief psychotherapy, I am aware that I am involved in the telling of a story from my own point of view, and that I will be consciously selective about material included and omitted. In other words, I will be sometimes consciously and perhaps a great deal of the time unconsciously engaged in fuelling my own bias.

The frame

The communicative approach to psychoanalysis has a unique characteristic, which is the intense consideration given to the psychotherapeutic frame. The methodology of the communicative approach relates to the diligent attention given to the client's unconscious requirements, which communicative therapists suggest is organized by the frame, secured or deviant. The term 'frame' refers to the therapist's management of the basic conditions of treatment, the therapeutic relationship and interactions. The frame can be seen in terms of a contract, the setting out of how the work is to be conducted: in other words, the laying down of the ground rules which will constitute the therapy. Langs (1992) describes the frame as the backbone to the communicative approach. Smith concurs with this view, suggesting that 'consistent unconscious reactions to the frame indicate that it does not function as a mere backdrop to the real business of psychoanalysis. The structuring of the frame, the management of the ground rules, is the real business of psychoanalysis' (Smith 1991: 164). According to Langs (1992, 1992b, 1993, 1995, 1996) and Smith (1991), components of the secure frame are as follows: consistency of the setting; set frequency of the sessions; set duration of the sessions; set fee; punctuality; free association; privacy; absence of physical contact; anonymity; confidentiality and neutrality.

Establishing the ground rules of therapy at the outset of treatment and then allowing them to fade into the background is not good enough. The ground rules – the frame – must be continually attended to, managed and maintained by the therapist; also any modifications to the frame by either the therapist or the client will need rectification by the therapist. Langs (1995: 45) suggests that a therapist 'who fails to monitor the state of the frame . . .

operates in a world that is severely constricted by his or her limited vision'.

Also I hasten to suggest that the therapist needs to be aware at all times of her or his own attempts to modify the therapeutic frame, and the implications of her or his frame modifications. However, when therapists find themselves having to establish an altered frame from the outset of therapy due to circumstances out of their control (for example brief psychotherapy or brief psychotherapy practised within a general practice surgery), what then?

The altered frame of brief psychotherapy

Langs (1992: 191) states that a deviant frame 'creates an inherently dangerous image of the therapist'. Langs suggests that when the boundaries are blurred, it can create feelings of mistrust, of not being contained; the therapist could be seen as an unreliable manager and poor role model. However, in spite of the indicative problems affirmed by Langs when there are deviations from the standard communicative psychotherapy setting, I postulate that therapy which occurs within a frame which has been altered but fixed at the outset of therapy, need not be deviant therapy and it can have secure-frame moments. The fixed altered frame, I suggest, needs the therapist's ongoing attention and management, just as does the standard communicative secure frame.

Let us now look at the altered ground rules of brief psychotherapy and the imposed alterations to the frame when practising brief therapy within a medical setting. I hasten to remind readers that the communicative approach affirms that there is a single optimal way of structuring the frame. Therefore my proposal of an altered fixed frame for brief communicative psychotherapy needs to be understood as an experimental concept and purely conjectural.

Listed below is the formulation of ground rules which I postulate could be the altered fixed frame for brief communicative psychotherapy, a frame that I have been attempting to structure and maintain in my clinical work within a general practice surgery. I have juxtaposed my proposed fixed altered frame of communicative psychotherapy against the standard communicative secure frame, allowing the reader to see how a number of the ground rules of the standard communicative secure frame have been altered for the purpose of practising brief communicative psychotherapy within a general practice surgery.

Components of the secure-frame	Components of the fixed altered-frame
1 Patient's responsibility for termination	Therapist sets the termination date; number of sessions are stated
2 Use of the couch	Seated face to face
3 A set fee	No fee; it is noted by the therapist that the service is funded and payment is received
4 Total confidentiality	As confidential as possible within a medical setting; the therapist does not view or write in patient's medical file; all appointments are made with the therapist and recorded separately
5 Total privacy	Private office to be used only by the therapist; a separate waiting area to be available
6 A consistent setting	Consistent setting; two easy chairs, low table between the chairs, a desk and office chair
7 Free association	Free association
8 The therapist's neutrality	The therapist's neutrality
9 No physical contact	No physical contact
10 The therapist's anonymity	The therapist's anonymity
11 Set frequency and duration of sessions	Set frequency and duration of sessions; once a week 50-minute sessions

With the knowledge that the frame is altered but fixed, my proposition is that the main task for a therapist practising brief communicative psychotherapy is no different from the responsibility when practising open-ended communicative therapy: which is, as I have mentioned previously, to manage and maintain the frame. However, with a fixed altered frame, part of the therapist's management is being aware of the triggers/adaptive contexts pertaining to the alterations to the secure frame. For example a therapist practising brief therapy would be aware of an important adaptive context and would listen for an allusion to it in the patient's stories. This adaptive context or trigger would be, for example, the restricted time of brief therapy, or the pending termination of the brief therapy contract.

Management of the frame

To manage the frame appropriately we need to attune our listening to a level which enables us to hear the unconscious ideas in the patient's manifest comments. Communicative therapists refer to these latent meanings of conscious communication as derivatives.

A derivative complex is a network of encoded messages that centre primarily upon unconscious perceptions of the adaptive context.

Communicative therapists believe that everything a therapist does constitutes an adaptive context. Every ground rule explained, established and then managed, the physical setting offered by the therapist, the therapist's silences and interpretations, all are adaptation-evoking contexts for the client. Therefore it stands to reason that it is the adaptive contexts or triggers which should occupy much of the communicative therapist's thinking. Two tasks to keep in mind when decoding a derivative are '(1) to translate the derivative into a decoded perception of the therapist and (2) to identify the specific adaptive context that contains and implication that is correctly perceived (identified) in the derivative image' (Langs 1992: 278–9). My efforts at implementing these two tasks when endeavouring to decode a client's derivatives will be demonstrated in the clinical material presented in this chapter.

Before commencing with the clinical presentation I need to stress that communicative therapists opt for silence, as do other psychoanalytical therapists, rather than questioning the client or giving clarification, confrontations or reflecting back the client's manifest material. However, the restricted time in brief psychotherapy can influence therapists to abandon a number of psychoanalytic principles. One principle many proponents of brief psychoanalytical psychotherapy maintain needs to be forsaken is the therapist's silence. Abandoning this principle for effective brief treatment encourages therapists to reconstruct their role mostly into an active role, one which focuses on goals and on the lack of time. In fact the lack of time can often be highlighted to such an extent in some brief psychotherapies that it becomes the therapy itself. In other words, it manages the therapy.

In communicative brief psychotherapy work, the lack of time is not treated as the key precept, but is, instead, listened for as an adaptive context. To listen for adaptive contexts or triggers, a therapist practising brief psychotherapy also needs to opt for silence. The therapist's silence gives the patient full freedom and encourages the client to 'create the therapeutic session on a manifest and latent level, a prerogative that is entirely the patient's due' (Langs 1992: 382). Langs (1992) believes the therapist's silence – silent waiting – is the most critical intervention available to the therapist; it shows the client that the therapist has faith in the client's ability to take the starring role in the therapeutic interaction. It is however a difficult intervention and certainly one that I struggle to maintain when practising brief therapy. This is apparent in the clinical material illustrated in this chapter, clinical material extracted from three sessions of an eight-session psychotherapy contract.

Psychotherapy and the medical setting

The practice consists of two inner city surgeries, staffed by three male doctors. I am located at one surgery and see clients from both surgeries. On commencement of my post I was located at the smaller of the two surgeries and shared with the practice nurses their consulting room with all their relevant medical information on view – not an ideal setting by any standard. I have since moved to the larger surgery, which simultaneously moved to new and purpose-renovated premises. My office, which I requested be used only as a counselling room and only by myself, is situated on the first floor away from the main running of the surgery. Clients come straight to an adjoining waiting room; they do not register at the reception desk.

Clients are referred to me by the doctors and the practice nurses; however, the clients make their appointments directly with me. It is suggested to clients that they can contact me at a given time at the surgery. The doctors and the nurses keep discussion with clients about therapy simple and basic. If I am not available when a client contacts the surgery, the client has a choice of leaving her or his telephone number for me to return the call or the client can try again at the given time. No messages are taken by the receptionists: if the client asks for information, it is suggested that they can talk with the therapist when contact is made. Informing clients that a therapist is available at the surgery and then leaving it up to the client to make the initial contact gives the client a choice about therapy rather than it being experienced as yet another prescription from the doctor which the client may feel pressured into taking up. This simple step also encourages a more autonomous therapeutic relationship (Hoag 1992). A separate appointment book is maintained by me and kept in my room; a book for clients' names and telephone numbers is kept at the reception desk. Separating the psychotherapy service from the medical service in this way helps to create a degree of confidentiality for the client within the medical setting.

It must be noted that, although every attempt has been taken by the doctors, surgery staff and myself to establish a fixed altered therapeutic frame in the medical setting, maintaining the ground rules is very much my responsibility. This presents me with not only the task of adhering to the client's request to rectify any modifications to the frame but also the continual challenge of dealing with the conscious and unconscious desires of the doctors and surgery staff to modify the fixed altered frame. Of course my own conscious and unconscious attempts to modify the ground rules must not be eliminated from this equation. Once again we are brought back to frame management and all its complexities.

Turning now to the clinical material, the complexities of frame management and my attempts to maintain a fixed altered frame within the medical setting are all evident.

Clinical example

The client in question sought psychotherapy at her general practice surgery because of persistent chest pains and a feeling of being unwell.

The patient is a 34-year-old Nigerian woman, married with three daughters of 14, 10 and 4. The 10-year-old's twin brother died at birth; the surviving twin has respiratory problems and is frail and needs constant care. The client miscarried a fourth daughter at 20 weeks, a month before her self-referral for therapy. The client received a number of investigative medical tests during her two-day hospital internment after her miscarriage, to ascertain the cause of her chest pains: no cause was found. Further tests were undertaken two weeks later, when the client was readmitted to hospital, again with strong chest pain; again she was informed that there was nothing physically wrong with her. It was suggested to her on a visit to her GP for the same complaint, that she was probably suffering from depression due to her recent miscarriage and that she could contact me for therapy.

All the above information was formulated during two initial interviews with the client. The interviews were difficult; the client's command of English was very limited. My response to the client's difficulties and reluctance to communicate was to take over, to manage the client instead of paying attention to managing the therapeutic frame. I found myself probing and directing the client, benevolently reflecting back some of the client's comments, and patronizingly explaining what therapy meant. As my anxiety mounted and the more active I became, the more withdrawn and silent the client became.

After the two initial interviews with the client, I experienced strong feelings of having bullied the client into taking up a brief therapy contract with me. I tried to alleviate my uneasy feelings by analysing the client. The client, I conjecture has an unconscious fear of becoming pregnant again; the fear relates to conceiving another daughter. Her husband desperately wanted a boy and there was conscious and deep unconscious shame for not being able to give her husband his much longed-for son. While the client was suffering with the pain, sexual intercourse wouldn't take place (the client had informed me that sexual intercourse was difficult and her husband was reluctant to force the issue). These assumptions of mine could perhaps be viewed as valid, in the search for meaning. However, what I had not done was give any meaningful thought to my part in this therapeutic interaction.

Reflecting on the two initial meetings and the client's reluctance and difficulties in communicating, I became aware that this had sharpened my anxiety around the restricted time of this therapy. In defence I turned to activity in the attempt to fend off my anxieties. The unconscious and conscious concern around lack of time, or the sense of accelerated time, brought up a strong desire to control the time, to put it to good use, by impregnating our meetings with my words. Keeping in mind that I had time to reflect before the following session, let us now turn to the first session of the brief therapy contract.

First session

The client arrived on time; she was extremely nervous. She sat on the very edge of the chair. Her coat was wrapped tightly around her body secured with her bag, and she gripped and re-gripped her hands. The client didn't acknowledge me in any way; she sat in silence. My anxiety once again triggered me into proceeding as I had done in the previous interview, and then I stopped and remembered my reflections. I waited in silence. Five minutes passed before the client spoke. She said:

> *Client:* I begged and begged my friend to bring me here. I had to go on and on at her, she didn't want to bring me. She is pregnant and it is hard for her to get behind the wheel of her car. She did bring me after I begged her so much. (*Pause*) When I went home last week after seeing you and when my husband came home, he made me sit down on the chair and tell him everything that had happened here. He said I should tell him what I had said to you and what you said. I told him what had happened. He needed to know, he likes to know everything, always. He says it is important that he knows what is going on, what is happening to me. (*The client shrugged her shoulders and sighed deeply. Pause*) He can be very, what is the word, umm, strong at me, bossy. (*Lengthy pause*)

I intervened at this point. I will from now on refer to myself as the Therapist.

> *Therapist:* You told me how you begged your friend to bring you here and although she didn't want to, she gave in to your begging and did bring you here. Also you said your husband demanded to be told everything that was said between us last week. You said you told him everything because he needs to know and it is important to him to know everything. I am wondering if perhaps in telling me these things, what you are saying to me is that the same thing has been happening here. That I have begged you to talk and you, like your friend, have gone along with me. Perhaps you, like your friend, didn't want to. Also maybe you are saying that I, like your husband, have been pushing you, forcing you to tell me things because it is important to me. Maybe you are saying that I have been bossy with you like your husband bosses you.

The client's reaction was one of surprise, she seemed startled. She looked at me for the first time. Until that moment the client had kept her eyes averted from mine, even at times covering them with her hand to prevent any eye contact between us.

Something I had missed in my verbal intervention was the client's reference to her friend not being able to get behind the steering wheel of her car with comfort due to her pregnancy. This may have been a derivative representation of something getting in my way, hindering my ability as a therapist, as it hindered the friend's ability as a driver.

Let us see how the client responded to my interpretation.

> *Client:* I wouldn't think of you like that. (*Long pause*) My friend is from Africa, not from my country, but it makes us friends, nearly the same because she is African and understands. She is so pregnant, so heavy with her baby. I worry for her. She doesn't know how hard it is to have a baby, to look after it, they cry and get sick. I have the pain now, it is bad. (*Pause*)
>
> *Therapist:* I am wondering when you talk of how you worry about your friend and how she is going to take care of her baby, if you are wondering if I can take care of you. You said that you are feeling the pain now, perhaps you are concerned about how I will manage, how will I know what your needs are, just as you are wondering how your friend will manage a crying and sometimes sick baby.
>
> *Client:* I will help her with the baby and that will be help for her, it will help her.

I believe I had been given a slight validation. The client had said she was friends with her friend more by accident of nationality than through choice. This could be how she perceived me and the therapy. Also, she said she would help her friend, meaning perhaps she would help me to help her.

This interaction had taken up 17 minutes of the 50-minute session. The client for the rest of the session sat in silence. I found moments of the silence extremely difficult, being acutely aware of time ticking away and experiencing a strong desire to break the silence during those uneasy moments. However, for much of the 33 minutes of silence there was a calmness within the consulting room. I noted that the client's hands rested quietly in her lap, an indication that she felt more at ease. I terminated the session saying I would see the client next week.

I had concerns about the length of the silence and questioned myself about the appropriateness of such a length of silence. I also questioned the moments when I felt the need to counterbalance the silence, and questioned how in fact I had given in to part of that need with my closing remark, begging the patient to return next week. However, in retrospect and after much deliberation, my belief was that the silent intervention had been appropriate and that the client had created and asked for my silence. In fact it was possible that the client's silence was a way of helping me to rectify the frame.

If silence has been used appropriately, Langs suggests, it will be supported in the client's material in three ways. The client's communicative resistance will decrease and meaningful material will be disclosed, through 'a well-represented adaptive context and a coalescing derivative complex' (Langs 1992: 379), and the client's derivatives will have images of well-functioning people. Also clients will not manifestly comment on the therapist's silence nor will there be derivatives pertaining to missed interventions (Langs 1992).

Moving on now to the second session, we will hear how my silence was perceived and whether it was considered an appropriate silence by the client.

Second session

The client arrived on time. She entered the counselling room, unbuttoned two buttons of her coat and placed her bag on the floor at her feet. Both actions demonstrated a confidence that had not been there on previous meetings. She looked at me and smiled. The client opened the session, saying she had felt more relaxed since Friday (the client's therapy sessions were held on Fridays); as she spoke she pushed her hand deeply between her breasts, where she felt the pain; it was an expressive action. I had a strong desire to say how happy I was that she was feeling better. However, I realized that much of my pleasure stemmed from being pleased with myself. I resisted the temptation and waited. The patient continued:

> *Client:* I like doing homework with my daughters, very much. (*Pause*) I am thinking of my children, of picking them up from school. I am going to do this today, I cannot do it very often, my pain. When we get home we will work together. I did some work with my smallest daughter yesterday and the day before, because I feel better. I taught her the letter A and what it is for. A is for apple and aeroplane. B is for ball and bounce and C . . ., I will do L with her today. L is for ladder and learn and lessons. It is hard, very hard for me to help my children with their homework. I try, it is not easy for them to understand me. To know what I say. (*Pause*) Lessons are done as the school sets them out. It is hard, sometimes it is very hard.
>
> *Therapist:* You said that you have been feeling more relaxed this week. Then you went on to say how you enjoy doing homework with your daughters but you also find it difficult helping them with their homework. Maybe you are saying this is how this therapy seems, how it feels here. You told me how you teach your youngest daughter the ABC. L is for ladder, learn and lesson, ladders are often not easy to climb. There seems to be something about lessons, something perhaps I need to learn. You said your daughters find it difficult to understand you. I am wondering if you are saying I may have difficulty in understanding you or I will need to learn how.
>
> *Client:* I didn't go to school in Nigeria, I don't tell this. I talk to my children in my language; they talk to me in English. I think always in my language. I do not speak English at home. My husband speaks to me in our language. It is hard for me to speak in English. My children speak English, they do not speak Nigerian. I think it would be better for my children to speak Nigerian and English, they will need a Nigerian teacher. (*Pause*) To read my language is hard, I do not read; I do not write. My children do not know I did not go to school. (*The client seemed embarrassed, she spoke shyly and hesitantly.*)
>
> *Therapist:* When you tell me that you think in your own language it makes me think you are saying something about

what I have asked you to do. To talk about what is on your mind. Perhaps when you say it would be better if your children spoke Nigerian as well as English, maybe you are saying it would be better if I could speak and understand Nigerian. Could it be that you are perhaps telling me it would be better for you if your therapist understood your language, when you talk about what comes to mind. Maybe you are telling me that it will be to difficult for me to learn to understand you and you need a Nigerian therapist, just as you say your daughters need a Nigerian teacher.

Client: You do not have to speak Nigerian . . . No. (*The client shook her head in disbelief and she laughed, the indication in her laughter was that I had said something very funny. She was laughing at me; her laughter subsided. After five minutes of silence she continued*) My oldest daughter wants to be a doctor and take care of people and make them well. She gives me a massage. A massage for my pain, it helps the pain. Her hands are very gentle but they are strong hands. She will be a good doctor, I know that.

The session terminated after a few minutes of silence.

A communicative therapist does not allude to a client's positive images of the therapist, instead she acknowledges them in silent appreciation. The client's encoded validation is the positive representation of her daughter. When a client produces positive derivative imagery, it is understood to be 'an unconscious appreciation of the positive, insightful qualities of the intervention' (Smith 1991: 143).

Being given the space to express herself in a meaningful way gave the client the opportunity to be the 'star', an active participant in the therapeutic relationship, instead of the passive client I had been forcing her to be in the initial meetings. The silent interventions may also have given the client time to modify her defences in order that difficult therapeutic work could take place at her pace. As Langs (1992: 183) states, 'It is essential to allow the patient to lead the way, and to permit him or her to work at his or her own pace. Psychotherapy sessions should be first and foremost the patient's creations. So should the therapist's interventions. These are the precepts of sound therapeutic efforts.' Difficult work did take place over the following weeks and in no way could I say that the client had a communication problem due to a language barrier. I hasten to say that I was the one with the language problem. This was certainly how the client perceived me. Nor could I think of her as 'the silent client', my label for her after our first meeting. Turning now to the client's last session, we will witness how the client leads me to end the therapy.

Eighth session

Client: My middle daughter, the tube has been taken away, I knew this would happen, the hospital has been getting her ready for weeks, she will not need to be looked after so much now. It will be better for her at school and when she is home. This makes me happy, I am pleased. (*Pause*) When I come to see the doctor for me and for my daughter I know you will be here. (*Pause*) I will not see you. (*Long pause*) I was thinking of the baby, my miscarriage. I told my husband I wanted to see her, he thought it would make me sad and I would cry, he said it was best not to see. I did not cry. (*Pause*) I am happy about my daughter, but I feel very sad about the baby, she was dead, I know that. They did not say anything to me. My other baby was dead.

The client began to cry saying she was thinking of her dead baby and how she would have looked after her. She said that she had not cried for this baby, but she had cried for the other baby. After five minutes, when the client's crying had diminished, I intervened with

Therapist: You told me that your daughter had her tube removed and how it will be easier and better for her at school and home without it. You said you are happy about this. You seemed sad when you said how you will be coming to see your doctor at the surgery but you will not be seeing me. Maybe this reminded you of other sad times, your miscarriage, of that sadness. Perhaps this is how it feels here today on our last day, some sadness and some good. You told me how your daughter has been getting ready at the hospital for weeks to have the tube removed. You have been coming here for weeks and perhaps there is something good about the thought of managing without the therapy, just as it is for your daughter to manage without the tube.

The client started to cry once more, deep sobs, she held herself tightly and rocked herself backwards and forwards. Her painful keening continued for some time. I waited. The temptation was to pacify, to murmur soothing words. I resisted these urges with difficulty.

After some time the client removed a large handkerchief from her bag, wiped her eyes and blew her nose loudly and carefully returned the handkerchief to her bag. She adjusted herself in the chair, she sat up straight and made eye contact with me. She said:

> *Client:* My husband did not want the baby, we knew it was a girl. I did not want the baby, I think the baby knew that. I think in my language about not wanting the baby. There are things and ways to think. It was best that I did not have this baby. (*Pause*) My mother died when I was a baby. I stayed mostly with my father's sisters or my mother's mother, they did not want me. I wish my mother could be with me, not having a mother has made me so unhappy. (*Pause*) My mother could not say goodbye, she could not say goodbye because she ran away, she ran away from us. She is there, she is alive but did not want to see me. She did not say goodbye or try to see me again, ever. It is hard for me to think this.
>
> *Therapist:* I think when you talk of being left by your mother, her not wanting you, your family not wanting you, and you and your husband not wanting the baby, you could be saying something about the end of this therapy. Perhaps this is how you see me, not wanting to continue therapy with you. When you told me that I would be at the surgery but I wouldn't be seeing you, perhaps it made you think of how your mother is alive but has chosen not to see you. Maybe you are telling me that I have chosen not to see you, that I decided when to end your therapy, this being the best for you, just like your husband decided it was best for you not to see your baby. Also it was your mother's decision not to see you, not yours.

The client nodded her head in agreement, she stopped crying and said:

> *Client:* Today I know that I will not have any more babies, I will speak to my husband, he will be all right, then I will speak to Dr S. I know my oldest daughter will be pleased that I will not have more babies. She has been such a good daughter and helped me with my daughter when she was sick and looked after my smallest daughter when I needed to be with my daughter when she was sick. My oldest daughter loves her baby sister, she says that it is good to have girls. My girls are clever and they have lovely faces. My husband loves his daughters and is proud of them. (*Pause*) I am proud of my daughters, you know that because I speak of them that way. When I think of my mother I think she would look like all my daughters. I like to think my mother looks like

> all my daughters together. Maybe I look like my mother,
> I think
> *Therapist:* It is time for us to finish.

The client said goodbye shyly, as she opened the door she turned to me and said; 'I am going to school and will learn English there.'

My first verbal intervention in this last session is, I suggest, a clear example of how difficult it was for me to hear the client's perception of me. The client gave me a wonderful bridge to therapy, when she talked about me being at the surgery but not being able to see me. Then she continued with a story about not being allowed to see her dead baby. I, however, stayed with the client's story of her daughter having the tracheotomy removed. My need was for the therapy to end with me being seen in a positive light. A little sad for the client, but she was pleased that the therapy was coming to an end, therapy had served its purpose, just as the daughter's tracheotomy had served its purpose. However, the client wasn't having this interpretation and she gave me a second chance, responding to my interpretation with strong derivatives, which I couldn't ignore. My second verbal intervention was validated by the positive imagery of her eldest daughter. Holding and containing (managing the frame), states Langs (1992: 295), 'provide overall ego strength to the patient, and communicative interpretations and reconstructions are the avenue to the specific resolution of intrapsychic and interpersonal conflicts and their pathological consequences – symptom formation, disturbances in self and identity, and the like'. Perhaps it could be said that there was a resolution of intrapsychic and interpersonal conflict when the client stated that she would not extend her family and would be seeking information from her doctor about sterilization.

I was moved by the client's beautiful reference to her three daughters, herself and her mother being one, and I silently accepted, rightly or wrongly, the client's closing affirmation about learning English as a gift from her.

Conclusion

Although the fixed altered frame of brief therapy sets up active adaptive contexts, and can shape the client's conflict derivatives, the fixed altered frame can also be viewed more benignly. Each adaptive context has a plurality of meanings and each of these meanings has different levels of importance and different functions for every client. According to Langs (1992: 116), 'In psychotherapy, a patient unconsciously selects those implications of the therapist's interventions that are most pertinent to his or her madness.' My client selected meanings carried by the adaptive context which were pertinent to her unconscious memories, along with her current pathological dynamics and self needs, for example the pain and hurt of being abandoned by her mother, and subsequently her perception of the worth of her gender and the worthiness of herself and her three daughters.

I suggest that although the therapist is aware of particular adaptive contexts because of the fixed altered frame of brief therapy, and that each client's response will be different, these known adaptive contexts should be used only as a guide to decoding the client's manifest communications. Langs (1992: 280) suggests that the patient's 'primary responses are to the definitive interventions of the therapist'. It is this theory of Langs's – that clients react mainly to the actualities of the therapeutic relationship and interaction – that brings me to suggest the communicative approach is a valid model of psychotherapy for the practice of brief psychotherapy.

I hope that I have illustrated in this chapter that brief psychotherapy can be non-active and psychoanalytic, and that the communicative model makes this possible, because of the technique of listening to the unconscious meaning of the moment. While a client's conscious system can and often does look elsewhere, the unconscious system is always centred on the present situation. This suggests to me that each session is in effect a brief therapy.

References

Hoag, L. (1992) Psychotherapy in the general practice surgery: consideration of the frame, *British Journal of Psychotherapy*, 8(4): 417–29.

Langs, R. (1980) *Interactions: The Realm of Transference and Countertransference*. New York: Jason Aronson.

Langs, R. (1992) *A Clinical Workbook for Psychotherapists*. London and New York: Karnac.

Langs, R. (1992b) *Science, Systems, and Psychoanalysis*. London and New York: Karnac.

Langs, R. (1993) *Empowered Psychotherapy Teaching Self Processing*. London: Karnac.

Langs, R. (1995) *Clinical Practice and the Architecture of the Mind*. London: Karnac.

Langs, R. (1996) *The Evolution of the Emotion-Processing Mind*. London: Karnac.

Smith, D.L. (1991) *Hidden Conversations: An Introduction to Communicative Psychoanalysis*. London and New York: Tavistock/Routledge.

Chapter **7**

Student counselling: a consideration of ethical and framework issues

Kitty Warburton

Introduction

This chapter illustrates some of the ethical and clinical difficulties which may arise when student counselling takes place under conditions paying insufficient attention to the ground rules of therapy. It considers the importance of the frame in psychotherapy and the implications for work in an institutional setting. It also looks at the changes that may be made in the way the counsellor functions in the institution, in order to secure the best conditions for effective counselling work with students, based on the author's personal experience.

Student counselling services in institutions of higher education (HE) have mushroomed since their modest beginnings in the late 1960s and 1970s. Large increases in student numbers, hand in hand with a belief that a counselling service benefits both the institution and its students, have led to a corresponding expansion in counselling provision (Jonathan 1989).

There is, however, little consensus on the role of the counselling service in such institutions. Bond (1992) has identified two models: the integrated and the differentiated. In the former the counsellor is 'so integrated into the educational organisation that the role requires guidelines on ethics and practice which are quite specific to this situation and distinct from the practice of counsellors in other settings' (Bond 1992: 51). In this model, the counsellor's primary responsibility is to the institution. It follows that, ultimately, the client is the institution and it operates on the assumption that the interests of the institution and the student client are basically the same (Noonan 1983; Bond 1992).

In the differentiated model, on the other hand, the role of the counsellor in HE is seen as essentially similar to that of the counsellor working in any other setting; therefore they should work to the same ethical and professional guidelines (Bond 1992). This model stresses the importance of maintaining appropriate boundaries for counselling. As Bond points out, the blurring of roles where counsellors are working within an integrated model may have ethical implications, which may not have been adequately addressed.

Whether student counsellors find themselves working within the integrated 'educational' model or the differentiated therapeutic model – or somewhere in between – will depend on a number of factors, such as the background and previous training of the counsellor, the counsellor's theoretical orientation, and the size, type or stage of development of the institution (Jonathan 1989).

Some time ago I took up a post as student counsellor at a college of higher education which, although it had increased its student numbers by 100 per cent over the last few years, was still, by higher education standards, a small institution, with a tradition of teacher education, now diversified into a modular degree structure. Although the post was described as 'student counsellor', it was open to those with a formal training in either counselling or psychotherapy. While HE institutions differ in whether they consider the service they offer to students to be counselling or psychotherapy (with the former much more common), I am using the terms interchangeably in this chapter as, in common with counsellors working in other sectors, for example GP practices, the work may be done by someone who considers herself or himself to be either a 'counsellor' or a 'psychotherapist' (Hoag 1992). May (1988a, 1988b, 1988c) has also considered the issue of counselling versus psychotherapy in a college setting.

I came into this post with a background in education but also with several years' experience as a counsellor/psychotherapist in private practice. Much that I had taken for granted in terms of the management of the boundaries of time, place, privacy and confidentiality were suddenly thrown into sharp relief – I found myself working in a context where these ground rules for therapy could not be assumed. Inevitably this generated a considerable amount of anxiety for me as I took on a new role in a relatively unfamiliar setting. Part of the challenge for me came in trying to disentangle this web of anxiety: how much was my own anxiety and how much belonged elsewhere? I found that I kept returning to thinking about the

importance of the ground rules or the frame within which counselling and psychotherapy traditionally takes place, and their implications for work in a college setting.

The importance of the frame in psychotherapy

The term 'frame' – referring to the ground rules in psychotherapy –
was first used by Milner, who used the analogy of the frame of a
painting to define the therapeutic or analytic space, as opposed to
the outside world of the client (Smith 1991). However, the concept of
the frame goes right back to Freud, and there are references to ground
rules in many of his papers on technique (Smith 1991), even though
Freud himself broke many of his own ground rules, for example by
touching patients, confiding in them and even conducting sessions
in the park (Cooper 1993). The importance of the frame or the management of the ground rules in psychotherapy has been given vary-
ing degrees of attention by analysts and therapists since. Of these,
Winnicott's notion of the analytic space being used to 'hold' or contain the patient in a maternal way has been very influential (Smith
1991; Cooper 1993). Bleger (1967: 514) went further than Winnicott
in seeing the frame in the psychoanalytic situation as the depository
of 'the psychotic part of the personality, i.e. the undifferentiated and
non-dissolved portion of the primitive symbiotic links' (with the
mother). For Bleger 'the psycho-analyst's frame must help to re-
establish the original symbiosis in order to change it' (p. 518). However, American communicative psychoanalyst Robert Langs has
placed the greatest importance on the frame in psychotherapy.
Indeed, to a communicative therapist, 'the structuring of the frame,
the management of the ground rules, is the real business of psychoanalysis' (Smith 1991: 164).

According to Langs, a sound (or 'secured') frame offers opti-
mum conditions for a climate of safety and trust to develop in which
the client feels free to communicate openly. It offers 'the opportunity to resolve the patient's symptoms through insight and understanding, rather than through a mode of cure designed for
action-discharge, immediate relief and pathological gratification
and defense' (Langs 1982: 326).

The 'secured frame' referred to (Langs 1982) consists of a way of
managing the ground rules of the therapeutic encounter, in order to
offer:

- *Total confidentiality* – there should be no discussion of the client
  with any third party. This would extend even to whether or not
  the client was coming to sessions.

- *Total privacy* – clients should not be observed by third parties as they arrive for, or leave their sessions. There should be a sound-proofed room, free from interruptions. Appointments should be made directly with the therapist, not through a third party such as a receptionist.
- *Predictability and consistency* – counselling should take place in an appropriate room which will not change; there should be a fixed and unchanging session time; an exact length for all sessions, and a set fee which is not altered.
- *Therapist neutrality and anonymity* – neutrality requires that the therapist should not give advice or opinions, or touch the client. The therapist should not intervene in the client's life outside the sessions.

  Anonymity is demonstrated by refraining from self-revelation or the forming of a relationship with the client outside of the therapeutic encounter, whether prior to, during or after therapy.

When any of these ground rules are broken by the therapist, Langs (1982) refers to this as a 'frame deviation'.

According to Langs, the patient responds to such deviations by producing associations which reflect unconscious judgements on the therapist's behaviour or actions. These unconscious judgements are 'derivative' or 'latent' communications which are adaptive reactions to the therapist and to the therapeutic setting (Langs 1982). Langs abandoned the term 'countertransference' to denote the therapist's emotional responses to the patient in favour of the idea of 'therapist madness', thus putting the therapist's psychopathology firmly 'centre-stage'. According to Langs, the patient's unconscious communications to their therapist will reflect their therapist's madness back to them. As Smith (1991) points out, it is in their management of the therapeutic frame that therapists most clearly express their madness or sanity. However, there does need to be enough of a secure frame to contain the anxieties of both therapist and client (as well as the anxiety of colleagues and the institution) in order for the therapist to

> adequately manage inner and outer conflicts and tensions, fantasies, and perceptions in order to maintain a core relationship and set of conditions under which the patient may safely and meaningfully communicate the manifest and derivative material through which his or her neurosis may be insightfully resolved.
>
> (Langs 1982: 326)

Clearly, working in any institutional setting (as opposed to private practice) is going to pose a considerable challenge if these conditions are to be met. My own initial experience, as I struggled to make sense of my own anxieties, my clients' issues and the demands of the institution, seemed to suggest that at times the work did lack the necessary safety and containment. At times I also wondered whether my ability to work within the Code of Ethics and Practice of the British Association for Counselling was being compromised (BAC 1992). A number of papers have looked at the difficulties and opportunities for counsellors and psychotherapists in securing the frame and managing the ground rules when working in a primary health care setting or clinic (Cheifetz 1984; Phillips 1991; Hoag 1992; Milton 1993), and much of this discussion is relevant to counsellors working within a college or university setting. However, less has been written regarding the management of the frame specifically in an HE setting, although Jonathan (1989) is an exception.

Indeed, it is widely accepted in the field of British student counselling that it is inevitable and even desirable that the boundaries of traditional therapeutic practice should be abandoned. Noonan (1986), for example, describes a 'three person' therapeutic relationship involving not only the student and the counsellor but the student's tutor as well. Noonan (p. 129) argues that this can be done 'without contravening ethical principles through ensuring that the student knows what and why information is being exchanged' and believes that 'it is useful and necessary that academic and therapist speak together so long as the exchange is in aid of furthering the joint education and health aims'.

However, she acknowledges that this kind of collaboration 'does, of course, materially alter the concept of confidentiality and of what is admissible information in the therapeutic work. Confidentiality becomes an institutional matter' (p. 128).

A similar view has been taken by HMI Elizabeth Jones in a debate within the BAC on how the work of a counsellor in education may be assessed: 'The counsellor's client can be considered to be the educational organisation and the individuals who seek counselling as consumers of a service offered within that organisation' (cited in Bond 1992: 52).

It does seem to me that there are profound ethical and therapeutic implications for this 'integrated' model which, as Bond (1992) points out, have not yet been adequately explored by those who advocate this model. In HE, where students are adults, I have not yet been convinced of the justification for such a blurring of ethical and professional boundaries. It is interesting that these matters tend to be seen differently in the American context. May, for example, notes that if we do not separate, for the most part, administrative and clinical matters, then we run the risk of being disabled in our central function. Once we can no longer assume, or once we wrongly assume, that a student has come to the psychotherapy service because of conflict or pain, that is once the student is in our office to get a course extension, a medical leave, or a letter to the draft board, then we can no longer function as psychotherapists.

(May 1988d: 16)

Pursuing this argument, Gilbert (1989) has offered useful guidelines for counsellors working in a college context. He acknow-ledges that 'a psychological service agency in higher education has responsibilities to individuals, institution and profession and all too often finds itself caught between the rock and the hard place of these conflicting loyalties' (Gilbert 1989: 477). He maintains, however, that it is vital to face these issues and to draw up consistent policies and guidelines concerning boundaries in order to 'protect the agency's capacity to carry out its central mission (however defined) and not improvise on a case-by-case basis' (p. 478). The guidelines he suggests are that:

1 The limits of confidentiality should be defined by legal statute and professional ethics, not by the needs of the insti-tution as defined by deans.
2 Counselling Centres should be administratively neutral in order to provide effective counselling to students and useful consultations to the College.
3 A student's status at the College should depend on his or her behavior and not on whether he or she is in treatment.
4 The Counsellor's job as consultant to staff is essentially simi-lar to his/her job as a therapist.

(Gilbert 1989: 484–6)

These four points seem to me to offer a clear ethical framework within which to make decisions involving institutional issues.

Jonathan (1989) has looked at some of the implications for the secure frame in counselling in a college setting. He discusses prob-lems around privacy, confidentiality, and so on. His conclusion is that 'the setting of a college counselling service may be of such a nature that it may be difficult or even impossible to establish, main-tain or re-establish a secure frame' (Jonathan 1989: 91); he suggests that further research is necessary to 'assess the impact of frame modi-fication on the therapeutic interaction'.

In the rest of this chapter I look at my own experience in a col-lege setting. In the first few months a number of issues served to highlight these ethical and boundary issues. My new supervisor was a communicative psychotherapist and therefore particularly interested in frame issues. With her help (as well as with my colleague at the college) I attempted to find my way through the many ethical dilemmas and frame issues which arose.

Management of the frame in the student counselling context

One of the first issues we had to consider was the question of how students would actually get appointments to see me. Reception arrangements are obviously crucial in a counselling service, and when the counsellor is based in a student health centre the implications are similar in many ways to those facing counsellors based in a GP surgery (Hoag 1992). The counselling service at the college had the services of a receptionist, and the existing system required students to make an initial appointment with the counsellor through her. The receptionist kept the counsellor's diary and knew when she was free and when she was seeing clients. An attempt was made to safeguard client privacy and confidentiality by entering appointments as initials rather than full names. The receptionist also dealt with enquiries for the rest of the Student Services team based at the site which included Careers, Welfare Advice, Financial Advice, Accommodation Service, and a medical practice. Students wanting an appointment with the counsellor had to explain this to the receptionist, whose duties included some initial 'screening' (for example identifying students needing 'urgent' appointments, students who would be better advised to see the welfare officer, etc.) If a student came in 'in crisis' the receptionist would try to get hold of the counsellor immediately. It can be seen that this system, although administratively convenient, breaks the basic ground rules of confidentiality and privacy for the client, who had to explain his or her request (and perhaps justify it) to a third party, the receptionist. Hoag (1992) and Jonathan (1989) looked at the implications for the therapy of this type of frame deviation.

My post, which was a new one, was based mainly at another college site a couple of miles away: decisions had to be made as to how students would make appointments to see me. Initially a number of appointments had been made for me by my colleague, who had only been able to have initial sessions with students because of her existing workload. Moreover, because those sessions had taken place in my colleague's room, it was assumed that I would continue to use that room to see these particular students, despite the inconvenience to my colleague. These were the circumstances under which I saw my first few clients: I felt distinctly uneasy because of the major breaks in the therapeutic frame, certainly compared to what I had taken for granted in private practice.

The frame issues raised were those of confidentiality, privacy, set place, and so on. Hoag (1992) refers to Langs's statement that 'unless the therapist works with fixed appointments, for which he or she and the patient are responsible, the relationship is too tentative, and a proper therapeutic hold is not established' (Hoag 1992: 423). In an attempt to establish a more secure frame within which to work, we decided that

- I would see all clients in my own room on one site, and that students should travel to see me, rather than vice versa.
- All appointments should be made by students directly with me, rather than through the receptionist. To facilitate this I was able to acquire an answerphone. My telephone number and availability were publicized on leaflets and posters; times were set aside for dealing with calls, but students were free to call at any time.

These arrangements have not solved the problems but they have helped to increase what Langs (1982) describes as 'secure frame moments' in which the client (and therapist) can feel safe and contained.

The use of the answerphone seems to work quite well: most students either leave a message for me or speak to me directly in order to make an appointment. A continuing issue has been the understandable anxiety of the receptionist, or sometimes other members of staff who have referred students, to know if the student has been seen. Staff in the institution who have dealings with distressed students or potential clients quite naturally find this anxiety difficult to deal with. They want the student to be seen 'immediately' by the counsellor, or at the very least, staff like to be reassured that an urgent appointment has been made – staff are clearly not happy at the lack of feedback from the counsellor. Menzies Lyth (1988) has described the unconscious processes in institutions which make it difficult for staff to contain such anxieties. She suggests that the operative model of many educational institutions may be inappropriately based on some version of the family:

> The institution may become too permissive, too nondirective, and lacking in firmness and boundary control. The staff may, in fact, both lack for themselves and fail to give to clients the firm, authoritative management which is a necessary feature of both staff support and client therapy.
>
> (Menzies Lyth 1988: 230)

That the college tends to operate as an anxious family, and a rather 'enmeshed' one at that, quickly became apparent as the following case examples may illustrate.

When M, a young man who was one of my first clients, came to see me he was having difficulties both with coping with his teaching course and in his interpersonal relationships. He was angry and defensive and distrustful of counselling, but it seemed to be his last hope. Between his second and his third session his tutor contacted my colleague to discuss her concerns about him. My colleague then reported this conversation to me as he was my client. When M came to his third session he began by saying 'I suppose you've been hearing things about me.' He had decided that counselling was not going to help after all, and that he would 'just try to get on with things'. He left the session early and has made no further contact with me since. However, I have had several phone calls from tutors anxious about M who want to know what can be done, feeling that he needs 'help'. Although I was careful not to discuss my ex-client in any detail, I nevertheless felt uneasy at these conversations and very aware of a powerful and uncomfortable conflict between my own anxiety to be seen to be doing a 'good job' in the eyes of my colleagues and my wish to work within the boundaries of the therapeutic role. Hoag (1992) vividly describes similar conflicts in her work as a practice counsellor. In the circumstances I have attempted, as May (1988d: 19) suggests, 'to reflect on and help contain anxieties, rather than to internalize the fears and rush to fulfill the initial request'. In attempting to allay the anxiety of staff I have tried to suggest that it may not be possible to do anything if the student (who is an adult) does not want help. The staff then need to take a decision regarding his continuing on the course on academic and behaviour grounds – something they plainly find very hard to do. There is a need, as May (1988d) points out, to distinguish between the 'administrative voice' (which needs to be able to say 'no' on behavioural or academic grounds) and the 'psychotherapeutic voice' (which suspends judgement, listens and attempts to understand).

In another case example, the contentious issue of the counsellor writing notes for examination boards was highlighted. It has been customary at the college for occasional requests to be made of the counsellor to write a letter to support requests by students for extensions of deadlines for essays, dissertations and so on, or to plead extenuating circumstances at examinations boards. There are no guidelines laid down about how these requests should be responded to and my colleague had (albeit reluctantly) acceded to these requests when she felt the circumstances to be justified. However, it seems to me that to comply with such a request undermines the ground rules of confidentiality, privacy and neutrality and is also ethically dubious (see, for example, the BAC Code of Practice – BAC 1992: B,2,4). It seems to me that there is a contradiction in offering a 'confidential' counselling service in which students are encouraged to engage in a process of self-exploration and then using that process and the material shared to make judgements which will affect the student's academic career. Although to do so may be seen as 'supportive' to the student in a superficial way, it involves stepping outside the boundaries of the therapeutic relationship in order to intervene in the student's life and thus may be antitherapeutic. In my view the student is most likely to be effectively helped through the therapist maintaining her neutral stance, and passing the responsibility for the decision back to the student and to the administration. Klein makes the same point that

> in our roles as college psychotherapists we are, as much as possible, neutral in relation to conflicts between student clients and the institution. If a student feels he deserves to live off-campus or not to fail a course, for reasons which are emotional in nature, it is for him, not his psychotherapist, to make that case convincingly to the Dean.
>
> (Klein 1988: 39)

Gilbert (1989) refers to the demands for such notes as an abdication of academic disciplinary and gatekeeping responsibilities and describes this as 'a dangerous situation that tends to pull the counselling centre into the institutional vacuum and creates a temptation for the agency to directly perform these functions itself' (Gilbert 1989: 483).

Gilbert is clear that

> the counselling centre must not be viewed as a place where confidentiality is easily breached and where dispensations of various kinds are either provided or withheld. These realities are in fact synergistic. Students can safely trust that their revelations will remain contained within the therapeutic relationship. At the same time they cannot expect their counsellor to step out of those boundaries to directly influence day-to-day matters in the client's domestic or academic life. So doing contributes to that part of the client yearning for a regressive experience in counselling, rather than for work and growth.
>
> (p. 485)

In Gilbert's view, 'willingness to suspend neutrality' in this way poses difficulties for the therapeutic work itself and for the counselling service when such dispensations are granted to some students and not to others. He points out that consultations with third parties may damage treatment 'perhaps by replicating family dynamics in some fashion' (p. 485).

An interesting example of this occurred when a student client, J, who had been sexually abused as a child, possibly with her mother's collusion, requested a letter from the counsellor to support her request for an extension to the deadline for her dissertation, on the grounds that she had 'personal problems'. In fact she did not initially make the request of me but of my colleague, who had previously written a note for her supporting her request for an extension of essay deadlines. It appears that J saw her relationship with me (as her counsellor) differently from her relationship with my colleague, who had not only written a similar note in the past, but had also earlier facilitated a three-way discussion between J and her tutor and herself. This appears to support the view of communicative psychoanalysts that patients unconsciously know how the frame should be managed in psychotherapy (Smith 1991). In fact, this particular client seemed to know instinctively what was appropriate at a conscious level.

However, on this occasion I was requested by the Dean to 'support' this student by writing a note as her counsellor. This involved a number of phone calls, discussions and so on between the student's tutor, the Dean, myself, my colleague and the student, so that the whole situation became chaotic and – in my view – 'mad' and abusive to the client; for whom the situation now reflected the abuse by supposedly 'caring' adults that she had suffered as a child. My own role had been undermined. I had stated one thing (I am your counsellor and it is not appropriate for me to act on your behalf) and done another, thus demonstrating my basic untrustworthiness (or in Langs's terms, my 'madness') to my client, who is used to having her trust abused.

These intrusions into the therapeutic space destroy the boundaries of the therapeutic relationship and foster reactions such as mistrust, regression and acting-out. They impair the intimacy necessary in a therapeutic relationship and will cause both patient and therapist to defend against the consequent loss of closeness. This defensive reaction can lead to erotic and aggressive fantasies without movement towards insight, and can destroy the therapeutic atmosphere and potential for progress (Hoag 1992: 420).

Conclusion

Boundary and frame issues will always be present when working therapeutically in an institutional setting. Minor 'frame deviations' can be worked with and interpreted. Gross violations, however, like the chaotic situation described above, may make it impossible to work in a therapeutic way with clients. It is therefore vital for the therapist or counsellor working in an institution to do his or her best to ensure that as secure a frame as possible is offered to the client. My colleague and I are attempting to develop a college policy whereby counsellors are not required to make interventions such as those described above on behalf of students they are counselling. One way round this would be for the Examination Board to decide that only medical certificates would be acceptable as mitigating circumstances. The issue of tutors requiring support from counsellors for extending essay deadlines is another example of the blurring of the distinctions between administrative/academic decisions and psychotherapeutic ones.

Clearly there is still much to be done in terms of developing staff and institutional understanding of these aspects of the counsellor's role. Smith (1991) provides a useful analogy taken from education to illustrate the importance of the frame in demonstrating the type of relationship that the counsellor wishes to establish with clients:

> It is obvious that the way a teacher structures a class – the way that he or she manages space, time, resources, and so on – will reveal the type of relationship that she is attempting to establish, consciously or unconsciously with her pupils. It will also reveal a great deal about the teacher's inner resources: her strengths, weaknesses, blind spots, biases, and so on . . . A teacher who manages the setting chaotically is likely to have a class which behaves chaotically. The chaotic situation will, in turn, reinforce and exacerbate the inner chaos which led the teacher down this path in the first instance. It seems legitimate to extrapolate from this to consider the role of the frame in psychotherapy.
>
> (Smith 1991: 167)

While this much seems self-evident, there are many issues which have been raised in this chapter which would benefit from further investigation and study. These include the clinical implications of the different models of counselling service in educational settings; the correlation, if any, between model of counselling service and the stage of development of the institution; how the counselling service can contribute to dealing with anxiety in the institution; staff development for tutors and others; and the relationship between personal tutors and the counselling service.

I am also very aware that I have said nothing in this chapter about the undoubted satisfactions of working with student clients in an institutional setting. However, as May (1994: 19) recently reminded us, it is a 'time-honoured psychoanalytic assumption that we learn more from obstacles and difficulties than we do from the placid times when all goes smoothly'.

Acknowledgements

I would like to thank Carol Holmes, my supervisor at Regent's College, for her support and encouragement in writing this chapter; David Livingston Smith for reading and commenting on a draft and my colleague, Jenny Greenard, for her help and support as we struggled with the issues described here.

References

Bleger, J. (1967) Psychoanalysis of the psycho-analytic frame, *International Journal of Psycho-analysis*, 48: 511–19.

Bond, T. (1992) Ethical issues in counselling in education, *British Journal of Guidance and Counselling*, 20: 51–63.

Bond, T. (1993) *Standards and Ethics for Counselling in Action*. London: Sage.

British Association for Counselling (1992) *Code of Ethics and Practice for Counsellors*. Rugby: BAC.

Cheifetz, L. (1984) Framework violations in psychotherapy with clinic patients, in J. Raney (ed.) *Listening and Interpreting: The Challenge of the Work of Robert Langs*. London: Jason Aronson.

Cooper, J. (1993) Different ways of structuring the frame: according to Winnicott, Khan and Langs, *Journal of the British Association of Psychotherapists*, 24: 23–35.

Gilbert, S. (1989) The juggling act of the college counselling center: a point of view, *The Counselling Psychologist*, 17: 477–89.

Hoag, L. (1992) Psychotherapy in the general practice surgery: considerations of the frame, *British Journal of Psychotherapy*, 8: 417–29.

Jonathan, A. (1989) 'Counselling in a college setting. Considerations of the frame', unpublished MA thesis. Regent's College, London.

Klein, S.M. (1988) Psychological consultation in a college community, in R. May (ed.) *Psychoanalytic Psychotherapy in a College Context*. New York: Praeger.

Langs, R. (1982) *Psychotherapy: A Basic Text*. New York: Jason Aronson.

May, R. (1988a) Brief psychotherapy with college students, *Journal of College Student Psychotherapy*, 3: 17–38.

May, R. (1988b) Introduction, in R. May (ed.) *Psychoanalytic Psychotherapy in a College Context*, 11–18. New York: Praeger.

May, R. (1988c) The scope of college psychotherapy, in R. May (ed.) *Psychoanalytic Psychotherapy in a College Context*, 57–100. New York: Praeger.

May, R. (1988d) Boundaries and voices, in R. May (ed.) *Psychoanalytic Psychotherapy in a College Context*, 3–21. New York: Praeger.

May, R. (1994) The centre cannot hold: challenges in working psychodynamically in a college or university, *Psychodynamic Counselling*, 1: 5–19.

Menzies Lyth, I. (1988) *Containing Anxiety in Institutions*. London: Free Association Books.

Milton, M. (1993) Counselling in institutional settings – secure frame: possibility – or not? *Counselling*, 4: 284–6.

Noonan, E. (1983) *Counselling Young People*. London: Tavistock/Routledge.

Noonan, E. (1986) The impact of the institution on psychotherapy, *Psychoanalytic Psychotherapy*, 2: 121–30.

Phillips, M. (1991) Violations of the ground rule of confidentiality in a counselling centre: the contribution of Langs, *Counselling*, 2: 92–4.

Smith, D. (1991) *Hidden Conversations: An Introduction to Communicative Psychoanalysis*. London: Tavistock/Routledge.

Chapter 8

Therapist illness: a communicative exploration of an interrupted therapy

Gabrielle Gunton

Introduction

It came as a shock to find myself suddenly incapacitated and unable to move. I awoke one morning with searing pain in my back and leg. Unable to walk or move, I lay helpless. The GP suggested there was nothing serious, just a pulled muscle. He was wrong, and from such a humble beginning stemmed a dramatic series of events that has totally altered my way of being. There is no need to go into the events of the illness as such here, except to say I had a spinal problem that even now leaves me in constant and continual pain, and affords me very limited mobility. I have had numerous surgical procedures, diagnostic procedures, scanning procedures, nerve-blocking procedures, complementary procedures and have had to learn to come to terms with the many changes it has brought to my life. More significantly I have had to come to terms with the debilitating misery of long-term constant pain.

The impact of sudden illness and of being temporarily paralysed caused great disruption in every area of my life. Like most people I had no contingency plans and I therefore had to deal with situations as best I could. When ill, one is faced with awesome uncertainty. When the calamity of serious illness strikes, one confronts one's own mortality and the healthy denial that death will only threaten in the future.

I had been seeing Ms W for once-weekly psychotherapy sessions for nearly two years when my illness suddenly hit and I unexpectedly did not return to sessions after the Christmas break. I was absent for six months.

Literature documenting therapist illness

In trying to understand the significance of such a situation I was surprised to find that the literature connected with suddenly leaving a patient was sparse and a relatively poorly researched area. Current literature contains no systematic study of this issue. Instead there seems to be personal vignettes that highlight the various idiosyncratic reactions by analysts to their illness, and further vignettes to show the impact of a therapist's absence and illness on the client.

The paucity of comprehensive work on a therapist's illness in the literature suggests that this is connected with expressions of avoidance and denial that is invoked in the therapist when faced with the anxiety, guilt and vulnerability that accompany the incapacitating illness. Similarly, therapists' countertransference discomforts and the technical ambiguities involved bring about a suppression of clinical study (Searles 1979; Abend 1982; Dewald 1982; Halpert 1982; Silver 1982; Lindner 1984; Guy and Sounder 1986). Such suggestions, though, seem insufficient if one considers that illness, however insignificant, is likely to impinge on the working life of almost every therapist, and it is likely that as the ageing process takes its toll one's health will be affected. This is particularly so because most therapists qualify at a more mature age than in most other professions.

Lasky (1990) offers insight into this predicament. He accepts that the mechanism of denial is enforced but suggests it is more than that. Catastrophic illness is not a common experience, he states, and unless forced to do so therapists prefer not to contemplate the issue. Indeed in my research I could find very few papers which were written by therapists who had not undergone serious illness (Halpert 1982; Rosner 1986). Lasky does not consider this to be denial but, rather, a 'counter-phobic' state. Similarly, he states that those who have had contact with severe illness but not experienced it themselves feel unqualified to write about it. However, those who have undergone and suffered catastrophic illness, Lasky suggests, are too traumatized by the event and its aftermath to write about it. It requires a considerable passage of time before one feels sufficient distance from the experience to analyse it with any confidence about the conclusions.

Interestingly I could find no writing by Freud about the effects of his illness on his work, even though he was a prolific writer and had to suffer cancer of the palate for 17 years, enduring 33 operations, severe pain and discomfort, difficulty in speaking, and deafness. Yet he made no mention about the effect of his illness, on transference, countertransference or his ability to work (Halpert 1982). Other than the Wolf Man's post-analytic encounter with the ailing Freud (Brunswick 1928) I could also find no specific reports in the first half of this century of an analyst's illness.

The two main foundation papers in this area, Dewald's 'Illness in the analyst' (1982) and Abend's 'Serious illness in the analyst: countertransference considerations' (1982) are milestones in this area. These papers mainly concentrated on whether to tell one's patients about one's situation and, if so, how much or how little information to give. On the whole other therapists have since followed this format: consider the question of what the patient should be told and examine their reactions.

Lindner (1984) gave his patients a full account of his illness and further updated information by letter or telephone. He described his patients as having an almost 'ghoulish interest' in him. Kriechman (1984) did the opposite. He gave his patients no factual information at all. Silver (1982) chose to give her private patients a selective description of her illness and her psychotic institutionalized patients a much more forthcoming description, sharing with them her emotional life and even crying with them. Goldberg (1984) found that the question of how much information to give about her illness became intertwined with her own feelings of helplessness and her need to be cared for. Chernin (1976) felt guilt at abandoning his patients and apologized to them, thus recognizing his own previous unrecognized assumption of omnipotence. Wong's (1990) dramatic account of his catastrophic esophagoscophy and stomach rupture was extraordinary. He analysed many of his countertransference issues with sensitivity and insight, yet in resuming patient care he used such understanding mainly to concentrate on how his absence affected his patients and what to tell them. Similarly, Arlow's (1990) powerfully moving account of his heart condition concluded also by wondering what to tell his patients. He did not relate the countertransference issues – of his own defensive distortion of his experience – to the analytic situation.

Countertransference issues

My particular interest in researching the literature was to consider analysts' countertransference reactions to their illness and how this affected their patients. Certain life situations, I felt, might be so threatening to the analyst that his or her strategic retreat could be considered adaptive. I wished to consider how these anxieties affected the analysis.

The need for analysis of countertransference reactions seems imperative. Wong (1990) stressed the importance of careful self-monitoring, ideally in conjunction with a colleague. He also emphasized the importance of post-illness ongoing self-analysis. He concluded: 'Finally the analyst must not underestimate the impact of his own illness upon the patient and the need to eventually deal with this issue even when a response may not be forthcoming for months after the intrusive event' (Wong 1990: 44).

The work of Robert Langs (1975a, 1975b, 1976, 1978, 1988) and those who have followed his approach (Anisfeld 1984; Brown and Krausz 1984; Smith 1991) gave me the insight into how I could use my patients' narratives to help clarify my countertransference issues within the therapy. Their work recommends how therapists could learn to understand and use patients' unconscious guidance as a constructive approach to their work. They reinforced clearly that unconscious advice was provided by patients to their therapists.

Finally, Whan (1987), a Jungian therapist, offered a fascinating paper which suggested that when the therapist represses his own wounded nature, he projects it onto the patient, who comes to incarnate it and offer insight to the therapist. Whan implored the therapist to acknowledge his woundedness and also recognize that projection and dissociation by the therapist could lead to a schizoid position. He suggested the therapist would have introjected the 'good' healing part and 'projected' the bad wounded part onto the other. Because of projective identification the patient may be kept in the role of the 'ill' one of the pair. The patient, he stated, was increasingly perceived in a depersonalized way and the therapist compensated for his denied woundedness by grandiosity and over-estimation of himself. Thus the therapist defended against the experience of guilt, anxiety and depression which may be engendered in the psychotherapeutic relationship.

The psychological effects of the illness

After six months I was discharged from hospital. I could now move again with effort. My mobility was poor and my pain level extremely high. Such things were physical, I believed. I was surely well enough to spend one hour per week with one patient. Although I was unable to sit in one position for 50 minutes I felt able to concentrate for that amount of time. I was well enough to see Ms W again.

Although I felt intellectually able to return to working with Ms W, part of me knew that emotionally and physically I was not ready.

However, I was unable to acknowledge this aspect or recognize that I had many unresolved concerns connected with my illness that I needed to address. I denied the effects that my illness and my lengthy hospitalization had brought about. I ignored how severe pain had created an emotional anguish where rational thought was normally absent and where my state of being was one of helpless stupor. My illness created a tendency to panic and become anxious at the unexpected; I found it extremely difficult to be with people, whether it be friends, colleagues or even my family. I did not seem to be in the world. There was a sense of depersonalization, of being separated from the spiritual nourishment that comes from being in relationship with others. I was separated from a desire to experience life. In a way I did not exist – and therefore did not have to feel. The world as I had known it no longer seemed familiar. I ignored life because I was too tired and in too much pain to care. My state of confusion and fragmentation was revealed in my sleep through disturbing dreams. I was dismayed at the primitive representations in my dream world. They were disconnected, chaotic, difficult to recall when awake, and had a nightmarish quality about them. My illness challenged and shattered all my previous defensive structures. I had desperately wished not to be helpless, passive or dependent – but had ended up as all of them.

Intense pain is so strangely 'painful', so ungraspable that I was unable to describe what I was going through. Pain is quite incomprehensible to those who have not experienced it. If I could have readily described the pain I was feeling some of the torment I was undergoing might have been understood. I feel, even now, quite illiterate about my pain. I am unable to deal with it rationally, often becoming panic-stricken when it is at its strongest. Yet all these things were flung aside at my need to return to 'normality'. I had felt many things at abandoning my patients so dramatically. Although they were offered other therapists they preferred to wait for my return even though I didn't know when that would be. This added to my sense of guilt and brought about an urgency to return to work as soon as possible.

Case study

Ms W was a divorcee aged 38. Her background was unsettled and she rarely saw her parents together. Her father came to England from Afghanistan. He was intolerant and a bully, an austere man. Her mother was a care worker, and Ms W described how her mother was often away at conferences and meetings. Her sister was a year younger than her, and Ms W felt she was spoilt and that she had many tantrums. Ms W was emotionally close to her maternal grandfather, who died when she was 7 years old.

When Ms W began therapy she was in a relationship with a 50-year-old executive, which had since finished. They owned a house but she often felt like running away in the hope that everything would then be all right. When she was in an argument or in a tight position she had a strong urge to run under a train or run in front of a car.

She hated men and found them difficult. She didn't trust people. She described crying most days at school until she was about 15 years old and of buying friends with money and sweets. She now worked as a consultant; she was doing well and was ambitious.

Ms W talked avidly and with interest about her job where she was doing well, working extra hours and expecting promotion. Part of her job involved booking other people's excursions. This enabled her to link with her phantasy of escape, where she would be happy. The real world felt persecutory: she was off in her mind on holiday, being in a depersonalized state with others. She experienced objects as invasive and persecutory. She held internal dialogues with herself which created an increasingly self-absorbed world into which she was withdrawing. It became evident in our early sessions that Ms W found it difficult to communicate with me. She would come to sessions as if she had already designed the total script and interaction for the forthcoming session in her head. She was unable to relate to any of my comments and would continue with her account as if I were not present.

An interrupted therapy

Within the therapy I very carefully monitored my own input. I registered my own philosophical model where the significance of the therapeutic relationship was vital. I carefully monitored components of the therapy I considered important: empathy, the therapeutic frame, trust, autonomy, ethics, and so on. I tried not to undermine the components required by the therapist and closely looked at my own countertransference issues, both in evaluating the sessions and in my weekly supervision. I can find no evidence in the session narratives or in supervision feedback that any deep countertransference issues were mobilized at this stage of the therapy.

It was at this point that I unexpectedly and dramatically suffered my serious illness and left Ms W without warning for over six months.

A therapist's illness per se does not automatically damage the basic trust between therapist and patient (Counselman and Alonso 1993). It is the way in which the issues created by sudden illness are managed that have the enduring effect upon therapy. It is the management of the broken frame that is vital, as is the need to address matters that frame infringements have brought about. The management of such issues must be taken seriously, and although I consciously did not feel there was any huge dilemma in starting the therapy again (that I could not iron out within my own therapy), my state of denial about the seriousness of my own illness set the stage for an unconscious collusion within the therapeutic relationship. Abend (1982) emphasized the vulnerability of the analyst's judgement, under the stress of being (or just having been) ill; and it is my experience with hindsight that my understanding of the frame infringement in Ms W's therapy was superficial and ineffective.

The communicative approach

The communicative approach offers a philosophy and technique through which such countertransference issues can be explored. The work of Langs has altered radically the conventional view of the analytic situation and consequently offers an alternative view concerning the stimuli that bring about a patient's unconscious communications. By considering the therapeutic situation as a bipersonal field where both therapist and patient interact, Langs has made it clear that reality stimuli brought by the analyst evoke in the patient an unconscious response that needs to be analysed. The communicative methodology stems from posing the question, 'How can we tap the deep unconscious and acknowledge the patient's unconscious response?' The therapist therefore needs to understand the language of the deep unconscious and be able to identify the unconscious communications. These unconscious communications communicative therapists call 'derivatives'. Derivative communications follow a form. Firstly, derivatives are not, on the surface, about therapy. The scene is elsewhere where other people and situations are described. Secondly, derivatives are expressed in concrete images that can be visualized. Thirdly, derivatives are discontinuous: the patient jumps around and often changes the subject.

Non-derivative information is intellectual and rudimentary, with talks about the therapy. It is often analytical, logical or very general and abstract. The communicative approach ignores the non-derivative communication and concentrates solely on derivative communication. These unconscious communications expressed through derivatives are considered to be responses from a 'here and now' stimulus (normally the implications of the therapist's behaviour). They are an encoded reading of the implication of the stimulus. In order to know what to do with the patient's derivative material the communicative therapist needs to decode the trigger of the stimulus in order to reveal the unsuspected unconscious meaning, and then to respect the insight that the decoding offers. A type of translation procedure is required. The therapist uses what the patient unconsciously gives and treats it very seriously. The trigger of the stimulus for the derivative will be related to the therapeutic situation itself and the 'here and now' context. A form of displacement takes place, and the therapist or therapeutic relationship is represented by something else in the patient's narrative. These disguised pictures or derivative representations of the trigger are often difficult for the therapist to pick up yet unless the therapist understands the trigger, the patient's narratives are just abstractions. Often, however, the patient will allude manifestly and in passing to the trigger and then offer a rich network of derivatives which inform the therapist how the patient has processed the trigger. The patient will offer the therapist an interpretation of what is going on, through the themes in the narrative material. The therapist needs to understand what the narrative is a response to, then he or she extracts the themes of the narratives in order to gain understanding; the theme needs to be taken out of the picture and applied to the therapeutic situation.

The derivative themes contain the patient's perceptions of the therapist's behaviour. There are three basic categories – relationship, function and environment themes. Relationship themes are used to convey unconscious perceptions of the quality of the relationship between the therapist and the patient. Smith (1991: 200) describes how patients tell their therapists about their 'abusiveness, seductiveness, deceitfulness and destructiveness as well as their constructiveness, creativity and contactfulness'. Themes of function and dysfunction usually express patients' unconscious awareness of how well or how poorly their therapists are functioning. Environment themes almost always unconsciously depict the state of the therapeutic frame.

In order for the communicative therapist to understand every facet of what the deep unconscious is telling and report back to the patient, he or she must understand the basic essence, the phenomenology of what is happening. The trigger, derivatives and an indicator must be present before the therapist acts.

It was this 'unconscious awareness' by the patient that I wished to explore. I wished to see whether Ms W's unconscious guidance could offer insight into my countertransference issues. I was unaware however, that it was not only the countertransference issues that needed to be addressed. Ms W's derivatives would point unmistakenly to deviant frame issues.

Returning after a six-month break

I resumed sessions with Ms W after a six-month break. The therapy continued for a further two years. I now retrospectively and with communicative insight explore the second part of the therapy. In our first session back after my absence it was as if, from Ms W's point of view, there had been no break at all. She did not refer to my absence, ask me about my illness or in any way indicate that there had been missed sessions. She talked about a partner who represented someone helpful and supportive but who was frightened to engage emotionally, who was not yet secure, and who had found an absence traumatic. She was concerned about a new relationship that was going well but a poor work situation. She recounted how well she had been doing with a course she had been following but told of insecurity in her relationships. She mentioned several times that something awful had happened at Christmas. She also questioned whether she should be having sessions, for surely, she thought, there were people more ill than she. Towards the end of the session Ms W announced:

> *Patient:* Oh. And my dad had a heart attack, I forgot that. I forgot that had happened. He's in America now under observation or something but I didn't feel a thing, it didn't mean anything to me.

Communicative supervision

Throughout the session I made interpretations linking her narrative to our break and I interpreted that she felt insecure in our relationship after such a break. I suggested she felt let down by me and that she seemed to distance my absence from her by having no interest or feeling about it. What I did not do, however, was to examine how Ms W's narrative could have assisted me in my self-analysis of the countertransference issues that had been mobilized by my illness.

There is no doubt that Ms W's derivatives suggested I was unknowingly preoccupied with my own concerns and did not attend to hers. Her derivative themes again and again showed her perceptions of my behaviour. From the communicative point of view Ms W saw my actions as 'mad'.

Langs states: Our techniques are constructed out of our madness. Things that they, the therapists, don't see as mad, their patients unconsciously see as mad. Patients are unconsciously aware of many mad elements in what we do. They understand how our interventions are self-serving, self-gratifying seductive, narcissistic and so on.

(in Smith 1991: 115)

Communicative supervision showed how Ms W had offered me derivatives alluding to my needing to leave, interpersonal conflict, and the break – all the things about which I was anxious. I was especially anxious about my relationship with Ms W after my abandonment of her during my six-month break.

I had also totally blocked out that I had left her at Christmas – for Christmas was when my illness had struck. Communicative supervision also showed that I had not picked up her derivative in which she said that it was not sustainable for people to be in two roles. Nor had I seen that in the way she had forgotton about her father's heart attack she described exactly my denial of my illness, both to myself and within the therapy.

Frame issues

Communicative supervision also showed me how my illness had affected my management of the therapeutic frame, for towards the end of the first session I told Ms W about having a further month's break, and a change in the day and time of future sessions. I blamed the hospital for this break and the changes, citing refurbishment that the hospital was undergoing as the reason for the break.

Communicative theory states such changes are major frame infringements and must be addressed appropriately. When dealing with frame issues, Langs considers that there can be a psychotherapeutic 'conspiracy' in which both patient and therapist collude to avoid the anxiety brought about by a secure frame. Both honestly enter therapy but the anxiety of the frame is such that both try to avoid it, and its particular existential meanings.

In communicative terms the secure frame evokes basic primitive anxieties. With my serious illness I had already had to face such anxieties, I felt lost and wounded and was unable to take on further assault. My paralysis had already made me confront some of my death anxieties. I was not strong enough to face them again. In retrospect there was no real reason for me to have taken a further month's break. It was the summer, but the hospital was open (although undergoing refurbishment). I was not going on holiday, nor was Ms

W; I could easily have seen her for sessions and begun to address our frame issues. I didn't.

In the second session after the break Ms W began by telling me that she was ending the relationship with her partner. She referred to him as being a 'know-it-all', having an answer for everything and making statements that were not warranted. He took her for granted. So too did his family, expecting her to go off on holidays with them and have Christmas with them. Her narrative themes also included the need to clarify things, that there was unfinished business to attend to, that someone would like to be different but they were unable to manage it now, that someone lacked self-esteem and was threatened by the presence of another.

I interpreted the transference issues to her, suggesting that she felt I also took her for granted, that she thought I'd just expected her to wait for my return and that she felt I didn't appear to listen properly to her either. Supervision again showed that I was unable to hear in her narrative that she felt I had an investment in keeping the therapy going, and that with my badly timed interpretations I was trying to grab onto her and absorb her. I was not able to interpret that she felt I was using her for my own ends. This helped me recognize that within myself I had secretly felt my illness might mean I was unable to complete my psychotherapy training, that I would lose my job, my family and friends. In my mind I unconsciously needed Ms W.

The therapeutic relationship

Generally as in any other deep interpersonal experience, both participants have motives to maintain the experience. The patient has a deep need for this relationship, since she has finally achieved the type of parental response for which she has been searching. Within it she also resolves the transference areas where previously possible gratification was minimal. Yet there are times when the therapist also wishes to maintain the relationship. Although the therapist functions parentally there is also an unconscious demand for the satisfaction of her own personal needs and desires. It seems then, in the decoding of Ms W's narratives, that the motivation to preserve the therapeutic experience was mine.

Unconscious guidance for the therapist

In the communicative approach it follows that a patient can offer supervisory guidelines for the therapist through models of rectification. These come in the terms of 'should' statements. As the patient tells his story he tells what should be the result, or what should happen. Ms W offered me a model of rectification in her story about her colleague Pauline: 'If she wasn't well she shouldn't come into work and that was it. If you're not well enough to do the job, stay at home.'

I recall with some sardonic humour the statement from the Wolf Man (Brunswick 1928: 445) 'How agreeable it is that I, the patient, am really healthy, whereas he, the doctor, has a serious illness.' Communicative supervision showed how I ignored totally Ms W's model of rectification alluding to the termination of the therapy and that I was unable to address my inability to confront our situation. How was I to retrieve the situation in the few sessions we had left before we ended?

I wanted to keep in mind the communicative point of view that patients prescribe their treatment and that the therapist needs to wait and integrate what is said. I wanted to bear in mind that I had been breaking the ground rules, and when I left them uncorrected Ms W gave derivatives about betrayal, resentment and anger. The communicative approach demands that when a therapist makes an error she needs to understand why she has felt the need to do so, in order that she does not keep repeating the error. I was aware that previously I had not resolved the issue of my neediness within myself. Thus Ms W had seen me as greedy and devouring. In breaking the ground rules Ms W unconsciously saw me as fulfilling my own pathological needs but failing and traumatizing *her*. Although I considered I was helping Ms W, she instead unconsciously saw me as attempting to help myself. I did not want there to become a stalemate in treatment which Searles (1975) suggests comes when the therapist receives a kind of therapeutic support from the patient and clings to it without the conscious knowledge of either. It was therefore with some caution that I approached our next session.

The final stages of the therapy

Two months before the agreed ending of the therapy, Ms W announced she was leaving her job and her home, and that she intended to end therapy a month early. Mindful of my countertransference issues and the need to monitor Ms W's derivative material very closely, I was aware that I must let her tell me the issues through her stories and that I must be sensitive to the moment in the last few sessions.

Ms W clearly felt there should be consistency in relationships, codes should not be broken when agreements had been made. I was again reminded that I had already broken my agreement once – I had left her for six months. She unconsciously wanted me to keep our official ending. I kept in mind this supervision of hers, for we were in the final stages of therapy.

However, in the first session after Ms W's announcement that she wished to end therapy a month early I was uncharacteristically five minutes late. This is a deviation of the frame expressing my own anxieties, and I could predict that Ms W's derivatives would respond to this lateness and to my offer to put the five minutes onto the end of the session. Indeed, her first narrative theme suggested just that – she told a story in which someone was given extra time but the time seemed pointless as nothing subsequently would go according to plan.

The trigger of my lateness and our previous session's unresolved ending regarding her announcement were prominent in her narratives. A model of rectification was offered – people shouldn't be dropped in favour of others, she said. People should not leave others in the lurch.

Validation

I interpreted to her that she was telling me she did not want me to end a month early for it would seem that I was abandoning her and going off with someone else. The communicative approach gives clear implications about the truth or falseness of an interpretation, and clear implications about whether the therapist has gained the correct understanding of the derivatives. If the therapist's intervention is correct the patient will respond with validating imagery. As Smith (1991: 214) advises: 'A communicative intervention is considered appropriate only if it is followed by constructive derivative imagery. If the patient responds with negative imagery after the intervention the communicative therapist concludes that his efforts were seriously flawed.' I was rewarded with a validation – a story which told of her ambivalence to something at first but then a sense of 'that's great, this is really good'. Her story told of her reluctance to go to art class the night before. She used to go to art class years ago, she explained, but she never took the exams. She had started art again now but she really hadn't particularly wanted to. Once she was there and got started it was really great. Now she wanted to get her exams and her teaching certificate. The validation continued in the story she then told about Samantha. She was seeing more of Samantha now. They propped each other up and gave each other confidence. She could talk to Samantha much more now. Everything between them was fine.

However, the validation in the story about Samantha contained some supervision for me too; Ms W told about Samantha seeing a married man: 'It's not her I blame; it's him – he's got commitments, he shouldn't cross the boundaries; he's got a duty and he shouldn't break it. If she's foolish enough to want that, okay, but he shouldn't break his code.'

Ms W clearly felt there should be consistency in relationships, codes should not be broken when agreements had been made. I was made conscious that I had broken my agreement more than once – I left her for six months and I then altered and extended our original ending date for the purposes of my training. She unconsciously wanted me to keep to our official ending. I kept in mind this supervision of hers, for we were in the final stages of the therapy.

Dramatically, four weeks prior to the 'official' ending time but on the day of Ms W's revised ending date, she finished the session 15 minutes early, leaving for me – to receive once she had left – an extraordinarily huge bouquet of flowers and a handwritten note saying she would make contact again.

She did not attend the following three sessions, but she wrote again before the 'final' session reiterating that she would not be attending but thanking me profusely for helping her and expressing a profound sense of loss at never seeing me again.

Unless she came to that 'final' session there would be no ending as such. She did not attend.

Although the huge bouquet of flowers was a gift at the end of four years' therapy, I also felt it represented her anger and aggression at our unresolved frame issues. Leaving me 'holding the flowers' enabled her to transpose roles so that this time she left me, and left me powerless, holding a representation of her anger. I speculate that my enforced break and temporary disruption of the therapy recalled Ms W's emotional deprivation during childhood and that my nursing demands represented her depressed mother and my absence her unobtainable father.

Whitaker and Malone (1981) suggest that a patient's impulse to separate from a therapist stems from three general areas. Firstly, that the patient is able to deny his patient status. Secondly, that there is a new insistence by the patient of her status as a separate person, and thirdly, that there is some subtle acceptance by the patient of her new therapeutic role.

In the ending with Ms W she seemed to suggest there was an element of all three areas. There also seemed to be an increase in the importance of her real needs (beginning her new job positively) and an ability to gratify those needs as they interlinked with her phantasy needs outside of the therapeutic relationship. Although she wrote in appreciation of the symbolic parent relationship, her need for such a relationship seemed no longer to have the compulsive and repressive quality it once had. It seemed Ms W was able to obtain some real gratification even though there were still unresolved issues.

In conclusion, then, following the communicative framework with communicative supervision, and with hindsight, I was able to identify adaptive contexts within the therapy. While the therapy was in its final stage I attempted to address the adaptive issues that had been raised.

The outcome of the work

The outcome of the work falls into two categories: the outcome for the patient and the outcome for the therapist. The outcome for Ms W seemed positively toned despite therapeutic disruptions.

She no longer held the same worries concerning the main conditions outlined in her initial assessment. She no longer felt the urge to run away from frightening situations by running in front of a car or jumping under a train. She didn't any longer dislike sex nor find it difficult. Although there were still unresolved issues about what sex represented, there had been a shift in her feelings of sexuality. The strong sense of depersonalization and fragmentation that was first shown in sessions had changed, and there was an integration that allowed her to view herself more passionately and with interest. There was less self-absorption into fantasy and with her change of job she had chosen to lessen her escape into holidays. She no longer designed the scripts for interaction with other people and was able to distinguish between reality and fantasy in her interactions with others. She no longer withdrew into a self-absorbed world in the same way or had such an invasive sense of hostility and threat in her close relationships.

The outcome for me was as follows:

1 My absence through illness caused significant frame deviation that severely affected the therapy.
2 My illness brought about strong countertransference issues that impaired judgement and self-analysis.
3 My impaired judgement and countertransference difficulties meant that the frame issues were not appropriately addressed.
4 Following the communicative framework I recognized that the patient had extensive unconscious perceptions of my difficulties.

5 In decoding the patient's narratives according to communicative technique, I was made aware of function and relationship issues in regard to the therapy as well as frame infringements.
6 Addressing such issues through supervision and writing this chapter has had a beneficial effect upon me.

Stemming from such outcomes I offer the following guidelines to therapists who find themselves returning to patients after a period of absence resulting from chronic emotional or physical illness.

• Serious illness can impair judgement. It affects one's thinking in a number of ways, even to the extent of the timing for returning to clinical practice.
• Countertransference issues are likely to affect self-analysis and the way one monitors clinical material.
• Lengthy absence causes frame infringement, and the therapist must be vigilant to address such frame infringements throughout the remaining therapy.
• Regular supervision with a colleague who will listen particularly for countertransference and frame infringement issues will help address the therapist's impaired judgement, however.
• Working within a communicative framework will clearly show therapists their patients' unconscious perceptions of their analytic behaviour.

Often the fact that the therapist is human gets lost, yet traumatic illness reminds the therapist and the patient that the therapist is a very vulnerable human creature indeed. I quote from Wong (1990: 45):

> because I must continue to live with the residua from my illness, and face the eventuality of more surgery, I have found it helpful to re-examine and try to understand and analyse those traumatic moments of my life. I have had to acknowledge the aftermath of the illness upon my work. I hope to focus further attention on an important and much neglected area with which all analysts must come to grips one day.

In Ms W's final letter to me, she thanked me profusely for her care. How can I explain that it was she who also unconsciously cared for me?

References

Abend, S.M. (1982) Serious illness in the analyst: counter-transference considerations, *Journal of American Psychoanalytic Association*, 30(2): 365–79.

Anisfeld, L.S. (1984) The therapist's disability as an adaptive concept, in James Raney (ed.) *Listening and Interpreting: The Challenge of the Work of Robert Langs*. New York: Jason Aronson.

Arlow, J.A. (1990) The analytic attitude in the service of denial, in H.J. Schwartz and A.L. Silver (eds) *Illness in the Analyst – Implications for the Treatment Relationship*. Madison, CT: International Universities Press.

Brown, R.D. and Krausz, R. (1984) The patient's unconscious perceptions of the therapist's disruptions, in J. Raney (ed.) *Listening and Interpreting: The Challenge of the Work of Robert Langs*. New York: Jason Aronson.

Brunswick, R.M. (1928) A supplement to Freud's history of an infantile neurosis, *International Journal of Psychoanalysis*, 9: 439–76.

Chernin, P. (1976) Illness in a therapist – loss of omnipotence, *Archives General Psychiatry*, 33: 1327–8.

Counselman, E.F. and Alonso, A. (1993) The ill therapist: therapists' reactions to personal illness and its impact on psychotherapy, *American Journal of Psychotherapy*, 47(4): 591–602.

Dewald, P.A. (1982) Illness in the analyst: transference, counter-transference and reality responses, *Journal of American Psychoanalytic Association*, 30(2): 347–63.

Goldberg, F. (1984) Personal observations of a therapist with a life threatening illness, *International Journal of Group Psychotherapy*, 34(2): 289–96.

Guy, J.D. and Sounder, J.K. (1986) Impact of therapist's illness or accident on psychotherapeutic practice: review and discussion, *Professional Psychology: Research and Practice*, 17: 509–13.

Halpert, E. (1982) When the analyst is chronically ill or dying, *Psychoanalytic Quarterly*, 51: 372–89.

Kriechman, A.M. (1984) Illness in the therapist, the eye patch, *Psychiatry*, 47: 378–86.

Langs, R.J. (1975a) Therapeutic misalliances, *International Journal of Psychoanalytic Psychotherapy*, 4: 77–105.

Langs, R.J. (1975b) The therapeutic relationship and deviations in technique, *International Journal of Psychoanalytic Psychotherapy*, 4: 106–41.

Langs, R.J. (1976) *The Bipersonal Field*. New York: Jason Aronson.

Langs, R.J. (1978) The adaptational interactional dimension of countertransference, *Contemporary Psychoanalysis*, 14: 502–33.

Langs, R.J. (1988) *A Primer of Psychotherapy*. New York: Gardner Press.

Lasky, R. (1990) Keeping the analysis intact when the analyst has suffered a catastrophic illness: clinical implications, in H.J. Schwartz and A.L. Silver (eds) *Illness in the Analyst – Implications for the Treatment Relationship*. Madison, CT: International Universities Press.

Lindner, H. (1984) Therapist and patient reactions to life-threatening crisis in the therapist's life, *International Journal of Clinical Experimental Hypnosis*, 32: 12–27.

Rosner, S. (1986) The seriously ill or dying analyst and the limits of neutrality, *Psychoanalytic Psychotherapy*, 3(4): 357–71.

Searles, H.F. (1975) The patient as therapist to his analyst in tactics and techniques, in P.L. Giovaccini (ed.) *Psychoanalytic Therapy, Vol. II. Countertransference*. New York: Jason Aronson.

Searles, H.F. (1979) *Counter-transference and Related Subjects*. Madison, CT: International Universities Press.

Silver, A.L. (1982) Resuming the work with a life-threatening illness, *Contemporary Psychoanalysis*, 18(3): 314–26.

Smith, D. (1991) *Hidden Conversations: An Introduction to Communicative Psychoanalysis*. London and New York: Routledge.

Whan, M. (1987) Chiron's wound: some reflections on the wounded healer, in N. Schwatz-Salant and M. Stein (eds) *Archetypal Processes in Psychotherapy*. New York: Chiron Publications.

Whitaker, C. and Malone, T. (1981) *The Roots of Psychotherapy*. New York: Brunner/Mazel.

Wong, N. (1990) Acute illness in the analyst, in H.J. Schwartz and A.L. Silver (eds) *Illness in the Analyst – Implications for the Treatment Relationship*. Madison, CT: International Universities Press.

Chapter **9**

The two parts of myself: decoding a video-recorded session between 'Kathy' and Rogers[1]

Ivan Thorpe

Introduction

This chapter examines the video-recorded therapeutic session between Carl Rogers and 'Kathy' from the perspective of Robert Langs's understanding of the nature and focus of unconscious communication. It does not seek to denigrate the work of Rogers, but to explore the hypothesis that there may be two levels of interaction in any therapeutic interaction between any therapist and any client: the conscious dialogue and the unconscious attempts by a client to communicate her reaction to a therapeutic situation which is less than perfect.

Langs's work is rooted in the detailed examination of client–therapist interactions, and emphasizes clients' perceptions of the therapist within the therapeutic encounter, communicated in narrative form. The client is seen as unconsciously attempting to cure the therapist of the perceived 'core madness' they exhibit in their interventions in therapy. I will seek to show how Kathy attempts to educate Rogers in this way in the stories that she tells during their meeting. The curative efforts of the client monitor what are perceived as the self-serving communications of the therapist, since these are understood to threaten the 'secure frame' which, Langs (1980) claims, is unconsciously demanded by clients.

It is important to explain some of the terms that Langs uses before I go any further. I introduced the term 'core madness' above in the context of client–therapist interaction. Langs (1985a and 1985b) uses the term 'madness' to describe a potential way of responding to essential fears created by the human condition in all of us. By this he means our apprehensions of our limitations which include vulnerabilities such as aloneness, mortality and limitations of our power. When he refers to a therapist's madness, he is referring to the way in which a client may contact some of these fears within the therapist, causing the therapist to express or avoid these emotional conflicts, in the way they respond to the client's material.

Langs (1985a) describes three interrelated sources of madness. The first arises out of the very nature of the human mind, and of life itself, and he calls this *psychobiological*. The second derives from the inescapable disturbances we experience in our relationships with others. The third stems from the hurtful and disturbing aspects of human growth and development, and from random, unexpected life incidents that are physically and mentally harmful. In order to live with the growing knowledge of these threats to our existence, we require healthy forms of denial, and an ability to live without constantly thinking of these potentially paralysing realities. The self-condemning agencies of the mind are kept out of our consciousness by our system of defences, in order to avoid constant anxiety, and to preserve a faith in the purpose of existence.

Langs uses the term 'madness' in order to emphasize that disturbances in thoughts, behaviours and feelings overtly displayed by either the client or the therapist, are always an interface between an external stimulus and an internal response that has been perceived as dangerous. The symptoms, which may be expressed by the client or the therapist, are a maladaptive form of communicative defence designed to express and at the same time to keep from direct awareness, the threatening, raw feelings, images and thoughts that the stimulus has generated.

'Core madness' therefore is universal to us all, and 'expressed madness' is the emotionally founded disturbance that is particular to an individual patient, and contains his own unique attempt to manage dangerous, unconscious images created in him by external stimuli, but kept outside of his direct awareness. The most serious forms of madness, with which we find particular difficulty in communicating, are those where there is a disruption in the contact that the client has with objective reality. These forms of madness are often called 'psychotic', with symptoms of false beliefs and false sensory experiences such as delusions and hallucinations. They may also include loss of self-control, as in states of excessive desire, sexuality or aggression, and senseless behaviour. These behaviours can be considered as maladaptive defences against disorganized inner states. However, they may contain encoded expressions of unmastered primitive responses to threat. When learned, 'healthy' defences fail, we fight to avoid the kind of madness previously described by trying to express our madness in various ways.

Langs (1985a) says we do one or all of the following:

1 express and discharge behaviourally what might otherwise be experienced as terrifying and disorganizing inner states;
2 place ourselves in 'mad' situations, or relate to openly mad individuals in order to cover over and seal off our own insanity;
3 develop psychosomatic symptoms.

It follows, therefore, that madness is a form of contagion, and the therapist who lives in its presence has a natural inclination to mobilize communicative defences (conscious ways of communicating and interacting) against the client's expression of madness, and the client will welcome the therapist's help in defending them both against direct awareness of his unconscious conflicts.

I believe that we see in the encounter between Rogers and Kathy both participants defending against a conscious awareness of the madness contained in their attempt to do therapy in front of a video camera. Kathy has put herself in a treatment situation which she eventually sees, unconsciously, as characterized by her perceived madness of the therapist, Rogers. Her own problems are gradually sealed off from awareness as their encounter focuses, unconsciously, more and more on her reactions to the madness of the conditions under which Rogers is attempting to counsel her. Kathy begins to express indirectly, through encoded messages derived from these unconscious factors, her perceptions of Rogers's self-serving behaviour.

Langs (1985b vol. 2), argues that there are three modes of listening present in a therapeutic encounter. The first is *manifest listening* in terms of the consciously intended context: this means the surface aspect of the client's conversation, the direct and self-evident meanings which seem obvious to client and therapist alike.

The second is *Type 1 derivative listening* (Langs 1985: 7 ff.) in terms of the context of the client's hypothetical intrapsychic world: for example, stories, memories, dreams, or reflections that may give insight to the client's internal world. The meaning of this material may not be self-evident to the client or the therapist, but will contain a disguised or encoded theme within it. The term 'derivative' was coined by Freud to indicate a manifest content that simultaneously expressed a disguised meaning, the implication being that the hidden, raw (dangerous) image, feeling and thought, is perceived as too frightening to be expressed directly. This is also called an *encoded* message or hidden communication which occurs when we find ourselves in a situation that we perceive as dangerous and anxiety-provoking. Hiding our communication, within a narrative for example, offers us the opportunity of providing a dual-meaning form of communication from which we can disassociate our awareness. In this way a message with implications reaches conscious expression by way of themes that it shares in common with material already in conscious awareness. The client moves from one story to another, a dream, a story, a memory, each containing clues to the theme of the displaced communication.

The third type of listening (*Type 2 derivative listening*) focuses on derivatives which are stimulated as an adaptive response – an unconscious reaction to a *trigger* or reality stimulus, present in the context of therapy. It is by consistently listening for narratives and displaced communications of this nature from clients that therapists can gain insight into clients' perceptions of their (therapists') functioning in the session. The client's unconscious mind becomes the supervisor of the therapist's clinical practice. With this approach it is possible for the therapist to evaluate from intervention to intervention the accuracy and appropriateness of their interventions and their client's perceptions of their management of the therapeutic frame or context.

Countertransference is constantly monitored on the basis of the client's disguised supervisory comments. This modality of therapy is essentially client-centred, since it encourages silent holding of the client and allows the client to move freely from one form of communication to another. Langs argues that depth psychologists may see this lack of confrontation and probing of a particular subject as allowing resistance in the client. I feel, however, as does Langs (1985a, 1985b), that the pressure on the therapist to disrupt the client and to interrupt them without invitation, relates more to the therapist's agenda than to the client's. The communicative approach makes the assumption that clients want to communicate and have a need to express themselves when the conditions are right and when the responses they perceive they get from their therapist are appropriate.

Langs (1985b) goes on to divide the types of communication taking place in the client–therapist encounter into three types. The first – *Type A* – is communication which attempts to convey truth. This may be colourful narrative, as in dreams, containing the potential for disguise, inference and evaluation. In the session with Rogers you will hear a story about the client's ex-husband which, I maintain, conveys a truth about her unconscious perception of Rogers that she wants him to hear.

The second form of communication (*Type B*) is that which has the purpose of discharging tension and is triggered through interactional pressure: like the desire to rescue, persecute, give advice, engage in a theoretical teaching session, make suggestions or be a victim with the client. In the session discussed later you will see how Rogers provokes Kathy into a behavioural response by using a tissue to blow his nose which is closely followed by her using one to wipe her eyes, and by her derivative response to a suggestion made by Rogers that he does care about her.

The third form of communication (*Type C*) has no latent content and may be characterized by clichéd ritualistic forms of communication and dead metaphors. This form of communicating has the flavour of pass-times, diary descriptions and reportage. Langs argues that the purpose of this type of interaction is to avoid and deny truth. This can take place as a form of resting between periods of other forms of communication. Within this framework the possibility of having straight communications between client and therapist which convey truth without innuendo, inference, displacement and disguise, is not considered as a possibility by Langs (1985b, 1988).

Langs sees only four forms of intervention by the therapist as legitimate within the session. The first is an interpretation, which is a verbal intervention that attempts to offer the therapist's perception of the themes contained in the client's derivative material, connected to the trigger or stimulus for the production of these images, and including the bridge to the therapeutic context which is seen as the invitation to make the intervention in the first place. This is a process intervention that centres on 'you-me' talk, and deals with the client's unconscious perceptions of the therapist.

The second type would be the reflection or playback of selected derivatives from the client's material, which are thought of by the therapist as containing possible communications as to the adaptive context or trigger which is as yet unknown or unrepresented.

The third intervention is silence.

The fourth is framework management, which means the setting or securing of necessary boundaries to the client–therapist interaction which work towards an appropriate, 'holding' frame. This is a core concept in communicative psychotherapy and issues involved in this will be discussed later as they apply to Kathy's meeting with Rogers.

The therapist's responses to the client are made only when the client indicates a need to be heard and recognized. The therapist also listens for material provided by the client of a type which seems to be based on the adaptive context of the therapy and contains possible clues to the therapeutic trigger that sparked the derivative story. Lastly, the client will have provided a bridge to therapy by a direct or thinly disguised reference to the adaptive nature of the therapeutic interaction and context.

When the intervention is made by the therapist it should contain the following: a playback of connected derivatives produced by the client in the session; a hunch by the therapist about the client's perceptions of him or her contained in them; a sharing with the client of the therapist's logic in connecting the bridge or reference to therapy to the other narratives; and last, but by no means least, the therapist should identify, in a tentative way, the interaction or communication between them which he/she considers to be the source or trigger for the derivatives provided by the client. If this is an error by the therapist it can be acknowledged in a non-defensive way and rectified.

Communicative theory suggests that the client will 'validate' the therapist's appropriate behaviour if the therapist's intervention is seen as correct by the client by providing a displaced or introjected reference to someone who is helpful, or a story with a theme which is positive. The client may give a selected fact, previously withheld, which makes a difference to the understanding of the client (this may be a previously repressed memory). Equally, if the intervention made by the therapist is perceived as inaccurate, showing him to be unaware of the encoded communication contained in the client's discourse, the references in the new material may be negative, and the client may stay silent, repeat material or offer the type of material that is manifest in content.

Encoded messages have manifest meaning, immediate implications, and transformed meaning. The most distinctive feature of the transformed level of meaning is that it is created by the unconscious use of the mechanism of displacement. An encoded message is an adaptive response to a stimulus or trigger. It is the product of an interactional experience and can be understood only in light of a specific stimulus and the interactional context that has provoked it. The client's reaction to these perceived stimuli, however, is strongly shaped by their previous experience and the internal structure of their personality.

The frame

Central to the communicative approach is the notion of the secure frame. The communicative therapist hopes that by listening to the encoded messages present in the client's stories, and thus guided by the client's unconscious mind, the therapist can so manage the frame that a curative 'secure frame moment' can be achieved. For

Langs the rules of the frame are quite specific and can be found in detail in his literature, including *Rating Your Psychotherapist* (1989). They include the following: a secure comfortable private space free from interruptions and observation; a fixed fee; a fixed appointment time; the careful observation of time boundaries; the same environment each week; no touching; no self-disclosure on the part of the therapist other than is relevant to specific interactions between therapist and client which take place in the therapy room. Included under the heading of confidentiality would be consideration of such issues as the audio recording of sessions, appropriate sources of referral; ownership of and access to client notes; supervision. The dress of the counsellor, and the decoration and objects present in the therapeutic space would be relevant to the issue of therapist neutrality.

A communicative therapist struggles with these issues, and has to be aware that the client will communicate, through encoded messages, their unconscious perceptions of the therapist's competence, as demonstrated by his provision of these requirements. At the same time as the client is unconsciously telling the therapist how to secure the frame, it is likely that, consciously, clients feel threatened by the experience of contacting their inner fears and their 'existential angst', and may prefer to seek the comfort of fraudulent, inauthentic and illusory therapy. The therapist has to contend with his own panic, 'core madness' and self-doubt, and may well be frightened into deviating from a secure 'holding' environment (Davis and Wallbridge 1981: 106).

It was with these theoretical guidelines in place that I examined the videotaped encounter between Kathy and Rogers. I wanted to use a session in the public domain to examine the approach so that others who might be interested may themselves observe the evidence.

Theory into practice

The dialogue of the encounter between Kathy and Rogers has been transcribed verbatim from the video *Three Approaches to Psychotherapy II* (1972) which I have watched numerous times, and have presented in various training workshops over the years. I have great respect for the person-centred approach of Rogers, and would argue elsewhere that a counsellor practising within a secure frame, offering limited self-disclosure, accurate reflection, appropriate silence, and 'immediacy' interventions, could ensure a client a therapeutic experience which might be helpful. In fact, what becomes apparent when analysing the Kathy and Rogers interaction is that it is Rogers'

appropriate and reasonably accurate 'immediacy' or process interventions at the end of the session that, inadvertently, offer a form of
communicative intervention which relates Kathy's subjective experience of her public performance as client to the adaptive context of
the counselling session and its limitations. The whole interaction
can be seen as Kathy's attempt to communicate to Rogers the 'madness' inherent in their recorded session.

   Both of the videos made by Rogers, one with Gloria in the early
1960s and the other with Kathy in the 1970s, were made for training
and promotional purposes. Gloria and Kathy volunteered to be
clients and may have been 'seduced' by the prospect of exposing
their psyches to the famous therapists of the time. Gloria and Kathy
could have declined to participate in these sessions, but their self-
sacrifice or self-interest has provided us with a record of influential
therapists (Rogers, Perls, Ellis, Shostrom and Lazarus) in action.

   What I find most interesting about these interactions from a
communicative viewpoint is that, despite the decisions made by the
client's conscious mind, unconsciously she is not allowed to 'get
away with it'. Kathy is in a situation where the potential for fraudulent therapy is encouraged, but there is also the possibility that some
real contact between her and Rogers might take place. Consciously
Kathy may decide to play the game of the 'good' client for Rogers, but
the derivatives generated by the session, when decoded, show us
that, unconsciously, she is far from happy with the situation and
attempts not only to 'tell it like it is', but also 'how it should be'.

   Rogers, a man of humility and empathy, openly shares his own
reservations about their situation, but his attempts at being authentic in this 'deviant'[2] frame environment increase Kathy's unconscious perceptions of the madness inherent in their meeting.

   The deviant frame of the session between Kathy and Rogers sets
the scene for the themes which dominate their interaction. The communicative approach argues that an appropriately timed intervention by the therapist which communicates an awareness of the
meaning of the derivative, and of the part the therapist has played in
triggering that specific derivative, will elicit a validating statement
from the client. According to Langs this may take the form of a further derivative which contains a more positive theme or a reference
to a therapeutic object, or a new theme or piece of information.
There may also be a greater inclination towards 'you-me' talk
between the client and the therapist. The experience of the therapist
and the client participating in a mutual struggle to secure the therapeutic frame can promote, at one and the same time, the feelings of
heightened authenticity, excitement and fear for the client which
may result in a resting period after a successful *secure frame moment*.

Rogers is not a communicative therapist and therefore he is unlikely to use this formula. However, Rogers does use 'you-me' or 'immediacy' talk, and shares with Kathy his perception of their relationship, paraphrasing her own words and metaphors. I see these moments of immediacy as the most meaningful interactions between Kathy and Rogers in the session, but they seem to occur more by coincidence rather than as a planned response by Rogers to an invitation by Kathy to share his perception of his contributions.

The session

The session begins:

> *Rogers:* Hi, Kathy, I'm really glad to meet you. (*As he says this he crosses his legs.*) I feel a little uptight under these lights, but I do not feel that it will last very long.
> *He finishes his introduction by saying that he would be glad to hear whatever Kathy would want to say.*
> *Kathy:* I don't know where to begin, but, umm . . . (*at this point fleetingly looking at the camera and away down to her right.*)
> *She tells Rogers about the death of her husband and the awareness that she used this as a shield against beginning new relationships with men. Then, while looking at Rogers:*
> *Kathy:* I feel very frightened of new male relationships.
> *Rogers reflects this statement back to her.*
> *Kathy:* In going out with other men lately . . . it is very strange, I'm very uncomfortable, so . . .
> *Rogers again reflects this statement clarifying Kathy's meaning of the feelings of loss. Kathy joins in to help Rogers understand what she had said.*
> *Kathy:* I became aware of how very lonely I'd become. I have not been dating much over the last four years. I think I'm keeping myself in a no-win situation where I'm really lonely. I'm keeping myself there . . . a guard around me, and I'd like to break out of that. (*Here she indicates a semicircle with her hand which may be a reference to the set, cameras, carpet on the floor, etc.*)
> *Rogers:* You are in some way responsible for your aloneness.
> *Kathy:* (*different tone of voice – quickly*) Yes, I know that, yes. I'm very, yes I am . . .
> *Rogers:* Like to break out of that shell or that safeguard you've been hiding behind.
> *Kathy:* (*smiles at Rogers*) Part of me does (*looking at Rogers*), part of me says no way!

Rogers introduces the notion of Kathy's ambivalence to being guarded or breaking out, Kathy nods and Rogers goes on to share a hunch.
Rogers: More of a risk if you break out . . . is that part of it?

When the interaction so far is viewed from a communicative perspective Rogers acknowledges the lights, but does not refer to these as part of the deviant frame. He says he is glad to meet Kathy but crosses his legs. Kathy tells him she is frightened of new male relationships, possibly referring to this one with Rogers, and that she is very uncomfortable.

Other thinly veiled encoded messages commentating on the session may include the story Kathy tells Rogers about dating: she tells him that she is in a double bind, that she has put herself in a no-win situation (perhaps, too, by agreeing to be Rogers's client) but she is very lonely and wants to break out of the situation she is in, which prevents real communication. Kathy has acknowledged the camera by looking at it, Rogers has mentioned the lights. Therefore the main focus of this session may be solely the frame violations present. I would predict that Kathy would make other references to cameras, being photographed or looked at.

For me there is another important dilemma for Kathy and Rogers: whether they should attempt real therapy in this deviant frame. Although Kathy's conscious judgement brought her to this session, unconsciously she feels: 'no way', 'this is crazy'. But she feels lonely, uncommunicated with, and wonders whether Rogers can be the one to help her break out of this bizarre, no-win frame that she has put herself into. Kathy tells Rogers that the knowledge of her process in relationships with men is not new, but that she doesn't go past the awareness.

Rogers: The knowledge is not new, the question is, what do you do about it?
Kathy: That's right, how can one stay safe and be open?
She shakes her head and grins at Rogers.
Rogers: The way you shake your head makes me feel you don't see any way.

Here I feel Rogers would have had a chance for a communicative intervention, provided by Kathy shaking her head and smiling at Rogers, which could be interpreted as a bridge to the therapeutic session. I will make an attempt at providing one, although it may be that it is too soon in the session to do so. I might begin:

And so, Kathy, we began this session in front of these cameras, which I mentioned made me a little uptight, and which we both seem aware of. You told me about the death of your husband, and how you used him to shield you against new male relationships, and how you'd like to break out of that loneliness. You'd got yourself into a no-win situation; the question seems to be: what can you do about it, and how can you stay safe and yet be open? When you shook your head just now in this session, I felt that you don't see any way that this could be, and I'm wondering if you perceive that you're in that same no-win situation here with me? I am, in a sense, a 'new male relationship', and I understand that you agreed to be my client, and I guess that brings an assumption that there needs to be some opening up taking place on your part, but now that you're here in this public situation, how can you stay safe and be open with me, at the same time?'

This is my attempt to include some derivative information, the trigger of the deviant frame, and a bridge to therapy.

Rogers's intervention is 'It seems unanswerable to be open with a person and yet feel safe.' What Rogers doesn't acknowledge in this reflection is his part in her concerns about the current situation. Kathy replies in a cold, 'matter of fact' way, that suggests Rogers had missed her displaced communication about the frame violation of the camera, and his self-serving expectation that she should perform for him.

> *Kathy:* I'm an open person to begin with, and everything is fine in a relationship to begin with, as long as the focus does not turn onto me.
> *Rogers:* I see, I see, if you can keep the focus on the other person you're OK.
> *Kathy:* That's right, and the focus on me, up to a certain level, but not in a romantic way, a friendship, I would value that.
> *Rogers:* But love at arm's length.
> *Kathy:* But do you know that's important though, if a person doesn't want to be your friend, how can you have him for a lover, no way. (*Grins at Rogers.*)
> *Kathy stops, looks at Rogers who stays silent. There is a few seconds pause.*
> *Rogers:* I'm not quite sure I get that – you mean friendship is a first step?
> *Kathy:* It is for me.

Rogers stays silent, and then takes a tissue from a box on the table between them, wipes his nose and puts the tissue down. The issue of tissues present in a counselling room can be perceived as a common courtesy to provide in a place where crying takes place;

however, their presence can also be seen as an invitation to cry. By blowing his nose, Rogers has drawn Kathy's attention to the tissues. He then puts his right hand on his chin and smiles at Kathy with an impish grin. Kathy looks down, smiles, looks at Rogers and starts to breathe deeply, Rogers stays silent and nods his head;

> *Kathy:* I've gotten to the point where I won't go beyond. I've laid the cards out, now that's all I want to play.
> *Rogers:* So that in this relationship, it's like in your other relationships, you go so far then stop, and this is as far as you want to go – to go any further is a risk? (*pause*) I think your eyes tell me you're feeling that risk right now.
> *Kathy:* So here I am.

This last statement from Rogers could be perceived as a clever observation of body language; however, in my view it invites, and perhaps provokes, Kathy to amplify her behaviour, and as a result Kathy takes a tissue and wipes her eyes. She laughs through the tears and says,

> *Kathy:* Well I've got this far, it's not so bad.
> *Rogers:* So let's laugh it off, it's very easy to run away from yourself.

In my view, Kathy is attempting to tell Rogers that he should treat her with some protection, and that he is the focus of this therapeutic frame. She tells him that she would become involved up to a certain point which she is in the process of negotiating with him, but she has told him not to romance her (seduce her) into giving more than she wants. She wants him to be her friend, although she sees the prospect of him being a lover, that is, having a more intimate counselling relationship, but for now to take it slowly. Rogers responds by providing two invitations to Kathy to take an emotional risk: the first is the 'tissue', and the second is to suggest that she might want to run away from herself.

> *Kathy:* I've made a bargain with two parts of myself . . . the part that understands, and the part that's scared silly, but the part that understands isn't going to force the part that's scared. When it's safe enough to be kind to myself I won't come out of my cave if there's a lot of pain to greet me. What's the sense? It's up to the best of me to make sure that there are nurturing people around me. (*At this point she looks directly at the camera.*)

This look at the camera is seen by Rogers who is watching Kathy intently. The look and the statement offer an opportunity to

Rogers to address the theme of the intrusive camera as a frame violation. However, Rogers chooses to press on and reflects the content of
Kathy's request. The fact that the latent content of the theme of her
communications so far is not addressed causes Kathy to go back to
the theme of friendship versus love and the assurances that she needs
before she can make herself vulnerable. Kathy then tells her first long
story.

> *Kathy:* ... I met a man on a trip who I had known years ago,
> anyway, he was such a lovely man, a kind person, and I went
> out with him. It was up in the mountains, and as I was
> driving back from his home I had that feeling that it was all
> right ... I don't know if you've read, like in the Carlos
> Castenedas books, the concept of the third eye, it was all
> right for my third eye to come out and be open and perceive.
> But when I came home from my trip I busied myself with
> working in the house. I was in the same predicament and the
> same environment, but I knew that I could consciously
> choose to focus in on things or not. He flew in to see me
> (*looks at camera again*) a couple of weeks ago, and because I
> had this memory of being open with him before, it made me
> feel more guarded.
>
> *Rogers:* Is that so ... having come out of the cave, you're afraid
> you might come out of the cave too easily.
>
> *Kathy:* (*delighted by this, grins from ear to ear*) That's right.

I hypothesized earlier that in this session Kathy is renegotiat-
ing her boundaries with Rogers. The interactions between Kathy and
Rogers seem to be constantly addressing this same theme. Kathy
refers to another Carl (Carlos) who knows about third eyes (think of
hidden messages: the camera, the previous videotape of Rogers that
she may have seen. Did Rogers fly in for the meeting?). Kathy is faced
with the conflict of coming to the session with a perception of Rogers
as being kind and wanting to be the good client, but now, unconsciously, sees him differently.

> *Rogers:* I guess what lives in this cave is your tenderest part.
>
> *Kathy:* My most tenderest part. (*she cries*) ... but you know, life
> is an existence without all of you (*smiles*).
>
> *Rogers doesn't hear this and Kathy has the presence of mind to lean
> forward and say it again clearly.*
>
> *Rogers:* I'm not sure ... life isn't an existence without ... Life is
> an existence without all of you ahmm.
>
> *Kathy:* We've reached another stop. (*She stops speaking, as if
> withdrawing.*)

Rogers: But you, but you, felt safe enough to let out a little bit more (*silence*).

What is Rogers saying here? On one level, I think it's an observation on the process of the interaction, but on the other it's an encouragement for Kathy to let out more: '*Please be good to me, if that wasn't so bad. How about some more?*'

Kathy's response, I feel, demonstrates that she heard the statement as a request to let out more and she gets angry with Rogers:

Kathy: (*laughing*) It's none of your business what I'm doing, you've got other things to do.
Rogers: I don't really care. It's just a story . . . (*pause*) But what if, what if I do care?

What kind of intervention is this, and whom does it serve? In my opinion it comes under the category of discharging tension and ritualistic communication. Rogers has to persuade Kathy to like him and to perform for him in this time-limited session. Rogers is under pressure, caused by the 'deviant' frame, and the contract he has to perform within it. His intervention appears to be altruistic but is, due to this adaptive context, self-serving. He cannot acknowledge the madness in himself at this time, or rectify the frame to help contain it and so it seeks expression through this ritualistic intervention. He draws upon a standard phrase, and by doing this he avoids the truth of the derivative communications Kathy has provided and attempts to seduce her to give more.

Kathy offers her commentary on his behaviour in the form of a derivative. She tells him that as a psychiatric nurse she used to give points to patients for talking in a group but that it wasn't the talking that was important:

Kathy: . . . anyone could do that – it was how it was received. That's a whole new ball-game, and the staff should get some demerits for 'not responding' appropriately.
Rogers and Kathy laugh together.
Kathy: Now I've talked.
Rogers: Now you rate some points.
How many demerits does Rogers rate?
Rogers: When you let out a tender part of yourself, does this person care, does it make any difference?

Kathy won't let her message to Rogers go, she won't let him off the hook; her encoded message gets closer to home:

Kathy: My husband once said he really cared, but it was words, just words. I think he cared as much as he could care but he

had so many conflicts inside himself, he didn't even see me
as a person. It's not that he didn't want to care, he couldn't,
he was too busy with himself.

Here she seems to let Rogers off the hook, having told him in a
derivative way that she sees him, like her husband, as self-centred,
fraudulent in his statements, and that he must have an inner conflict
or he wouldn't be doing this to himself and her:

> *Kathy:* But I understand that, and I understand that, with other
> people too, but I just can't go around revealing myself all the
> time to people who are just too busy with themselves.

I see this as another invitation from Kathy for an intervention
from Rogers that would let her know that her hidden conversation
has been heard; and by saying, 'other people too', she widens the
scope of people who act like her husband to include him. The trigger
for these derivative stories of nursing and her husband's failure is
Rogers's suggestion that he did care for Kathy and he would look after
her in this setting.

Let me try to construct a communicative intervention which
threads the strands of the various triggers, derivatives, and bridges to
therapy together.

> As I perceive it your husband used to say he really cared, but it
> was just words, and it wasn't that he didn't want to care but that
> he was too busy with himself and you mentioned you could see
> that in other people too. This reminded me of something I said
> earlier when I suggested that I might really care; in fact, I
> remember saying: 'But what if I do care?', and I am wondering if
> you perceive the same inconsistency in me as in your husband.
> Perhaps I am too busy with myself in recording this session to
> actually care about you and protect you in the way you would
> expect. Also, we joked earlier about your patients getting points
> for talking, but you felt staff should get demerits for not
> responding. I'm wondering whether you perceive me as not
> able to respond appropriately to you in this situation.

Kathy's invitation to intervene is not responded to by Rogers,
and she then tells him a story about dating after the death of her husband. When she met someone on a date, they would say they would
call later, and she couldn't bear to be let down so she stayed out.
Rogers responds by saying, 'A call isn't enough?' Kathy replies, 'No,
that would be enough if they would do that.'

I wonder if she is telling Rogers here that she doesn't want
absolute assurances of her safety in this session, which she knows he
can't offer. However, some show of caring would be enough:

> *Kathy:* As we are talking now . . . the focus of a relationship, it has to be this male–female kind of thing. I don't think I'm ready for this but I don't know how to come out too much without a man . . . it must be a man because that's where my fear is.
>
> *Rogers:* So that's where your fear is – a relationship with a man, is that it?
>
> *Kathy:* I feel like a little girl, I need someone to care about me, then he can ask for himself from the relationship.

Rogers reflects this back to Kathy and connects it to the cave analogy that she used earlier. Kathy tells Rogers that she doesn't want the sexual part of her used first.

> *Kathy:* If a man is interested in me he can keep coming back and eventually I could respond as a woman.
>
> *Rogers:* Can you tell him that?
>
> *Kathy:* I'm confused. This individual, yes I think I could tell him that. I know I could, but you know I keep putting him down.

At this moment I get the feeling that she has told the man about whom she is concerned, but she is confused because that man (Rogers) has not responded.

> *Kathy:* I'm the perfect nurse. I'll do anything for anybody but when I want to focus on my needs first I feel like a taker not a giver.

Again the reference to 'focus' would suggest that it is here in the therapy that Kathy is feeling these things and that by her consistent displaced communications she is trying to get Rogers to confront those aspects of this frame that are perceived by Kathy to be madness-provoking. Rogers reflects the manifest content of Kathy's communication and suggests that she needs to say, 'I'd like to care for myself first.' Kathy nods and smiles as if she feels that at last she has got her message across.

> *Kathy:* I feel wicked.
>
> (*Rogers and Kathy laugh out loud at this statement as if for a moment they are two naughty people not playing by the rules.*)
>
> *Kathy:* (*soberly*) There are people who would use you up and not even think about it.
>
> *Rogers:* You have respect for your instinct for preserving yourself. Not everyone would care.
>
> *Kathy:* I was thinking: 'but I care'.

Here the themes present in the derivatives given earlier are present again, and by using the words 'focus' and 'care' she encapsulates references to two active triggers in the session. These are the presence of the camera and crew, and Rogers's seductive yet challenging statement, 'but what if I do care?'. Kathy has unconsciously scanned Rogers's communications and has perceived them as self-serving. Kathy then returns to the theme of her conflicting needs of wanting to protect herself, but also of reaching out and taking a risk at the same time. She looks at Rogers and says:

> *Kathy:* If I could figure some way of doing that . . . – you were smiling – . . . that would be just great.

Here we have a very obvious bridge to therapy by a direct reference to Rogers and therefore an indication that these not so disguised communications may be about this context and also an invitation for an intervention. Rogers summarizes the content of this statement but doesn't acknowledge the deeper level of any of these communications, and does not take Kathy's inclusion of him into her statement as a signal for some 'you-me' talk.

> *Kathy:* (*trying again after a pause*) I feel like I want to ask you: how have you been lately; how is your wife. I need a rest for a while.
> *Rogers:* (*compliments her*) When you feel you need a rest in this session you will say so and take it.

This banter between Kathy and Rogers seems to me of a different level, and it is as if Kathy has given up on Rogers for a moment; now that the most blatant of her encoded clues have been ignored they move into pass-times and ritualistic dialogue to relieve the pressure.

What could have been said by a communicative therapist? A possible intervention would have been the following:

> You mentioned that you felt like you would like to put the focus on me for a while, maybe ask about my wife, and you noticed me smiling when you were talking about figuring out a way to protect yourself and take a risk at the same time. I'm reminded that earlier you mentioned that there are some people who use you up and not even think about it. Here we are recording this session together in front of cameras so that in one sense I can use you as a client to demonstrate my skills with the expectation that you may get something out of this too. Perhaps you perceive me as someone who may use you up and not think of you again, which activates your instinct for

preserving yourself here and now. However, I'm wondering if there is a part of you , the 'good nurse' you mentioned earlier, who wants to be an obedient client for me and care for me. Perhaps you're wondering how I would react in this context if you decided that it is just too risky to expose yourself here.

In the session Kathy then comes up with a piece of derivative material, just as Rogers looks at his watch.

Kathy: I had a dream one time, and I dreamt that I was on a sledge with two other girls on a snowy hill and they were going too fast. So I told them to stop, to get off because we were going to crash into a train station at the bottom of the hill and they wouldn't believe me. So I got off, and they went on, and I side-stepped in the snow all the way down the hill. But there were lots of trees one by one as I went down. When I got to the bottom of the hill the sled had crashed, so then I thought to myself that that's to do with me, part of me would go too fast.

Rogers: This morning has been an example of the fact that you're not going to go so fast that you crash, you'll go at your own pace, down the hill.

Kathy: That must be it.

Conclusion

The session ends with Rogers using Kathy's story: by relating it to the session he acknowledges Kathy's process of caution in it. What he does not do (as a communicative therapist would hope to do) is to search for, or to own, his contribution to the triggers present in their encounter. Kathy seems to tell him during the session that she perceives his sincerity as fraudulent in the context of this session, because it is a seductive ploy to get her to be a 'good' client in front of the cameras. In another session – with a different frame, perhaps – she tells Rogers, 'things may be different', as she is aware that he may be a caring person, but that both he and she are 'performing' in this session for what may be the wrong reasons. The interaction demonstrates to me that, unconsciously, Kathy will not let herself be fooled, regardless of the opportunity or the prestige of being with Carl Rogers.

In this examination of this session I have attempted to show communicative listening at work and have offered some examples of possible communicative interventions linking triggers to derivatives and to possible bridges to therapy. I have also highlighted the unconscious significance to Kathy of the 'deviant' frame of this interaction between Kathy and Rogers, and how Kathy, unconsciously, consistently attempts to communicate to Rogers her concerns about this in the stories that she tells. I have also shown how she provides a supervisory commentary for the therapist, in this instance Carl Rogers, offering him both insight into the harmful qualities of the interaction and derivative hypotheses about Rogers's personality based on the implications of what he said and did. I have argued the case for looking at the therapist's contribution to any interaction between therapist and client.

Notes

1 This is an enlarged and greatly revised version of an article entitled 'Kathy and Rogers decoded', which appeared in *Changes*, 11(1): March 1993.
2 'Deviant frame', 'frame deviations', 'deviance', 'a deviant . . .' – the term 'deviance' describes an act which transgresses a cultural custom and is a variation of what is defined in that culture as appropriate behaviour in the context the actor finds herself. In the context of the practice of therapy we have rules of practice which each theoretical orientation teaches its initiates and which form the basis of clinical supervision. These rules of practice usually cover the management of the interactive space in which therapy takes place, and also what is appropriate for the therapist to do or say in that space. They aim to be consistent with the chosen theoretical models and of the perceptions of the workings of the psyche of the client and of the therapist in this context. The aim is to provide the optimal conditions under which the psyche can be free to reconstellate. Langs argues that he has found these conditions through research and clinical experience. They constitute the mores of the emotional processing part of our mind; if we as therapists deviate from these ways of conducting ourselves, in what we say or do with our clients, we will be criticized for it by our clients. Many of the basic ground rules of psychoanalytically informed therapies are the same and form the basis of frame and boundary management. In this scenario one psychotherapeutic culture may be seen to take the high ground but it is a theoretical high ground not a moral one, it is consistent within its own theoretical paradigm. If therapists depart from the accepted and expected behaviour of their expressed form of practice they can be said to be working within a deviant frame.

References

Davis, M. and Wallbridge, D. (1981) *Boundary and Space*. Harmondsworth: Penguin.
Langs, R. (1980) *Interactions*. New York: Jason Aronson.
Langs, R. (1985a) *Madness and Cure*. Emerson, NJ: NewConcept Press.

Langs, R. (1985b) *Workbooks for Psychotherapists*. Emerson, NJ: NewConcept
    Press.
Langs, R. (1988) *Primer of Psychotherapy*. New York: Gardner Press.
Langs, R. (1989) *Rating Your Psychotherapist*. New York: Henry Holt.

Three Approaches to Psychotherapy II: (Kathy) part 1 (Carl Rogers), video, 1972.

Part **IV**

DREAMS AND STORIES

Chapter 10

Dream interpretation from a communicative perspective[1]

Marie-Luise Petersen

Introduction

The principles of the decoding and interpretation of dreams from a communicative point of view form the basis of this chapter; in particular I shall point out the importance of noticing the interactional context or trigger. Then I will show examples of the possibilities of a valuable use of this method in the psychotherapy of children and adolescents.[2] Beside the 'classical' application of the interpretation of patients' dreams another possibility is considered, that of using one's own dreams as a technical aid or, should the occasion arise, as a revision and as a resource for self-analysis.

In analytic adult and adolescent psychotherapy the patient is told at the beginning to say whatever comes to mind. This ground rule is given because free associations are considered to lead the way from the manifest to the latent content of the presented material, for instance symptoms or dreams. In child psychotherapy a modified ground rule is used. Normally a child is told to say or to play whatever comes to mind. The psychotherapist offers toys in order to help the child to communicate.[3] After a child has narrated a dream it is very unusual to get direct associations to the dream or its elements. Therefore the classical technique of dream analysis is assumed not to be suitable for child analysis. Anna Freud (1945: 1013) wrote:

> Children who have not yet reached puberty, at best pre-puberty, cannot or do not want to associate freely . . . Children dream during analysis and they are willing to tell their dreams, but they are not willing to associate to the dream elements,

that means to come up with the ideas that lead from the manifest to the latent content.

(my translation)

I hold the opinion that the difficulty on which Anna Freud focused is one of the reasons why dream analysis was, and still is, a less regarded subject in child analysis. The metaphor Kimminz (1937) created in writing *Children's Dreams: An Unexplored Land*, is still as apposite now as it was then.

Ever since Freud, dream interpretation has been regarded as the *via regia* to knowledge of the unconscious. One reason was formulated by Langs (1978: 545): 'Dreams are, indeed, a sign of a distinctive wish to communicate though I would add that recognition of this quality need not call for any special variation in technique.'

Langs stresses, in particular, that in dream analysis the intervention technique (which includes the ground rule of free association or free play) does not need to be modified. In this chapter I pick up this idea and show how one can get a valid dream interpretation without asking or waiting for associations to the dream, without changing the (communicative) technique of taking into account the interactional context or trigger.[4]

In other words: the method of dream interpretation presented below is nothing else than a special application of the communicative technique.

After having listed principles of dream decoding and interpretation from a communicative point of view I will present several examples of application and possibilities of interpretation.[5] I will especially clarify the suitability of this method for child analysis.

The importance of the interactional context or trigger

Freud (1900) wrote that dreams are initiated by unconscious wishes seeking discharge. These wishes can only find an indirect expression because they are unable to overcome the barrier imposed by the endopsychic censor. They use the indirect way of transferring their cathexis to inoffensive preconscious ideas. The latter are therefore unconsciously reinforced and viewed as representatives of the unconscious ideas or as the latent dream thoughts.

According to Freud, one has to trace back the whole process until the unconscious wish is detected, in order to discover the meaningful intrapsychic causes of a dream. The method is well known: at first one has to find the day residues and the preconscious thoughts connected with them. Then, one must try to spell out the

nature of the unconscious wishes that are displaced to the preconscious contents.

The day residues and latent dream thoughts connect the dream
with the dreamer's everyday life and his current experiences. In his
writings Freud considered that a special case of current experiences
are the here-and-now experiences of the psychotherapeutic session:

> We must . . . bear in mind that free association is not really free.
> The patient remains under the influence of the analytic situ-
> ation even though he is not directing his mental activities on to
> a particular subject. We shall be justified in assuming that
> nothing will occur to him that has not some reference to that
> situation.
>
> (Freud 1925: 40–1)

But, as we know, Freud did not integrate these thoughts constantly and consequently into his theory.[6] Still up to now 'the material [of a dream] is treated largely as a reflection of the patient's
fantasies and resistances, and valid unconscious perceptions and
introjections are excluded' (Langs 1978: 566).

It was Langs who used the concept of the adaptive context or
trigger in a strictly analogous way to the Freudian dream method and
the treatment of day residues in order to link unconscious material in
psychotherapy sessions to the *current* experiences of the dreamer. His
method is based on the statement that the unconscious concerns of
patients in psychotherapy centre to a large extent on the behaviour
of their therapists.

Example

A female patient, referred by a psychiatrist, came to a psychotherapist who is not a physician. The psychotherapist agreed to a treatment
according to the German public health sector regulations, which
require that at the beginning of a long-term treatment the psychotherapist has to write a report which will be sent, firmly sealed, to
the patient's health insurance. While a physician is entitled to hand
over the report directly to the insurance, a non-medical psychotherapist has to send it to the referring doctor, who reads the report,
makes additional comments and keeps a copy in his surgery (the
delegation principle). The health insurance sends the sealed envel-
ope (without having opened it) anonymously to an expert who has
to make a statement on the taking over of the costs.

In the first session the patient described her problems. Central
were her difficulties with getting into closer contact with men, being

afraid of having a closer relationship and her inability to talk to men. The psychotherapist offered treatment to the patient, mentioned the frame conditions and in doing so he informed her especially about the delegation principle. The patient agreed and a contract was made. Then there was a little pause, the patient smiled and mentioned that her mother was a good friend of a receptionist of the referring doctor. She added that over the time she had been in that doctor's treatment she had been afraid that this receptionist would get intimate information about her. She said how glad she was to be in psychotherapeutic treatment now. The session ended at that point.

In the following session the patient mentioned that her health insurance had confirmed the funding of the psychotherapy fees as applied. Then she stated several times that she had difficulties in talking and there were long sequences of silence. Normally, an analytical psychotherapist would begin to study his own feelings and inner responses. He might notice his being impatient and a need to help the patient out of the silence. He also might notice a tendency for his attention to be distracted to outer events because of the boring situation. One classical possibility is to interpret the patient's behaviour as a projective identification, that means as an attempt to let the psychotherapist feel the patient's inner states, in this case, for instance, the emptiness and helplessness. He might suggest to her that she does not only want to talk about her difficulties, but also wants him to put himself in her position and that she perhaps wants to see whether he himself is able to cope with these difficulties and to offer a solution, in this case, to show her a way out of the silence. A communicative psychotherapist might only play back what happened (the patient's comment about the funding of the fee, the reported difficulties in talking, the silence). Let's assume that the analyst intervened in this way.

After a little pause the patient began to narrate her dream: a man invited her to a rendezvous in a café. At first she was happy about that meeting place, because she was afraid to meet him alone. But when she came to the place, she noticed that she could reach the room he had designated only through a big entrance room where many people were sitting at tables. They all seemed to watch her. The room where she was supposed to meet the man was a comfortable room with one table and two chairs where the man had already been waiting. With a feeling of anger and disappointment she realized that it was not possible to close the door to this room because there wasn't one. When she wanted to speak to the man she noticed that, suddenly, there was absolute silence in the front room and everyone seemed to listen to what she was going to say. She couldn't talk and suddenly became aware of the fact that they both were naked. She was very ashamed and wanted to leave the café, but couldn't say that to the man because even these words would have been heard by the others.

She reported that in the morning after the dream she had awoken with a tight feeling in her throat, which she also felt right now. She added that she knew that man very well and explained that they had met several times when she had been in the tennis hall together with her sister. Each time there had been another man with him. She would have liked to talk to him, perhaps arrange a date, but for some reason she had never been able to take that initiative. 'Perhaps it has something to do with the other man. They are in the same tennis team and I don't want them to speak about me. It's so shaming if he is not interested in me. It's also embarrassing in front of my sister.' Then she slipped back into silence.

I want to offer two possible interpretations. Firstly, let me state that I do not want to offer my thoughts as definitively valid, but as hypotheses. There are always several aspects that need to be taken into account. To my mind, information on the validity of a previous intervention can only be given by the patient's reactions and the observable effects on him.[7]

1   *The dream as an expression of an intrapsychic conflict*: it is possible to interpret the dream – perhaps after having asked for associations to the dream – in the light of the genetically rooted intrapsychic conflicts of the patient and thus to try to explain her symptom of difficulties in establishing personal contacts. The dream might be interpreted as a portrayal of the patient's main conflict: on the one hand, the wish to get into closer contact with a man, in the dream image represented by the ability to talk to the man, an ability that was described as desirable; on the other hand, her anxiety about meeting a man alone, and about being observed by others, which might be understood as revealing the paranoid aspects of her neurosis. One might perhaps understand the detected nudity as her distorted view of talking, as revealing too much in front of others, and might also interpret the sexual quality of the main conflict, suggesting the meeting in the presence of others as a dissatisfying compromise. One might add that she thinks that she will be able to cope with her difficulties if she is able to talk, in particular to express her wish to meet the man alone; and that it would also be helpful if he agreed to her wishes in this respect. In light of this interpretation, the psychotherapist might think of the offered treatment conditions as adequate and helpful.

2   *The dream as an unconscious analysis of the meaning of the therapist's behaviour*: alternatively, pursuing the idea of the importance of the

here-and-now stimulus, the question is whether there is something in the analytic situation that could explain the patient's difficulty in talking, her silence and the tight feeling in her throat.

I suggest the following: the patient has been referred by a doctor who obviously knew the name and the address of the psychotherapist. In giving information about the delegation principle the psychotherapist himself reveals that he, like the doctor, works in the public health sector and that he will get into contact with the doctor, the health insurance and an expert. Additionally he expresses his willingness to offer treatment under these conditions although a detailed report has to be written and although the patient mentions that her mother is a friend of the receptionist.

The dream may be understood as a portrayal of the analytic situation. The patient shows the psychotherapist as someone who suggested that they meet in public; she reveals that this at first soothed her anxiety but then disappointed her because she feels observed under these circumstances: the analytic frame is open like the room in the café. Information is given to the receptionist, the doctor, the health insurance and the expert, a situation which she compares with the situation in the café where everyone present could hear what they were saying.

She expresses her concern that too much intimate information about the man and herself is revealed in public or, directly formulated, that sending out a report is like going naked into a café. The feeling of shame also occurs in the comment after the dream: again the man can be seen as a displaced perception of the psychotherapist, the sister as a family member of the receptionist and the team-colleague as the referral doctor or expert. They all meet at the same place – the tennis hall, which can be equated with the public health sector. The patient gives a model of rectification by expressing the wish to be alone with the man at another place: that means to meet the psychotherapist alone out of the public health sector.

Clearly one has to bear in mind that her anxiety about meeting him alone is not yet explained. She might not only have expressed her own anxiety but also the perception of the psychotherapist as being afraid of being alone with her. This may be the case because he accepted the requirement to reveal details from their interaction in a report which was sent to the doctor and the expert. Perhaps she will reveal after an intervention something more of her feelings about that topic or she might make manifest comments about the possibility or impossibility of a change of treatment conditions.

Altogether, if one follows these ideas, it is not surprising that the patient is silent. It would be more surprising if she was able to talk freely. It is understandable that she is not able to express her view of the situation directly because she is at the same time for some reason afraid of meeting the psychotherapist alone; she also probably expects him to be afraid to be alone with her and perhaps not to be pleased to hear her explanation. And in addition, if she told him, even that information would reach the referral doctor. An expectation that again causes silence and the tight feeling in the throat.

Thus if one centres the search for unconscious meaning on a trigger, very different results emerge.

Principles of dream decoding and interpretation

Now I will point out important principles of the decoding and interpreting of dreams. The decoding of triggers will play a central role, as I have already mentioned. The starting point is the manifest dream content which will be narrated by a patient or, in the case of an analyst's own dream, will be remembered. In the first case, one will collect the associations the patient spontaneously makes; in the second case, all the analyst's associations to as many factors of the surface dream as possible are gathered. Langs calls this network of dream and associations a 'whole dream' (1988b: 116).

When the patient does not make further associations (first case) or when the analyst thinks that he has enough material (second case), then it is time to move from the phase of collecting to the phase of working at the surface or facade of the dream. This means that the analyst has now to abstract the themes touched upon in the dream. In the example previously given I considered the theme of securing a situation despite anxieties and the themes of exposure, shame, of not being able to communicate in the presence of others.

Langs (1988b) suggested engaging in three questions while doing this work on the manifest content:

1 Who is involved in the dream?
2 What are the manifest themes?
3 What is the scene of action in the dream?

Afterwards one can start the work at the intermediate level of the dream, which includes the whole list of non-manifest content in three sorts of messages: 'Conclusions, symbols, symbolic actions' (p. 147). The analyst's job is to draw conclusions and to uncover the background, to decode symbols and to find symbolic actions. In doing so one will, in the case of one's own dream, get new associations. In both cases there will be a development of many possible different dream interpretations.

Up to now the method presented here has not basically differed from others. It is central to find displacements, symbolizations and condensations, as well as interferences, in order to undo the encoding of the unconscious mind.

The peculiarity of this method consists of finding the trigger and linking it up with the themes, symbols and symptoms. It is assumed

1   that dreams are stimulated by day residues and are answers or messages from a deeper unconscious level. Day residues are nothing else than emotionally occupied stimuli – in other words: triggers;
2   that the deep level of meanings can only be reached by including the trigger situations. 'Knowing the trigger situation will set natural and adequate limits to what we consider as an unconscious content to a certain problem or range of problems' (Langs 1988b: 147, my translation).

In other words: ambiguity of interpretations cannot be eliminated unless the decoding and interpretation of a dream is seen in the light of one or several triggers. As a consequence, the work in the next phase consists of seeking the triggers. Only if triggers can be found will one be ready to interpret the dream. If the dream is narrated in analysis one has to look for triggers primarily in the analytic situation itself, strictly speaking in the interventions of the psychotherapist.[8]

The presented phases are not always worked through with the same directness and completeness. I know from my own experience that if a trigger is found then there is a feeling of great evidence; associations and conclusions centre on the trigger; unexpected insights emerge that make sense at once. This is valid for patients' as well as one's own dreams. But in case of a patient's dream one will receive either a validation or falsification only by analysing the patient's reaction immediately after the interpretation. As a result, one is given evidence whether the relevant triggers have been discovered and put into the specific connections which are important for the patient.

When the work of decoding has proceeded this far, then one is ready to interpret the dream. Now it is the therapist's task to connect in an interpretation the trigger(s), the derivatives (themes, symbols) that are extracted from the dream and the present symptoms (in case of a nightmare the dream itself is a symptom) or resistance.[9]

For instance, in the example given, the *trigger* could be found in the analyst's acceptance or offering of a treatment in the public health sector under the condition that a friend of the patient's mother might read the report; as *themes* the securing of a situation despite anxieties, exposure, shame, not being able to communicate in the presence of others; and as *symptoms* the silence and the tight feeling in the throat as unconscious reactions to the trigger.

Figure 1 illustrates the presented method:

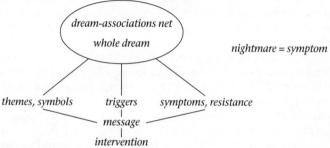

Figure 1

Dreams and (psychic) symptoms are both messages from the unconscious which are not understandable to the conscious mind, and according to Freud (1900) they are of similar structure.

It is widely agreed that symptoms are more difficult to decode than dreams since they appear in a condensed form. They also reveal less information about unconscious experiences of a concrete situation. It is therefore often helpful to rely on dreams to decode symptoms.

Langs gives the following reason for the validity of such a connection:

> Dreams as well as symptoms have manifest contents. Both are able to provoke a number of associations. Both are made by trigger situations, and if they happen nearly at the same time, they mostly express unconscious reactions to the same emotionally occupied stimulus.
>
> (Langs 1988b: 223, my translation)

The following vignettes are given to illustrate the method and to point out important applications of dream analysis.

Applications of dream analysis

There are two categories of dream narratives:

1 Dreams that were dreamt in the past and are coming up in the current session.
2 Dreams that were dreamt between the last and the current session.

Dreams from the past presented in the current session[10]

In this situation one has to find triggers for that spontaneous memory and to interpret the dream-images in the light of the expressed themes and present triggers. In addition, if one determines the circumstances in which this dream was dreamt, it is possible to add connections with early experience to the interventions as well.

For example, having been asked in his first session to narrate dreams, fantasies, experiences and so on, a boy told his female psychotherapist that he had had, in his early childhood, a dream that occurred to him very often: he was alone in his room, wanted to go to his mother in the kitchen, but couldn't reach her because suddenly he found a big crack in the kitchen doorway. His mother was so busy that she didn't see him. He fell into the crack and awoke with the feeling of falling down.

The psychotherapist came to the conclusion that the boy's dream narrative was a reaction to her intrusive asking. He perceived her as not seeing the patient and the danger he was in, unable to hold him, as distracted by something else (with her requirement, as a psychotherapist in the public health sector, to write reports) that she could not realize the dangers which were arising for him.

Much later the patient repeated the dream, this time in a situation of free association. Before that it had been a quiet and pleasant atmosphere. The patient had been busy with plans what to do in the next weeks (his holidays). Then suddenly the dream fragment occurred, followed by other stories and descriptions of experiences of not being held and not being able to reach anyone. This time he only remembered a dream sequence: wanting to go to the kitchen, seeing the big crack too late, falling. The mother did not occur in his narrative at all.

At first, no trigger could be detected. But then the patient pointed to the doorway of the consulting room and explained that the crack had been just as big as that doorway. The psychotherapist suddenly realized that this was the last session before her holiday, which she had announced very late. In this connection the psychotherapist developed a hypothesis as follows: the patient had told her by means of the dream that the coming holiday was announced too late, so that the feeling of a crack suddenly and unexpectedly occurred to him, that he was afraid of being unable to react early enough, which caused the anxiety of falling, crashing, not being held and not being able to reach anyone.

This is a completely different interpretation of the same dream. In both situations the dream narratives are memories with great significance to the present situation which throw light on the present unconscious difficulties of the patient.

Dreams dreamt between the last and the current session

Now I will present reflections to dreams that are triggered by the psychotherapy. I think that in most cases a dream which was dreamt between the last and the current session and is narrated spontaneously in the session is triggered by the psychotherapy.

At any rate, one has to wait for the patient's mentioning of the trigger that is the most significant for him at the moment, since connections to analysis which only exist as a figment of the analyst's imagination can be avoided and choices of less important triggers can be excluded.

The trigger as a single event may have happened in the current session or in one of the previous sessions (foreground), or it may turn out to be an ongoing constellation, now activated, that has to do with the setting, the frame as it was set out at the beginning of the therapy, or the personality of the analyst (background).

In any case, dreams that occur in analysis are comments about the analytic situation.[11] Therefore it is vital in the case of negative comments to consider carefully whether the patient's material shows which intervention could be the appropriate one and, if necessary, how to rectify the situation.

The following example shows a single intervention (the analyst's inappropriate silence) which is unconsciously worked through and commented on by the patient.

The dreamer is a little, cautious 6-year-old boy who suffers from severe anxiety problems (night fears, fear of strangers). The female psychotherapist frequently felt big and bulky in his presence. In the first sessions she also noticed with oppressive distinctness that he was uneasy in her presence (he exhibited shy, fearful glances, inhibited play). At the end of his tenth session he asked whether he could borrow a certain toy, a car, from the surgery. In response the psychotherapist asked him to give her time for consideration before letting him know whether he could take the car home or not. Internally she was prepared to wait for his derivative response to that reply.

In the following session nothing of special interest happened. The boy seemed to hesitate; he seemed to observe the analyst more carefully than he had done in other sessions. The psychotherapist did not make an interpretation because she was not aware of the obvious contradiction in what she had said ('I will think about it and let you know') and how she behaved (waiting for a reaction of the patient), and instead she was very engaged in thinking about the situation.

In the twelfth session the patient looked pale and tired. He sat down in an armchair in contrast to his normal habit. He told the psychotherapist that he had had an awful dream the night before. A huge figure had turned up raising one hand towards him. He hesitated.

> *Therapist:* You have been sitting down in that armchair today. In my opinion, this shows me that we must talk about something. And the dream has to do with it. You are very frightened, aren't you?

He nodded and then wondered why the figure had not spoken and why it approached him step by step. Then it came to his mind that the figure had been dressed in a green shirt. At that moment the psychotherapist remembered that she had been wearing a green T-shirt in the previous session. It became obvious that the trigger for that dream was hidden in the analytic situation of the last session. The psychotherapist assumed that the shirt was clearly hers and that she had been creepy, in some way, for the patient. She recollected the circumstances of the previous session, her silence and her deep engagement in considering the situation. At the same time the psychotherapist realized that she had kept the patient waiting for an answer. She had told him that she would think about his question and she had not marked an end of thinking, yet. And he had been waiting for the end of her thinking.

Because the patient expressed great anxiety and need of help she did not wait for further hints and began to interpret at once. She reported on her behaviour of the last session and also on his waiting for an answer.

> *Therapist:* When you described the frightening figure with the green shirt, I remembered that I had been wearing a green T-shirt in the last session. Then I remembered that I had not talked much to you in that session and that I watched you. I think you found that situation somehow creepy. In your dream you express how you experienced me, like a creepy figure that is coming closer and closer, that wants something but doesn't tell. I think I've understood what happened. You have been waiting for an answer, and I did not give it to you. (*He nodded.*) You kept on waiting; you couldn't understand what was happening; you were so tense, and finally I appeared big and creepy. But now you have told me the dream, and therefore I think that you also hope somehow that I can perhaps help you and that you can trust me. I will give you an answer. Among other things the figure in the

dream appeared creepy to you because of the outstretched
hand. You usually stretch out your arm when you want to get
something. I think you wondered what I wanted to get from
you.

She explained that he perceived rightly, that she had waited for
his reaction in contrast to what she had been telling him. She stated
that in any future case of such a question arising she first would wait
for him to say or play whatever comes to mind and that she would try
to understand what has to be decided.

> *Therapist:* In this case, the answer seems to be obvious now: if
> you borrowed something from me it would possibly stick in
> your mind since there is something that has to be given back.
> I believe that, on the one hand, you would like to borrow
> that car to play with. On the other hand, you find this
> situation too difficult and frightening so that you don't like
> it. That is why I should not and will not lend you any of my
> toys.[12]
>
> *Patient:* (*sighs*) The dream was awful but (*smiling*) last week my
> mother knew what I wanted. The two of us were alone, and
> she read out a beautiful story. At the beginning it was
> terrifying, but my mum took me in her arms, and then the
> story had a good ending.

Then he said that he wanted to go on the big water slide the last
time they went swimming, but his mother was against it. He said:
'That was OK because I was too anxious, indeed.'

This reaction validates the interpretation as the patient
describes a mother who is aware of his needs, who can hold him and
knows what is too much for him.

The reason why I have chosen this particular example is to
make clear that it is sometimes very difficult to see oneself as horror
figures like the one in the dream. At such times it may be helpful to
recall a statement made by Dr William Goodheart, who said in May
1993 at a London conference: 'It's the act, not the individual itself
that is represented in the narratives.'

Analysts' dreams

I will describe two dream images:

1 An image that offers a technical aid.
2 A dream that clarifies to what extent dream analysis makes a contribution to the analyst's psychohygiene.

Dreams as a technical aid

A 14-year-old patient made strong efforts to cope with his therapy on his own, i.e. without his mother's support. On the one hand he wanted to be independent, but on the other he wanted the psychotherapist to be available for him around the clock. The psychotherapist was concerned because as soon as he tried to differentiate himself from the boy, the boy answered with attempts to provoke the psychotherapist or regain control in a dangerous way.

The night after one of these sessions the psychotherapist dreamt of the patient as a little child and behaving like a fierce tyrant. In the dream the psychotherapist was aware that it was better not to make long explanations, and do no more than offer to take him by the arm, hoping that the patient would come to him instead of running away.

In the specific situation of that analysis the psychotherapist recognized only his feelings of insecurity (hoping that the patient will stay). It becomes obvious that a dream following a session reveals that something of great importance has been touched in the psychotherapist which has to be worked through (trigger: patient's behaviour). If one brings together the various elements (patient, tyrant, arm, hope . . .) one after the other and associates to each one, one will find the themes that are connected with the dream: perhaps helplessness, anxiety about separation, loss or feelings of responsibility are playing a role in this context. One has to find out.

To my mind, such a dream offers a solution to a situation in this way: the firmness of the therapist's grip (taking him by the arm) and the setting of limiting conditions can be regarded as a symbol of a secure frame. Offering and holding the frame was the solution, according to this dream. Offering and waiting are symbolic of preserving one's own boundaries and differentiation, allowing the child to choose whether to accept the offer or not.

After the analysis of the dream the psychotherapist decided to make no technical change. Emotionally much had happened: now he was aware of the fragility of the situation and of the fact that perhaps he might not have the power to secure the situation but that he did have the security to intervene according to his own convictions and possibilities.

Dreams as a contribution to the analyst's psychohygiene

I trust that the previous example shows how dream analysis can contribute to the psychohygiene of the analyst. A more far-reaching example of this application of dream analysis is the following: an analyst who maintained a private practice in his home dreamt of a building in which he was going to receive his patients.

The first patient rings the bell. As the psychotherapist goes to open the door he realizes that there are toys of his children spread out on the floor. As he picked up some of them he noticed several others; he felt angry and helpless that he had no hope of picking up them all.

It is obvious that the themes of the dream depict intrusion, violation of boundaries and futile attempts. The psychotherapist was surprised at this nightmare because he always paid attention to keeping his private and professional lives separate. Then he reflected on the previous day and asked himself if there had been any such intrusion. He remembered that when that particular patient came for his session he saw a ball belonging to his son on the way to the entrance of the practice (trigger).

He remembered that he had been slightly angry but then had forgotten about it. Now he knew what the dream meant: he realized that in trying to keep the private and the professional part of his life separated in one house he was condemned to fail, just as Sisyphus always failed to get the rock to the top of the mountain. The dream displayed his wish to find a lasting solution.

Notes

1 Parts of this chapter were originally published in *Analytische Kinder- und Jugendlichen-Psychotherapie*, 1994, no. 1.
2 In this text the two terms 'psychoanalysis' and 'psychotherapy' will be used synonymously.
3 Melanie Klein equated the free play with the free association of adults.
4 The precise definition of the terms 'interactional context', 'adaptive context', 'trigger', 'here-and-now stimulus' and the differentiation between them needs a careful examination which would go too far here. Essential is the different theoretical background: The term 'interactional trigger' is, for instance, connected with Sandler, Dare, Holder (see Mertens 1990: 189 ff.); the term 'here-and-now stimulus' refers to Gill (1982). All authors regard the interactional trigger or the here-and-now-stimulus as an explanation for transference. Both terms have developed into accepted and common psychoanalytical terms. The term 'trigger' as a specialist term is only used in the communicative approach. At the beginning Langs developed the concept of the 'adaptive context' and replaced this term in 1988 with 'trigger', 'a less unwieldy term highlighting the causal role of the stimulus' (Smith 1991: 111). An adaptive context or trigger is an event occurring in external reality which produces an intrapsychic response. In psychotherapy this is normally an intervention of the therapist which forms the stimulus for the patient's unconscious

responses. Langs (1992: 55): 'These triggers shape the derivatives to which they are a response; thus, derivatives can be properly decoded only in light of the implications of the triggers that have evoked them (mainly, the implications of a therapist's interventions).'

5 All examples given are fictional because I do not want to report from patients' sessions. I believe and hope that it is obvious to every psychotherapist that situations like the ones given here could have happened. I want to demonstrate how I would understand and handle such situations.

6 In the transitional period from the seduction theory to the phantasy theory Freud (1899) wrote in his essay 'Screen memories' that every childhood memory, which refers to a suppressed sexual wish of puberty, 'has the tendency to evade into a scene of the childhood; now add that this cannot be achieved/happen if there is not such a trace of memory whose content does not offer a point of contact with the phantasy, which comes to meet it. If such a point of contact is found . . . the remaining content of the phantasy will be modified by all valid intermediate ideas until new points of contact with the content of the childhood scene come out' (Freud 1899: 548 ff., my translation).

Here Freud postulated that a special occurring memory is activated by suppressed phantasies and tells these phantasies in an indirect and symbolic way. In other words, he put forward the hypothesis that infantile memories are representations of present importance which are projected back into the past.

Freud abandoned this theory with *The Interpretation of Dreams* and 'buried his concept of screen memories beneath a massive theoretical edifice emphasizing phantasy over reality, the past over the present, and transference over accurate perception' (Smith 1991: 78). Screen memories are no longer seen as having a primarily present importance. In 1906, for instance, Freud wrote that he 'has learnt to dissolve many phantasies of seduction as a defence against the memory of own sexual activities (early masturbation)' (Freud 1906: 152, my translation).

7 Positively toned emotional reactions and the appearance of good images as well as the disappearance of or the recovery from symptoms are important indicators for a good and helpful intervention. These validation criteria are based on a positive change as a reaction to an intervention. Following Langs, Smith (1981: 143) formulates: 'Validation occurs when the patient responsively produces positively toned constructive derivative imagery, reflecting an unconscious appreciation of the positive, insightful qualities of the intervention. Falsification, on the other hand, is revealed by patients' negative derivative imagery.' Elsewhere I (Petersen 1992) described that in case of an appropriate intervention the patient may also answer after a short positive reaction with narrating negatively toned images. This observation leads to a second type of validation Langs gives: cognitive validation is indicated by the 'emergence in the patient's material of a displaced and disguised . . . narrative or image that reveals an entirely new dimension of the patient's madness, a dimension that clearly extends the therapist's interpretation' (Langs 1988a: 82).

8 It is not my intention to postulate that to every dream in analysis a trigger can be found in the therapeutic situation. It is possible, for instance, that a patient who has the feeling of being held and cared for is busy on his own according to Winnicott's 'being alone in the presence of someone else'. In such a case (lack of symptoms and resistance pre-assumed) no interpretation is needed. The patient would probably judge it as an intrusive act.

9 As far as communicative psychotherapy is concerned, only symptoms and resistance are interpreted, i.e. if the trigger(s), the derivatives of unconscious proceeding, symptom(s) or resistance have appeared. (For a summarizing presentation of that topic see, for example, Smith 1991: 192 ff.)

10 In Freud's 1899 definition, that means as a memory that occurs to comment on the present situation.

11 In the case of a negative comment which is accompanied by symptoms or resistance an interpretation and, if necessary, a rectification is needed; in the case of a positive comment nothing is to be done.

12 In such a situation I would not consider including aspects to do with the past experiences of the dreamer in this interpretation if, for instance, I had corresponding information only from his parents and not from his own represented material. I also would leave out the aspect of intrapsychic conflicts (his own greed) because that would overtax him and, in addition, it would be less important compared with the interpersonal level that was included. The image of the green shirt led to the most important trigger.

References

Freud, A. (1945) Indikationsstellung in der Kinderanalyse. Schriften, vol. 4. Frankfurt: Fischer; or (1967) *Psyche*, 21: 233–53; (1968) Writings, vol. IV, *Indications for Child Analysis*, New York: International Universities Press, or *The Psychoanalytic Study of the Child*, 1: 127–49.

Freud, S. (1899) Über Deckerinnerungen, *G. W.* I. Screen memories, *S. E.* 3.

Freud, S. (1900) Die Traumdeutung über den Traum, *G. W.* II/III, The interpretation of dreams, *S. E.* 4, 5.

Freud, S. (1906) Meine Ansichten über die Rolle der Sexualität in der Ätiologie der Neurosen. *G. W.* V. My views on the part played by sexuality in the aetiology of the neurosis, *S. E.* 7.

Freud, S. (1925) An autobiographical statement, *S. E.* 20.

Gill, M. (1982) Analysis of transference, vol. 1: Theory and technique, *Psychological Issues*, Monograph 53. New York: International Universities Press.

Kimminz, C.W. (1937) *Children's Dreams: An Unexplored Land*. London: Allen and Unwin.

Langs, R. (1978) Dreams in the bipersonal field, in *Technique in Transition*. New York: Aronson.

Langs, R. (1988a) *A Primer of Psychotherapy*. New York: Gardner Press.

Langs, R. (1988b) *Die Sprache der Träume*. Munich: Heyne. (1990) *Decoding Your Dreams*. New York: Henry Holt.

Langs, R. (1992) *Science, Systems, and Psychoanalysis*. London: Karnac.

Mertens, W. (1990) *Einführung in die Psychoanalytische Therapie*, vol. 2. Stuttgart: Kohlhammer.

Petersen, M.L. (1992) unpublished paper, written work presented for examination.

Smith, D.L. (1991) *Hidden Conversations: An Introduction to Communicative Psychoanalysis*. London: Routledge.

Chapter 11

Dream psychotherapy and a fragment from a continuing story

Fiorella Gatti-Doyle

Introduction

Self-processing or 'empowered psychotherapy' aims to teach individuals to deal with their emotional conflicts by learning to become
their own analysts (Langs 1991, 1993). The approach has also
evolved into an innovative and exciting psychotherapeutic modality. The process unfolds through the decoding of dreams and of those
narratives which are also part of everyday communications. This
therapeutic modality has its origins in Freudian psychoanalysis,
although its theoretical structure has moved away from that paradigm in many respects. Most prominent in this divergence from the
classical model is the understanding of how we process emotionally
charged meanings, the concepts of unconscious functioning, and of
human evolution and adaptation.

Self-processing is an offshoot of the communicative approach,
which has been developed since the early 1970s by Robert Langs
(1973–4, 1976, 1978, 1979). Langs was dissatisfied with the consequences of his personal analytic experiences, and with the ways in
which psychoanalysts (and psychotherapists) were ignoring, dis-
missing, or placing pre-emptive and clichéd interpretations upon
many of their patients' communicative expressions – be these verbal
or symptomatic behaviours. Patients were often speaking by way of
dreams and storied associations – a language which, once decoded,
was conveying their unconscious perceptions of the therapeutic
interaction. In fact, patients were unconsciously monitoring and

selecting here-and-now situations and issues and reporting back their actual perceptions. These issues were unconsciously selected and communicated in encoded form because they were emotionally relevant to the individual patients. Their responses to these perceptions were never spoken directly. Significantly, more often than not they were in fact contradicting what was being communicated consciously. Invariably, however, these messages took narrative form. Dreams, memories, fantasies, anecdotes, the spontaneous recounting of apparently unrelated events, were all attempts, Langs realized, at communicating emotionally charged meanings. Langs made an in-depth study of these responses, and found that they invariably alluded to the therapeutic context and relationship (Langs 1978, 1979, 1980, 1982, 1986; Slavin and Kriegman 1992). This thesis is of central importance in communicative theory. A patient's storied associations almost invariably seem to reflect his or her experience of the therapist's presence and actions. The implications of such a thesis are, however, far wider reaching, since this mode of communicating unconscious meaning also applies to all our private relationships and interactions (Langs 1983).

In contrast with standard communicative psychotherapy (wherein the practitioner waits for the encoded messages to arise at their own spontaneous pace during the patient's free associations), the self-processing instructor (or therapist) directly solicits the production of storied material. The associations here are not 'free' but 'guided'. Rationalization and analysis are discouraged and frequently viewed as defence devices, which by their very nature will prevent contact with unconscious meanings (Langs 1993).

The self-processing space is charged with encoded (and therefore unconscious) contents. The language of our narratives and dreams reflects back to us our deep emotional hurts, our existential concerns, our most basic dreads. Its expressions are at once dramatic, poetic, uncompromising, amazingly unyielding and brutally frank – sometimes directly shocking compared with the cover-ups of conscious communication. These encoded messages aim at the preservation of our personal mental and physiological well-being. Ultimately, they have our interest and self-preservation at heart. The attempt to decode these hidden meanings, and to identify the stimuli which have provoked them, is the main aim of self-processing therapy (see Langs 1993).

As already pointed out, in any self-processing session the associations are 'guided', rather than being so-called 'free', as in conventional analysis. This means that the dreamer never strays too far from the focus of study. He or she keeps returning to that original source (the dream or story) until all its elements, or component parts, have been associated to. All associations are expressed, as much as possible, in storied form.

The characters which, by way of these narratives, inhabit the self-processing stage, communicate and enact the dramas of our current relationships, our inner conflicts, our fears, our personal history, our most pertinent needs. Dramatization is their mode of expression – displaced figures which often astound us with their unpremeditated entrance upon the stage of our daily interactions. Like Pirandellian embodiments, they demand expression and an audience. They want to tell their dramas, and present us with their inner hurts. If we allow them creative expression and don't deny them an audience, they speak to us a language of profound wisdom. When correctly understood and responded to, they acknowledge our efforts, but almost invariably protest when they sense an injustice.

Unconsciously, we communicate what we have encoded by way of displaced themes, enfolded and condensed within the narrative of dreams, fantasies, imagery (as well as within behaviours and psychosomatic symptoms). The triggers which have provoked the encoding, however, are usually nowhere to be seen with the naked eye. 'Last night I had a dream . . . Yesterday I met someone who . . . I saw a film once . . . When I was 10 years old . . .' The beginning of a narrative immediately halts the listener's attention. A message is passed on, to which the listener responds in two ways: one conscious, the other unconscious. Unless I am versed in decoding I will not hear its whispers. In fact I, the listener, may not want to hear it at all. As frequently occurs in therapy, I may want to shut you up, move you on to another topic, or stay with you, and take your story at face value. Unconsciously, however, I might perceive implications which are deeply disturbing, too disturbing for me to want to uncover them. Yet if I want to communicate with you at a level that cuts through the cover-ups of disguise, I need to learn how to decode these apparently random narratives – whether spoken by you or, unknowingly, by myself. The type of communication which results from this process touches us both at a highly powerful and influential level, since unconsciously communicated perceptions and meanings rule so many of our emotional responses and behaviours.

The self-processing setting is primarily a decoding forum. The self-processing approach to self-analysis consists of a structured methodology which owes its basic formulations to Freud's (1900) discoveries of those psychic phenomena by which we transform the latent dream-thought into its manifest representations (predominantly visual and auditory in nature). Here, however, communicative theory parts company with the classical model.

The self-processing message is an optimistic one, even when painful to bear. Its eventual insights are brought about by our unconscious attempts at rectifying those aspects of our environmental, personal and interpersonal lives which render us dysfunctional. Self-processing psychotherapy aims from the outset at placing upon the individual the task of learning to become his or her own healer. This work is never easy and it may not be suitable for everyone. Its difficulties must never be underestimated. As with all forms of therapy, self-processing demands a strict discipline, true commitment, and enthusiasm. Above all, it requires a deep desire to delve into unconscious meaning. This will no doubt reveal aspects of oneself that one may rather leave buried within. However, for the dedicated explorer, the rewards are many. The task is creative, adventurous and exciting. I have personally engaged in this activity for a number of years. The results of this form of self-analysis are, in my experience, far deeper reaching than any I have personally experienced through conventional therapy. I have found it interesting to discover of late that, following any particular relevant dream, I now seem spontaneously to carry out my guided associations and related attempts at decoding while still in a state of semi-sleep. I frequently awake from such an experience quite rested, usually with fresh insights. The changes I have observed in myself through this type of self-therapy have been truly astounding.

The other story

Langs's work on unconscious communication has led him to investigate the story of human evolution, and, more specifically, the evolution of human mental systems. Langs, as Freud (1900) did before him, assumes the existence of two main mental processing systems, conscious and unconscious, each with its separate subsystems. Langs wanted to understand how two main systems might have developed, within the same mental structure, separate and often contradictory modes of perceiving and processing information and meaning. Why, Langs asked, have we evolved mental functions which, within the same individual, are so frequently in contradiction with one another, such that, in our linguistic exchanges, for instance, we say one thing at one level (and mean it) while, at another level, we deny it (and mean that too)?

Until recently, psychotherapists and psychoanalysts have largely neglected to take into account the legacy of our Darwinian beginnings when formulating their theories. Our very survival as a species has depended upon our ability to adapt. It is clear that natural selection operates according to certain 'rules': what is selected is what works, is 'adapted to', or 'fits with' the environment (Slavin and Kriegman 1992: 295). Evolution and adaptation thus go hand in hand (Darwin 1859/1985; Dawkins 1989; Ornstein 1992; Smith 1995; Pinker 1998). So as we strive to make sense of who we are or how we function in the world – intrapsychically, organically and interpersonally – we cannot afford to disregard our evolutionary and developmental story (Plotkin 1994; Dennett 1995; Langs 1995, 1996; Nesse and Williams 1995). Nor, of course, should we forget 'the inextricable interplay of biology and culture' (Rose 1998: 43).

The communicative paradigm, in agreement with evolutionary theories, argues that the human mind is still in the process of evolving and, as such, it is still incomplete (Langs 1996). When the term 'mind' is used in communicative theory, this generally refers to emotional processing systems. These systems take the form of a complex structure which has been developed over millennia of natural selection, evolution and adaptation. It seems that our emotional responses cannot but function on a level which runs somewhat parallel with our physiological design. At the organic level we have developed an exquisite machine whose natural immune system has the potential to heal itself, yet at times that same system can turn against the very tissue which it is supposed to protect. 'That is, natural selection does not operate in a world without restriction' (Rose 1998: 42–3). It appears that many aspects of the design of our bodily systems, like those of our emotion-processing mind, can be both 'extraordinarily precise and unbelievably slipshod' (Nesse and Williams 1995: 5). In our battle for survival we are often faced with endless compromises, some of them extremely crude. At times, in fact, 'Even our behavior and emotions seem to have been shaped by a prankster' (p. 5).

If we wish to understand more thoroughly the diseases of the human organism we also need to be better able to understand the advantages of those 'apparent mistakes in design' that the organism presents us with (p. 20). The same might apply to the malfunctions which result from our psychological adaptations. If evolution demands a continual compromise, our emotional dysfunctions must also be, in great part, the products of such compromises. This may well be the price we pay for our own survival as a species.

Self-processing therapy can help us identify and modify some of these adaptational coping strategies which are the product of the schism between conscious and unconscious mental functions. One of the advantages of this model is that, as a form of self-therapy, its undertaking is not just therapeutic, but educational and, above all, preventative in nature. As a modality for self-study, this form of therapy can provide us with additional gains over other approaches, since it aims directly at training individuals to become their own analysts. As pointed out above (and as will be seen in the example which follows), its main feature is that it deals almost exclusively with dreams and storied associations. Any insight derived from it occurs through the decoding of unconscious (encoded) meaning and the identification of the triggers that have evoked the encoding. The meeting of triggers and themes will lead to some specific emotional response whose stimulus has been perceived and processed outside awareness. As validated through research in communicative psychotherapy and in self-processing therapy (Langs 1992, 1993), these communications will almost exclusively monitor our current relationships and our adaptationally derived concerns.

Communicative theory does not claim that it can correct the deficiencies which have occurred within the emotional realm in the process of natural selection and adaptation. The approach, rather, suggests a path for capturing and regularly bringing within awareness some of those adaptational issues which are at the root of many of our emotional ills.

Fragment from a continuing story

After ending her training in self-processing, Margaret kept up regular weekly appointments with herself, during which times she worked mainly on the decoding of her dreams. When she did not have a fresh dream to work with, a story or a daydream would usually come forward in her mind. This would then become the focus of the decoding process. She recalled how difficult she had found it, at first, to produce narrative material. She had later learned to entrust herself to the narrative stream as she engaged in her guided associations (Langs 1993, 1994, 1995).

Yesterday, on her way home from work as department manager with an advertising firm, she nearly had a car accident. She had felt irritable all day. On several occasions she experienced stabbing pains in her chest and feared she might be about to suffer a heart attack. She had these pains before when things had troubled her, and had learned that they were of a psychosomatic nature, since tests had cleared her of any physiological problems. The events of the last two days had consisted of a series of irritating incidents. Last night she had even succeeded in provoking an argument on the phone with her best friend. It was all rather uncharacteristic of her. This morning, as she awoke, she remembered a dream fragment. She focused upon it as the subject of her self-processing session. She sat quietly, and rewound the dream in her mind.

I am riding in a car with a man who is familiar yet a stranger. He
reeks of drink. It is dark. A female figure suddenly comes out of
the blackness and is running across the road towards our
speeding car. I shut my eyes. There is a loud thump. I know we
hit her. I shout to the driver to stop, but he ignores my pleas.
Instead he drives on, as though nothing had happened.

The near accident with the coach yesterday flashed back in
Margaret's mind. It had obviously triggered her dream. As she drove
home from work, a huge white coach had nearly squashed her
against the speeding traffic. It looked as though there were no pas-
sengers in it. The coach hit the side of her car and damaged one light
and her car bumper. She tried to memorize the registration number
as the coach drove away. Later, she decided not to pursue the incident with her insurers since she couldn't produce any witnesses to
the accident. In fact she considered herself lucky that she did not
suffer any personal injury.

On the surface it appears as though, in her dream, she had been
processing the incident from the previous day. The event had scared
her, and provoked considerable anger at the time, because the driver
of the coach did not stop to check the damage done. She had shouted
at him to stop from inside her car, and had pulled up by the roadside,
while the rest of the traffic, like the coach driver himself, had gone
by, indifferent to her predicament. Its emotional impact upon her
had appeared in the dream, transformed and displaced onto a more
dramatic and powerful context.

In her dream a woman is hit by a driver who does not stop and
who is unconcerned about the damage done. Now that she thought
about it the coach driver (like the driver in her dream) seemed to
have cut into her without slowing down, almost on purpose. Might
he have been drinking? The man in her dream reeked of drink. This
had not crossed her mind before now. Unconsciously she might well
have captured what she had not grasped, consciously, at the time.
Could that be the reason why the coach driver had not stopped?

She could leave it at that, and be satisfied with the hypothesis
reached on the cognitive level to explain away her dream. She had
gained a better awareness of her anger, and a perception (which
might or might not be accurate) that the coach driver had probably
been drinking.

Yet Margaret knew that her self-processing work had not yet
begun, and that she had only touched upon meanings which were
within the realm of the dream itself. She had learned long ago that,
in the dream world, nothing is ever as it seems.

As she began her string of associations to the various dream elements, she became aware that the man in the car bore a vague resemblance to John, her assistant and deputy manager. Margaret now recalled that, two days earlier, they had both attended a board meeting at which several people put forward proposals for planning a new advertising campaign. Afterwards she had lunch with John. They had been good friends for some time, and she had great respect for his opinions, and often confided in him. She suddenly felt very sleepy, and weak. She wanted to stop her associations and have a rest instead. 'Leave this room and go to bed.' She acknowledged this desire to escape as one of her favourite defence strategies at times of self-analysis. By this time she felt more apprehensive than usual. She looked round the room. Doors and windows were closed. The room felt safe. She lived on her own, there was no risk of interruptions, no phone in this room. Maybe she'd go and eat something, just to keep awake. 'Stop!' she said aloud, 'back to work'. During her training she had become very familiar with these claustrophobic fears of hers and understood their meaning. She also knew that running away now would only prolong the agony and bring about more erratic behaviours as well as physical discomforts.

She returned to the dream and began working with each of its elements in turn.

The woman running out of the darkness brought to mind an old lady she visited occasionally. She had been to see her a couple of days earlier. The old woman had been angry and bitter for some time because her daughter had been putting pressure on her to sell the house in which she lived. 'She wants my money before I'm dead. You see, then the state will be forced to keep me', wept the old lady. 'You see, if one day they have to put me in a home the government will take my house to pay for my keep, so when I die there will be nothing left for her. That's why she wants me to sell the house and give her the money.'

The woman being hit by the car brought to mind post-war stories coming out of Bosnia. Stories about betrayal, cruelty and torture. A newsreel showed a man whose fingernails had been removed. He had been his torturers' friend and neighbour. As children they had played together every day.

When Margaret was 11 years old, she now recalled, she had faked an illness because she did not want to go to school. She had been intimidated by a teacher who was bullying her and humiliating her in front of the class, making her look stupid and helpless. She had never told her parents about it, but she dreaded getting up in the mornings.

The driver ignoring her plea to stop the car brought to mind a board of directors' meeting, two days earlier. She had proposed a new idea which she had previously discussed with John, her friend and deputy manager. He had seemed very enthusiastic about her new campaign plan, and had in fact led her to believe quite clearly that he would support her proposal at the next managerial meeting. At that meeting, the following day, however, he had voted against her. Her proposal was rejected, and she had finally resigned herself to this majority verdict. Of course she was disappointed but had shrugged her shoulders, taken note of any critical comments, and put her disappointment to one side. Soon after that her thoughts had turned to fresh plans in which she might be able to incorporate some of her previous ideas. In fact, she thought at the time, this rejection might enable her to take time to modify the structure of her original project and channel it in a new direction. This would make a future proposal more appealing and marketable.

While lunching with John after the directors' meeting, she recalled that he had been his usual friendly self. He had been kind and thoughtful towards her. She found it a little strange at the time that he hadn't mentioned the reasons for his lack of support in backing her project. Then again, she dismissed this thought as an expression of her sometimes pathological need for approval.

As she thought back about that lunch date with John, she remembered recounting to him an episode in her life which was particularly private to her. That same story returned to mind now, as she associated to the dream. Somehow, as she and John talked, she found herself telling him about her father's death some years earlier. 'My father', she remembered recounting, 'had been terminally ill with cancer for some time. He had been living abroad. I should have been with him during the final phase of his illness, but I had just got this new job, my first managerial position, and my boss refused to release me. I was very ambitious and selfish at the time; I believed that my career must come first, no matter what. So my father died alone.'

She once more remembered this story, and was struck by the themes it contained. They were now taking her by surprise. Her father's story was about terminal illness, the ending of a relationship. It was also about abandonment at a time when that person was most in need of one's nearness. All this mainly for reasons of self-interest (one's career) and for personal ambition. Indeed, the sick person had been deserted and left to die alone.

Margaret realized now that the story she had narrated to her friend John was an encoded communication which spoke, in poignant and dramatic terms, of feelings which she had not consciously acknowledged and which she had not been aware of expressing at the time. In disguised fashion she was in fact saying to her friend, 'I feel that you have deserted me when I was most in need of your support, just as I let my father die alone when he was in need of me and

I should instead have been by his side.' As she verbalized this tentative interpretation to herself she began to feel a deep sense of relief. The stabbing pain in her chest eased, and the sense of apprehension which had been with her through the session suddenly lifted. She began to weep, at her father's pain, at her own feelings of guilt for having abandoned him when in need. She wept also for her own feelings of hurt at John's abandonment at a time when she had been in need of his support. She marvelled at the powerful images that, through her father's story, had so starkly and precisely represented how she had really felt during that lunch date after the board meeting.

Margaret knew that John had not been aware of her message, but then nor had she. She had now realized how deeply John's betrayal had affected her. The implications of John's behaviour had obviously touched upon a sensitive chord in her personal history. Was this what her dream had been all about or was there more? She looked back at her earlier associations, felt the urgent need to delve further into her stories.

She pondered over the themes in her earlier narratives. They were about lack of loyalty, cruelty, betrayal of people who were once close (herself and her father, the old lady and her daughter, the childhood friends in the torture story), of ruthless and violent behaviour towards them. The story of the bullying teacher appeared to imply public humiliation, a sort of torture, sadistic behaviour, abuse of one's position of authority or strength. The aims of the perpetrators of violence were, in these stories, to do with self-interest and power.

Her themes reflected a hurt which seemed to have reached much deeper than she had imagined. Margaret thought again about her dream. The dream image of the woman running out of the blackness towards the car flashed vividly back before her eyes. She could not tell whether the woman had purposely aimed at throwing herself under the car, or whether she had been running away from some danger and looking for help. Suddenly an incident came to mind, an argument Margaret overheard some days earlier in the office.

Strange how, till now, she had completely forgotten this incident. The argument was between John and a woman designer. She overheard the woman shouting: '. . . of course, John, I'm sure you'll get your way in the end, your type doesn't give a damn who they hurt in the process.' It was then that Margaret entered the office. To her surprise she now recalled twinges of jealousy which had gone completely unnoticed at the time. 'Why?' she now wondered. Was it the sight of those two figures together, arguing like two lovers? She felt puzzled by this realization, and by the oddness of that till now unacknowledged emotion.

Later that day Margaret had caught John whispering to the managing director in what appeared to be a conspiratorial manner. The following day she saw the designer rush out of the managing director's office in tears. After that episode Margaret found out that the woman had been dismissed.

This last story contained themes of a disagreement, of someone being accused of being ruthless, interested only in personal gains, of jealousy, of a possible secret affair, of apparent conspiracy, of possible betrayal leading to a dismissal (the ending of an engagement or relationship), and of hurt and damage.

Margaret suddenly recalled that when she was 8 years old she fell in love with the au pair's boyfriend. He was in the army. Every time he came to see the au pair Margaret believed he had really come to see her. She remembered how excited she felt each time he was due to arrive, how she checked herself in the mirror, and combed her hair over and over. How happy he seemed to be to see her, how he hugged her and joked with her. Then one day he stopped coming. She was brokenhearted, had felt rejected, abandoned, betrayed.

Margaret felt the dream had been trying to communicate layers of meaning which she had not quite grasped yet. Certainly her previous associations spoke clearly of her perception of someone who is ruthless and should not be trusted, of an infatuation which was not returned, of loss, self-deception, abandonment and of a relationship which came to an abrupt end.

She now turned back to her dream images. They spoke of someone who was in the company of a person who was familiar, yet a stranger (herself and the driver), of someone (a third person, a woman) who runs blindly from some possible danger (perhaps to seek help) only to incur serious injury, or death. The images also show the perpetrator of the damage as someone who had been drinking (the driver reeked of drink) and who was completely unconcerned about the damage inflicted.

So far all her stories seemed to lead back to the event of the previous day's collision with the coach driver. These stories, however, also evoked a perception that she might have been seriously injured, and even killed. She recognized that the incident must have aroused severe death anxiety in her. These stories were also telling her things she did not want to hear. They told her that John, whom she had thoroughly trusted, and who had proved to be a genuine and loyal friend, was being perceived by her, unconsciously, as someone who had no scruples about damaging or destroying others and who, therefore, could not be trusted. Yet the board meeting incident had been an isolated one. Consciously, however, she had accepted its outcome.

She felt an oppressive surge of panic as she thought about the soldier's story, about that hopeless infatuation, her sadness and sense of rejection and loss afterwards, when she realized that he did not seem to have cared about her after all. As a child, she had taken his affectionate embraces and jokes as a signal that he cared about her. She now smiled at the ending of that one-sided affair, and at the absurdity of her childhood fantasies.

Margaret now pondered over the implications of John's behaviour at the board meeting, and acknowledged the episode as the principal emotional trigger for the feelings of hurt, betrayal and abandonment she must have experienced at the time without quite dwelling upon them. None the less, there were certainly other triggers at work which she had previously forgotten or ignored but which were responsible for her dysfunctional symptoms and behaviours of late. She could point to at least three further triggers which had emerged through her associations. Until now she appeared to have managed to put them out of her mind.

There was the argument between John and the woman designer, the intimacy she had perceived between them, her own (at the time unacknowledged) feelings of jealousy and hurt. And, later, the conspiratorial manner in which she had caught John whispering with the managing director of the firm. Finally, there was the woman's dismissal. Margaret felt that these latter events must have had a powerful emotional impact upon her, since their implications had been strongly repressed, although perceived, processed and represented in an encoded form through her stories.

Besides the deep hurt triggered by John's lack of support at the board meeting, the second and probably most powerful trigger for her suppressed emotions was to do with her feelings of betrayal at finding out that John had probably been having an affair with someone else while, at the same time, leading her to think that their friendship meant more to him than just that. She had obviously been deceiving herself without realizing it. How foolish she had been. She felt again like an 8-year old child who had discovered that the soldier had never cared for her after all.

Furthermore, Margaret reflected, if John had been truly capable of conspiring to have the designer dismissed, this would mean that he would not hesitate to use or damage her either. It seemed now that her dream was condensing at least two individuals in the image of the car driver: John, and the driver of the coach with which she had nearly collided.

Perhaps, she thought, she was off the mark, and neither her dream nor her associations had anything to do with reality. All her deductions were just meaningless fantasies rather than unconscious perceptions. After all, John was still her friend. Perhaps her dream had nothing to do with him, and his affair with the designer had been a fantasy on Margaret's part.

Who was she to trust, then: her conscious mind, or this recondite wisdom system of hers, whose workings seemed to be far ahead of her rational self? She was coming to the end of her self-processing session. She sought out one last story. If she were really off the mark, she would quickly find out.

She ran over the dream images in her mind. She thought again about the man in the car who reeked of drink. From that image she allowed her mind to wander off onto some other context, thrusting forward her dream element like a rod thrown into a pond. A memory surfaced. She was sitting in a bus. A black man went to sit on the seat beside her; they were separated by the aisle. He carried a violin case. She recalled she had seen him earlier that day, sitting on a bench, polishing his instrument. He had short rastafarian hair and a smiling round face. There were several people in the bus. The man began to talk aloud, making intriguing philosophical statements about life, about people's relationships with one another in a city as crowded as London, in which one felt so alone. The audience the man addressed himself to looked away, tight-lipped, slightly embarrassed and somewhat fearful. Perhaps he was just another madman who at any moment might become dangerous, and wave a knife at them. Only Margaret nodded in his direction and smiled back. To her his philosophizing seemed to make a lot of sense. He noticed her smile and turned towards her: 'Do you know? I have this neighbour. We've been neighbours for many years. Every morning I pass by and say good morning to him. He never answers, never smiles either. Man, today I found him with his head deep inside the bonnet of his car. "Is there a problem?" I asked. "Yes", he muttered. "The bloody thing won't start." "Let's have a look", I said. I messed about in there for a while. I know a bit about cars, you know. "OK," I said, "try and start it now." He hesitated. "Go on," I said, "have a go." The car started like magic. He gave me a big smile, the first ever.'

This narrative about the black man would be the final step in her self-processing session. It would validate or invalidate the interpretation she had previously reached in decoding her dream. She set about unravelling her story. What was it all about? It contained imagery and themes which went from alienation and lack of communication to helpfulness and communication. They spoke about making connections. Margaret considered her last story as an encoded (unconscious) message whose positive outcome and imagery confirmed the decoded interpretation she had reached earlier.

The validation check is an inherent component of each self-processing session. The dreamer returns to the original source (the dream itself) and generates one or two fresh narratives from one of its elements. The themes emerging from this last procedure – according to whether they contain positive or negative imagery and outcomes – are then viewed as her validating or invalidating unconscious responses to the now decoded message as articulated by the dreamer herself. Conscious validation is not considered to be a reliable judge of trigger-decoded insight (Langs 1988, 1992, 1994). The conscious system is highly self-deceptive when deep emotional issues are at stake. The deep wisdom system – an unconscious intelligence that seems to operate within individuals – will speak out its true perceptions through communicative means: the storied medium. Metaphor bypasses conscious defences and aims directly at its target.

Several weeks after the above session Margaret discovered that John had been scheming to take her place as section manager with the firm, and that over the time they had worked together he had stolen and sold outside the firm several of her discarded ideas and projects without her knowledge.

She realized how hard it had been for her to accept and trust her own encoded perceptions, displaced as they were in the images of her dream and associations. She had not 'imagined' John's betrayal and destructive intentions after all. Rather, she had perceived with great accuracy their actual existence. She worked hard with herself to deal with that hurt and with the anger that accompanied it.

There were issues of boundaries being transgressed all around her. Not just in John's doings, but in her own secret aspirations for a more intimate relationship with him. His own dishonesty, as she realized later, broke the boundaries of both work ethics and friendship. Her own secret hopes collided with their work relationship. Similar transgressions emerged in John's relationship with the woman designer, as well as in his possible manipulations and betrayal which led to her dismissal. There was a frame break (transgression of appropriate ground rules) on the part of the coach driver with whom Margaret collided (a hit-and-run situation). The man did not observe the appropriate law which requires the driver to stop (check the damage done to her and the car, exchange insurance details, and so forth). Would he have behaved in the same way had she been seriously hurt, or even killed?

There were further layers, she discovered later, enclosed within those same dream images and in her consequent narratives. Their themes returned in future dreams. Many are still part of her narratives, of her fears, of coping strategies, of life itself.

References

Darwin, C. (1859/1985) *On the Origin of the Species by Means of Natural Selection*. London: Murray.

Dawkins, R. (1989) *The Selfish Gene* (new edition). New York. Oxford University Press.

Dennett, D.C. (1995) *Darwin's Dangerous Idea*. New York: Simon and Shuster.

Freud, S. (1900) The interpretation of dreams. *S. E.* 4, 5.

Langs, R. (1973–74) *The Technique of Psychoanalytic Psychotherapy*, vols 1 and 2. New York: Jason Aronson.

Langs, R. (1976) *The Bipersonal Field*. New York: Jason Aronson.

Langs, R. (1978) *Technique in Transition*. New York: Jason Aronson.

Langs, R. (1979) *The Therapeutic Environment*. New York: Jason Aronson.

Langs, R. (1980) *Interactions: The Realm of Transference and Countertransference*. New York: Jason Aronson.

Langs, R. (1982) *Psychotherapy: A Basic Text*. New York: Jason Aronson.

Langs, R. (1983) *Unconscious Communication in Everyday Life*. New York: Jason Aronson.

Langs, R. (1986) Clinical issues arising from a new model of the mind, *Contemporary Psychoanalysis*, 22: 418–44.

Langs, R. (1988) *A Primer of Psychotherapy*. New York: Gardner Press.

Langs, R. (1991) *Take Charge of Your Emotional Life*. New York: Henry Holt.

Langs, R. (1992) The self-processing class and the psychotherapy situation: a comparative study, *American Journal of Psychotherapy*, 46(1): January.

Langs, R. (1993) *Empowered Psychotherapy: A New Therapy for Self and Others*. London: Karnac.

Langs, R. (1994) *The Dream Workbook*. New York: Alliance Publishing.

Langs, R. (1995) *Clinical Practice and the Architecture of the Mind*. London: Karnac.

Langs, R. (1996) *The Evolution of the Emotion-Processing Mind*. London: Karnac.

Nesse, R.M. and Williams, G.C. (1995) *Evolution and Healing*. London: Weidenfeld and Nicolson.

Ornstein, R. (1992) *The Evolution of Consciousness*. New York: Touchstone.

Pinker, S. (1998) *How the Mind Works*. London: Allen Lane, The Penguin Press.

Plotkin, H. (1994) *The Nature of Knowledge*. London: Allen Lane, The Penguin Press.

Rose, S. (1998) Maybe I'm a machine, *New Scientist*, 2118: 42–3.

Slavin, M. and Kriegman, D. (1992) *The Adaptive Design of the Human Psyche*. New York: Guilford Press.

Smith, D.L. (1995) Free associations and honey bee dancers: the unconscious and its place in nature, paper given at the 1995 Conference of the European Society for Communicative Psychotherapy, Regent's College, London.

Chapter 12

Madness and reason: Shakespeare's *King Lear* and the psychoanalytic frame

E. Mary Sullivan

Introduction

In this chapter I investigate Shakespeare's *King Lear* from the perspective of the psychoanalytic frame, as developed by Bleger (1967/1990), exploring the consequences and processes following a breach of the frame in terms of communicative theory.[1] I propose that utterances of characters and their actions can be understood as derivative representations of the breach and its implications, that models of rectification are offered and go unheeded, and that the death and devastation by the end of the play represent the tragic termination of the relationships of the protagonists, together with the destruction of the frame which constituted their 'ghost world'.

Psychoanalysts have always found Shakespeare's *King Lear* fascinating, and it is perhaps only with post-Freudian clinical insight that many of the play's apparent inconsistencies make more sense than to earlier critics. For there is little doubt that Shakespeare was a phenomenologist – in his depiction of the characters, their behaviour and emotions in the play he was describing accurately what he had observed to be true, with what Cox and Theilgaard (1994) call his 'paraclinical precision'.

Bayley (1981) claimed that, in contrast to the modern spirit in its seriousness and sincerity, 'Shakespearean tragedy never begins at home'. He emphasizes the importance of the inner freedom this engenders in the poet, a freedom to perceive and to create 'which is denied to the tragic protagonists' (p. 14). Bayley claims that the mystery of Shakespeare's art in *King Lear* is that there is no point, no consciously driving message: so many of the personal observations, claims, discoveries and pronouncements in the play suffer from a lack of appropriateness, in terms of dramatic construction and unity. Bayley's view, if I understand him correctly, is that this is to do with a deeper verity, a more profound realism: 'The off-key note of everything human in *Lear* comes from the primal violation of family silence' (p. 27). I hold that this implies that the impact of the play upon its audience derives considerable force from Shakespeare's unconscious perception and poetic portraiture of 'real' family relationships.

I propose to investigate *King Lear* from a communicative perspective, looking at the possible origins and development of Lear's 'madness' in terms of the psychoanalytic frame.

The concept of the frame

Milner (1950) introduced the concept of the frame into psychoanalytic discourse:

> The frame marks off the different kind of reality that is within it from that which is outside it; but a temporal-spatial frame also marks off the special kind of reality of a psycho-analytical session. And in psycho-analysis it is the existence of this frame that makes possible the full development of that creative illusion that analysts call the transference. Also the central idea underlying psycho-analytic technique is that it is by means of this illusion that a better adaptation to the world outside is ultimately developed.
>
> (cited in Klein *et al*. 1985: 86)

Bleger (1967/1990) defines the psychoanalytic frame as 'the set of constants within whose limits the process [of psychoanalysis] takes place'. Institutions and the frame, Bleger maintains, make up a 'ghost world', of the most primitive and undifferentiated organization, which is never noticed until it is missing; there is no awareness of what is always present. He goes on to describe the frame as an implicit *meta-behaviour* on which depends the explicit behaviour which take place within it. Bleger refers to the work of Jaques (1955 in Klein *et al*. 1985) in showing how social institutions are unconsciously used as a defence against psychotic anxiety, and goes further, claiming that in them is deposited 'the psychotic part of the personality, i.e. the undifferentiated and non-dissolved portion of the primitive symbiotic links', which he designates the non-ego. The non-ego is the background or frame of the organized ego, and the two are dissociated. He concludes: 'Any variation in the frame brings the non-ego to a crisis, "contradicts" the fusion, "challenges" the ego, and compels reintrojection, re-elaboration of the ego, or stirs the defences to immobilize or reproject the psychotic part of the personality' (Bleger 1990: 424).

Lear himself set in hand the variation to the frame set out in Shakespeare's play: not only the polity, the taken-for-granted social and political institutions of Lear's Britain, but the power relations with his daughters. The result of his actions was to bring about, not only a profound crisis in the state, but a crisis in his non-ego, and the deaths of all his family and others closely associated with him. Lear's alteration to the frame took the form, for Shakespeare, of a breach in the contract – as it is set out by Cordelia – between father and daughters, from which flows the action of the play.

In communicative theory the sequence following on a variation in the frame conditions would, generally, be understood to take the following form: a 'breach' of the frame occurs, either initiated by the therapist, or passing unnoticed by her; the event is unconsciously perceived by the patient, who attempts to communicate her perception of it to the therapist through the derivative representation of the adaptive context or 'trigger'[2] and its implications, in a series of narratives, constructed through the unconscious processes of displacement, disguise and selection for representability. The breach may also be represented through behaviour which replicates the breach, in disguised or displaced form. As part of the derivative communication by the patient, a model of rectification – indicating to the therapist how she might repair or rectify the breach – will be offered. Should the therapist fail to hear, understand, interpret and/or act appropriately upon the patient's unconscious communication, the situation may well be 'resolved' by termination of the therapy by the patient.

I hypothesize that Shakespeare's *King Lear* can be understood in these terms: that the public ritual competition between Lear's daughters in Act I Scene 1 can be represented as a breach of the frame for which Lear is responsible.

King Lear – the play

King Lear is a play about family relationships and about kingship, or power. It also explores madness, not only from Gloucester's distractedness and the Fool's fooling, to Edgar's assumed madness as 'poor Tom', and to Lear's psychotic episode; but it even encompasses the malignancy and horror of the 'sane' behaviour of Lear's daughters, and of Cornwall and Edmund – the theme of 'reason in madness; madness in reason'.

The play can be read as a study of death anxiety, of Lear's attempt to come to terms with his approaching death, an attempt which goes tragically awry. As a king, Lear had known absolute power over his subjects, over life and death: one of the most fundamental properties of absolute temporal power is its capacity to corrupt its possessor. Lear's understanding of the nature of his power had become corrupted, and it was the subsequent distortion of his sense of reality in respect of his familial relationships which encouraged him to go about the arrangements for his 'retirement' in the 'deviant' way which set in train the action of the play.

The aged King Lear intends to divide his kingdom between his three daughters who must first, however, take part in a public love contest, the results of which will determine their share of the kingdom. His youngest daughter, Cordelia, refuses to take part in this contest and is summarily dismissed, or banished, from the king's presence, as is the Earl of Kent, who protests at the king's behaviour. As the play proceeds, Lear's elder daughters, Goneril and Regan, the kingdom divided between them, cooperate to exclude their father from power, and their attitude and his realization of his fundamental mistake bring out his madness. Cordelia seeks to rescue him and to recover for him the kingdom; she does the first, and he recovers from his madness, but they are defeated and captured by Goneril and Regan's forces; Cordelia is killed, and Lear dies. There is a parallel subplot in which the Earl of Gloucester is deceived by his illegitimate son Edmund into effectively banishing his legitimate son Edgar, who disguises himself as the madman 'poor Tom'. Gloucester is blinded by Regan's husband Cornwall and is dissuaded from suicide by the disguised Edgar; they are reconciled before Gloucester's later death and Edmund is killed by Edgar, who is left to assume responsibility for the kingdom.

King Lear[3] – the adaptive context

The frame and 'trigger' for the plot of the play are shown in Act I Scene 1, which introduces us to the characters and sets out the circumstances within which the action of the play is to unfold. It takes place in a state room in King Lear's palace. The context for this first scene is indicated by the prologuic interchange between Kent and Gloucester, which informs us, first, of the division of the kingdom – that there is a decision-making nodal point at hand is hinted at by

Gloucester's '. . . in the division of the kingdom, it appears not which of the Dukes he values most' (I.1: 3–5) – and second, in the curiously off-key conversation regarding Gloucester's bastard son, Edmund, of the parallel subplot underlining the intergenerational conflict theme.

The entrance of the king is signalled by a heraldic fanfare which emphasizes the full power and ceremony of this important moment. He states the agenda, 'our darker purpose' (I.1: 35): that the kingdom is to be divided, and the question of his youngest daughter's marriage resolved. Lear's manifest intention is to prepare himself for death, 'to shake all cares and business from our age . . . [and] Unburthen'd crawl toward death' (I.1: 38–40). We note a sense that Lear has delayed a decision about Cordelia's marriage: 'Long in our court have made their amorous sojourn' (I.1: 46), and wonder at the motivation for his hesitation. Some unconscious, 'psychotic' motivation towards chaos (*'apres moi, le deluge'*?) might be hinted at by the negative anticipation of 'that future strife/Must be prevented now' (I.1: 43–4).

The 'sensible' manifest motive is to be offset, damaged, even cancelled out, by the mode of his disposal of the kingdom, dividing it between his three daughters according to their competitive protestations of love for him: 'That we our largest bounty may extend/ Where nature doth with merit challenge' (I.1: 51–2). His youngest daughter Cordelia spoils the game – and it was a game, since Lear had already decided the division of the kingdom in his own mind: 'Know that we have divided in three our kingdom' (I.1: 36–7). When asked for her contribution to the love contest, she replies: 'Nothing, my lord' (I.1: 86), and refuses to deviate from this stance, referring him to the 'contract' between parent and child: 'I love your Majesty/ According to my bond; no more nor less' (I.1: 91–2). Cordelia therefore delineates the 'secure frame', the ground rules of the father–daughter–husband relationship; she attempts to secure the boundary, as does Kent, who protests on her behalf at Lear's extreme reaction against her, a reaction which betrays a desperate lack in Lear, and elicits the wounding: 'Better thou/Hadst not been born than not t'have pleased me better' (I.1: 232–3). Both are banished, and Cordelia's share of the kingdom given away to her two elder sisters, who have colluded with their father's frame deviation in order to gain power.

Thus the trigger for the action of the play is Lear's own decision to divide his kingdom between his daughters: he abnegates his own monarchical power in favour of his two elder daughters; he renounces the responsibility while retaining the privileges of the monarch in a flawed process which involve the public humiliation of the two elder daughters and the banishment of the third. It is possible that Shakespeare would have seen the 'premature' handing over of power in itself as a 'frame break', given belief in the 'divine right' of monarchs, but in any event the deviant way of doing it also in itself constitutes a frame break. By making the division of the kingdom contingent on a public spectacle and contest between his daughters, Lear was abusing his power both as a father and as a king – the rest followed from this. Cordelia's refusal to collude with his abusive behaviour brought about the premature and absolute termination of the filial relationship – Lear needed to 'kill' his daughter in order to compensate for the mortal wound she had dealt his narcissistic fantasy: his desire to end his life under her care, to make her as his mother. Had his elder daughters not reacted to their public humiliation by stripping him of his fantasy of post-monarchical power and sending him out, near-naked, into the storm, Lear might have been able to keep his 'madness' suppressed. But his exposure to reality, the harsh reality of his position, brought about by his own action, forces him into that different dimension of awareness which is the expression, the outward and visible sign of an inward, hitherto invisible, but deeply influential fissure in his psychic structure.

Derivative communications

In Act I Scene 3 we see Goneril complaining of her father's 'unreasonable' behaviour; plotting with her servant Oswald to reduce Lear's retinue, and to irritate and insult him, so that he will want to leave. She makes clear that she is of one mind with her sister Regan, to whom Lear will aim to transfer himself and his retinue, with the implication that he will meet with similar treatment at Regan's hands. Goneril's manipulation and her intention to humiliate Lear are open and frank; she justifies her behaviour in terms of both Lear's own ambivalent attitude to power, and by his advanced age:

> Idle old man,
> That still would manage those authorities
> That he hath given away! Now, by my life,
> Old fools are babes again, and must be us'd
> With checks as flatteries, when they are seen abus'd.
>
> (I.3: 17–21)

Her publicly humiliating treatment of her father is a corollary of his treatment of herself and her sister (she refers to her sister, 'whose mind and mine, I know, in that are one' (I.3: 16), which strengthens this link). She refers manifestly to the trigger ('those authorities/That he hath given away'); early in this scene she exclaims: 'By day and night he wrongs me', and refers (above) to his giving away his 'authorities'. As the action of the following scene unfolds, putting Goneril's plan into effect, the Fool's commentary insistently brings to mind the true meaning and effect of Lear's actions; Lear himself is utterly unaware, but the Fool could be said to function as his 'unconscious perception', offering disguised interpretations of his breach of the frame:

> FOOL: Why, this fellow has banish'd two on's daughters, and
> did the third a blessing against his will: if thou follow him
> thou must needs wear my coxcomb. How now, Nuncle!
> Would I had two coxcombs and two daughters!
> LEAR: Why, my boy?
> FOOL: If I gave them all my living, I'd keep my coxcombs
> myself. There's mine; beg another of thy daughters.
>
> (I.4: 100–7)

The Fool is pointing out Lear's 'folly' (the coxcomb is the 'badge of office' of the Fool) in his dealings with his daughters: he has done the opposite of banishing the two elder daughters, but they are intent on banishing him. He has done the third a favour, in that she is now Queen of France. He points out also that, in giving his daughters all his power, Lear does not even have the means to award himself the badge of office of a Fool, he must beg it of his daughters. Throughout this scene the Fool continues to interpret to Lear, in riddle, verse and doggerel, the folly and implications of his action in giving away power to his daughters, and offers a model of rectification: he should have banished the two elder daughters, and given the third his blessing as ruler of the kingdom in his place.

Goneril complains to her father, in an ironic, 'more in sorrow than in anger' style, about his failure to censure his followers; she implies a threat that his behaviour will elicit reproof, even punishment – punishment which in other circumstances would be shameful, but in this case would be justified. The speech is long (14 lines); her style is convoluted and indirect, but the Fool sums up her message succinctly in a powerful and brutal image:

> The hedge-sparrow fed the cuckoo so long,
> That it's had it head bit off by it young.
> So out went the candle, and we were left darkling.
>
> (I.4: 213–15)

He interprets that Goneril is like a cuckoo which, too much indulged, decapitates its foster parent; that her speech, though indirect in style, is nevertheless murderous in its effects. Indeed, Lear is utterly taken aback, and reflects the sense of the 'cuckoo' by asking: 'Are you our daughter?' (I.4: 216). She continues in a similar vein, in 'diplomatic' language, instructing him to come to his senses, in effect. Lear is disabled by her turning of the tables on him, her formal and indirect language, her use of the power he has handed over to her against him, her own father. He doubts his own identity, therefore: 'Who is it can tell me who I am?', and is answered by the Fool, 'Lear's shadow'. This response answers the question literally – the Fool is Lear's Shadow, his *alter ego*, in what could be taken as a Jungian sense; but he also means that Lear's self was inordinately reliant on his status as king; it is Lear's hidden, unconscious self which is needed to make clear to him who he really is. More of this ironic yet deadly serious interchange between Lear and the Fool goads Goneril into a direct statement of her complaint against him and his retinue: that they have turned her home into a brothel; and that he must reduce the size of his retinue. Lear in turn reacts by immediately threatening to leave; his imagery is extreme: 'Darkness and devils!' (I.4: 249) and 'Degenerate bastard!' (I.4: 251). As Albany, Goneril's husband, enters to try to calm matters down, Lear goes further: 'thou marble-hearted fiend,/More hideous . . . /Than the sea-monster' (I.4: 257–9), and 'Detested kite!' (I.4: 260). He claims his followers to be paragons of virtue (which may or may not be true) and, in a parenthetic moment, immediately realizes the magnitude of his own earlier mistake:

> O most small fault,
> How ugly didst thou in Cordelia show!
> Which, like an engine, wrench'd my frame of nature
> From the fix'd place, drew from my heart all love,
> And added to the gall. O Lear, Lear, Lear!
> Beat at this gate, that let thy folly in,
> And thy dear judgement out!
>
> (I.4: 264–70)

In other words, he manifestly refers to the frame break. Although he imputes the 'most small fault' to Cordelia, it is his own folly and lack of judgement that he berates; but the time seems not to be 'ripe' for insight, and he goes straight on to curse Goneril for her ingratitude: 'that she may feel/How sharper than a serpent's tooth it is/To have a thankless child!' (I.4: 285–7). I believe that, by displacing parent and daughter, we may infer that Lear was unconsciously expressing the hurt caused to Cordelia by his action. The terms of his continued cursing and renouncing of Goneril reflects the corollary of his attempted annihilation of Cordelia, and so another theme is repeated.

The Fool continues to reiterate his 'unconscious' veridical perception of the implications of Lear's behaviour towards the climax of:

> FOOL: If thou wert my Fool, Nuncle, I'd have thee beaten for being old before thy time.
> LEAR: How's that?
> FOOL: Thou should'st not have been old till thou hadst been wise.
>
> (I.5: 33–42)

This is another model of rectification, which forces Lear to a kind of realization, at an organismic level, of the conflict between his conscious and 'unconscious' reality and its implications:

> LEAR: O! let me not be mad, not mad, sweet heaven;
> Keep me in temper; I would not be mad!
>
> (I.5: 43–4)

The same theme of public humiliation is again repeated in Act II Scene 2, where the disguised Kent, the king's servant, is put in the stocks by Cornwall. The representative of the king is treated like a common criminal by the king's daughter. In Scene 4, when Lear arrives at Gloucester's castle, his daughter and son-in-law are refusing to see him. He insists, and Kent is released from the stocks; but Regan's and, later, Goneril's attitude is such that he begins to have symptoms of anxiety as he struggles to maintain control over his rage and fear. By the end of Scene 4, the king is, in effect, banished, or excluded, dislocated – as he did his daughter Cordelia and his faithful and truthful follower Kent – to the heath,

> the huge expanse of England beyond the reach of enclosing agriculture and the centralising state, a realm of wild growth and darkness without patrols or police, king's highways or lights . . . The heath is both a real place and a place in the mind. It is what the human world would be like if pity, duty and the customs of honour and due ceased to rule human behaviour.
> (Ignatieff 1990: 40–1)

Thus the theme of banishment and exclusion is repeated as Lear's story continues, but this exclusion is more fundamental: unlike Cordelia and Kent, who are simply banished from the sight of the King and from the country of Britain, Lear is excluded from the 'civilized world', or from 'sanity'.

Thus the stories within the play represent, through repetition of the themes of public humiliation and of banishment, the unjust behaviour of Lear towards his daughters at the beginning. The trigger is thus represented derivatively; in addition, Lear's own brief conscious acknowledgement of his fault is a manifest reference to the trigger, while his daughters refer a number of times to their father's ambivalent behaviour around his abdication of power.

A further layer of such derivative representations, to which I have not referred from considerations of space, lies in the subplot relating to Gloucester and his two sons. Gloucester has favoured the legitimate Edgar over the bastard Edmund. Edmund deceives his father into 'banishing' Edgar, and continues to deceive and betray his father paralleling Lear's treatment by his two elder daughters. Thus the themes of the subplot concerning the Gloucester family reflect, in a modified or displaced fashion, the themes of the main plot concerning the Lear family.

The Fool repeatedly offers Lear models of rectification, the last of which comes in the riddle of the snail:

> FOOL: Canst tell how an oyster makes his shell?
> LEAR: No.
> FOOL: Nor I neither; but I can tell why a snail has a house.
> LEAR: Why?
> FOOL: Why, to put's head in; not to give it away to his
> daughters, and leave his horns without a case.
>
> (I.5: 24–30)

He is pointing out that Lear should, at the very least, have reserved for himself some wealth, some property. The reference to horns may imply a degree of incestuous interest in his daughters on Lear's part, which is now frustrated, and/or it may originate in an animal image, for example the stag, and therefore resonate with the crown – Lear is still king, but powerless, without a kingdom.

Working towards resolution

The scenes on the heath, in this 'place . . . [where] pity, duty and the customs of honour and due [have] ceased to rule human behaviour' are at the core of the play. By the time we see Lear, we know that he moves in and out of his madness, but refuses to see his daughter Cordelia, who has come from France to his rescue, out of shame at his treatment of her:

> KENT: Well, sir, the poor distressed Lear's i'th'town;
> Who sometime, in his better tune, remembers
> What we are come about, and by no means
> Will yield to see his daughter.

GENTLEMAN: Why, good sir?
KENT: A sovereign shame so elbows him.

(IV.3: 38–42)

Cordelia has enlisted medical support to help the recovery of her father's senses, and the military support of her husband, the King of France, to help recover her father's kingdom. Lear appears, 'fantastically dressed with wild flowers' (IV.6: 80, Stage direction). If the reference in Act IV Scene 4 still holds good, it may be said that he wears his diagnosis: the wild flowers he wears have been detailed as follows:

Crown'd with rank fumiter and furrow-weeds,
With hardocks, hemlock, nettles, cuckoo-flowers,
Darnel, and all the idle weeds that grow
In our sustaining corn.

(IV.4: 3–6)

All of these plants fulfil the description by the Doctor of 'simples operative, whose power/Will close the eye of anguish' (IV.4: 14–15): fumiter (fumitory) was a sedative and hypnotic; hardock (dock) was used to build up strength in convalescence, being rich in iron; hemlock was a narcotic; nettles were a general tonic and regenerator of the blood, the seeds being a remedy for incontinence; cuckoo-flowers (cowslip) – an infusion of cowslip flowers – has a sedative action on nervous conditions and is used to combat headaches and migraines; and darnel (rye-grass) had narcotic powers (Palaiseul 1973). That the king is already wearing these remedies seems to indicate a sense of Lear's recovery lying within himself, rather than being reliant on the intervention of others.

His first words respond to Edgar's 'But who comes here?' (IV.6: 80), and to Edgar's evident astonishment and horror at the king's appearance. (A rather pathetic parody of Oberon, in *A Midsummer Night's Dream*, comes to mind, an association which resonates with the reference to 'coining' or counterfeiting, before 'I am the king himself'.) In this scene I surmise that Lear addresses himself to Gloucester, who can now (the Fool has disappeared) be understood as his 'shadow' or double, while Edgar stands apart as an observer. Lear gives, or seems to give Gloucester money three times, in three different contexts, and the themes of his discourse range around the notion of justice subverted by corruption.

The first theme is that of recruiting soldiers, which speaks to the king's concern for his own safety, a theme which recurs later in this interaction, and it is concluded by a request for a password, which Edgar answers with 'Sweet marjoram' (a remedy for diseases of the brain), a coded form of reassurance to Lear that he is safe with the present company, that no harm is intended to him.

Lear offers Gloucester 'Press-money', money paid to recruits when they enlist (Muir 1972). There follows a section about flattery; Lear has seen through the flattery, not only of his elder daughters, but of courtiers and followers, one of whom was his auditor, Glouces- ter. In response to Gloucester identifying the voice he hears as that of the king, Lear reverts to the theme of power and corruption: 'When I do stare, see how the subject quakes./I pardon that man's life' (IV.6: 108–9). He talks of corruption in sexual behaviour; despite teach- ing and commandments forbidding adultery, copulation thrives throughout the animal world, down to the smallest bird or insect. There is a profound and exquisite irony as he addresses Gloucester – apparently without identifying or remembering him – telling him that the bastard Edmund was kinder to his father than Lear's own legitimate daughters were to theirs, when actually Gloucester stands before him, blinded through Edmund's deliberate betrayal; and Edgar, too, is present.

Alongside the command to lust ('To't, Luxury, pell-mell!' – IV.6: 116) is the comment, 'For I lack soldiers', in contrast to the earlier 'I pardon that man's life'. From all-powerful to powerless – he has given away the military support necessary to preserve the essence of king- ship. His lack of soldiers and the themes of sexual corruption link to his daughters Goneril and Regan again, who have by this point already begun to compete in their joint sexual desire for Edmund, which will contribute to their undoing. Lear describes women as cen- taurs 'but to the girdle do the Gods inherit,/Beneath is all the fiend's' (IV.6: 125): above the waist is 'good', below the waist 'bad', and he is overcome by his disgust and horror as he contemplates 'the sul- phurous pit' (IV.6: 127) below. Not only his daughters' lust for Edmund and Gloucester's adultery with Edmund's mother come to mind as Gloucester listens to this, but we also infer Lear's own inces- tuous wishes (or perhaps behaviour) towards his daughters, more openly hinted at in reference to Cordelia. Gloucester intervenes at this point, seizing Lear's hand, and asks, 'Dost thou know me?' (IV.6: 134). Lear remembers what Gloucester has lost – his eyes; he remem- bers Gloucester's quality of not seeing, of not being able to perceive. In calling Gloucester 'Blind Cupid' (IV.6: 136) he again refers to Gloucester's adultery, and to his own abjuration of sexuality.[4] Lear's crude punning around Gloucester's lost eyes intensifies the poignancy of the moment, and connects again to the theme of money: 'No eyes in your head, nor no money in your purse? Your ayes are in a heavy case, your purse in a light: yet you see how this world goes' (IV.6: 143–6). He seems to be pointing out that one must lose position, wealth, even eyes, (perhaps, too, a sense of Gloucester's tendency towards compliance can be inferred from the 'ayes') in order to begin to see clearly the extent of injustice and corruption in the world, which he proceeds to describe. By being unable to see the outward signs of wealth and power, justice (judge) and thief are interchangeable – there is no difference between them: 'Look with thine ears: see how yond justice rails upon yond simple thief. Hark, in thine ear: change places, and handy-dandy, which is the justice, which is the thief?' (IV.6: 149–52). He points to 'the great image of Authority:/A dog's obeyed in office' (IV.6: 155–6)[5]. In that more grass-roots symbol of authority, the beadle, one finds the same sins or qualities as the whore he punishes. Vice is more visible in the poor: 'Robes and furr'd gowns hide all. Plate sin with gold,/And the strong lance of justices hurtless breaks./Arm it in rags, a pigmy's straw does pierce it' (IV.6: 163–5). Since all offend, it is unjust that only the poor, the powerless should be punished. As the king, Lear has power (he again offers Gloucester money) to buy off an accuser. Money would buy Gloucester glass eyes, which would allow him to pass for a 'politician'.

Glass eyes do not allow of weeping; Lear offers his own eyes to Gloucester in recognition of the latter's sympathy and pain. With simplistic wisdom, the direct and wounding perception of madness, he points out that human existence is inseparable from pain: 'Thou know'st the first time that we smell the air/We wawl and cry . . . When we are born we cry that we are come/To this great stage of fools' (IV.6: 177–81).

At this moment he becomes aware of the approach of Cordelia's searchers, and his mind returns to the military theme. His mood switches immediately, therefore, from profound 'reason in madness' to terror and the need to protect himself from those whom he fears would wish to kill him.

> This a good block!
> It were a delicate stratagem to shoe
> A troop of horse with felt; I'll put't in proof,
> And when I have stol'n upon these son-in-laws,
> Then, kill, kill, kill, kill, kill, kill!
>
> (IV.6: 181–5)

In his madness, Lear fears capture and death from all, he feels his existential aloneness, but still refuses to submit, to weep, to be humble; and he gets his would-be rescuers/captors off their guard by invoking his royal status; as they loose their hold, he slips out of their grasp and escapes.

In all of this, he describes his own abuse of power and his blindness to the reality of the corruption of power and wealth, but at the beginning and at the end of the scene he has the 'psychotic' fear of being killed, which is, of course, based on a real and accurate perception of his daughters' wishes. Within the military and pecuniary themes there is also the sense that kingship is exposed as being, not an innate and essential quality as he had supposed, but simply the expression of the 'ownership' of military power, and wealth.

Conclusion

The recognition and expression of his own responsibility for events – 'O! I have ta'en/Too little care of this' (III.4: 32–3) – enables Lear's later reconciliation to his human, rather than kingly self, and to his daughter Cordelia:

> I know you do not love me; for your sisters
> Have, as I do remember, done me wrong:
> You have some cause, they have not.

> (IV.7: 73–5)

But he is not 'redeemed'; he is happy in the illusion of possessing Cordelia, fantasizing contentedly about their future life in prison: 'We two alone will sing . . .' (V.3: 9), and 'Have I caught thee?' (V.3: 21). The 'contract' for their relationship articulated by Cordelia cannot be reinstated, and termination, or death, is the only rectification possible.

By examining the play through the prism of the 'frame' we gain a fresh perspective on its interactional dynamics. The public ritual competition between Lear's daughters is a breach of the frame for which Lear is responsible; the utterances of characters and their actions can be understood as derivative representations of that breach and its implications. Represented in the text of the play are a series of models of rectification which go unheeded by Lear, and the termination of the play represents the disastrous termination of the relationship between Lear and his daughters and their lives, and of the general social 'frame' of which King Lear was the keystone.

These remarks offer a communicative perspective on the genius of Shakespeare's representation of human interaction and its consequences. I claim to add nothing to critical studies of the playwright's work; rather, I hope to share my sense of a striking similarity of pattern between processes in psychotherapy and the dramatic process in the play, the theme of which I have elaborated as follows: someone who is responsible for managing a situation reneges on that responsibility; the public abdication of power is paralleled by an abuse of the father–daughter relationship – a breach in the familial contract, or bond. Rather than recognize and rectify that responsibility, he erects manic, psychotic defences against awareness of the true situation, despite many indirect, or derivative representations, in word and deed, communicated to him by those who are in relationship to him. The situation becomes more and more disturbed – more 'mad' – until all of these relationships are terminated – mostly through sudden or violent death.

I recognize this pattern, excepting (I trust) the death, as one which pertains in therapy, where there is a serious breach in what are understood to be the fundamental ground rules of therapy. When a therapist is unable to perceive and acknowledge her responsibility for such a breach, and attempts forms of manic defence rather than a rectification of the frame conditions, clients are likely to terminate that therapy 'prematurely'.

The central 'message' of *King Lear*, contained in the key interchange between Lear and Gloucester (Act IV Scene 6), is to do with a fundamental equality and interchangeability between individuals, whatever their status or power: strip away the conscious 'lendings' of social or clinical power, and what is left is an interaction between two 'unaccommodated' individuals. Social interactions are generally predicated on considerations of power: those with power exploit and abuse those without; this can be hypothesized as an expression of evolutionary survival strategies of cheating and deception (Smith 1995).

Communicative psychotherapy proposes that what Langs calls the 'deep unconscious wisdom system' of the human mind accurately perceives human interaction in this 'unaccommodated', fundamental and uncompromising way; that it detects and sees through human cheating and self-deception; that it conceptualizes human interaction in terms of the interactional 'contract', bond or 'frame' of sets of rules governing relationships between individuals and groups; that it represents in a derivative, often exquisitely poetic and dramatic fashion, the significance and impact of breaches of this frame, offering also models of rectification. We take this 'ghost world', this exo-skeleton of human interaction for granted, until it is breached, and then we perceive a glimpse of terrifying chaos.

Both in and out of therapy, the 'deep unconscious wisdom system' offers radical new insights into human social and personal interaction, but, as is so often the case, one makes such a discovery, only to find that Shakespeare got there first.

Notes

1 As, for example, set out by Smith (1991).
2 In communicative theory, the adaptive context or 'trigger' is the breach of the frame; the 'deviation' is from the ground rules of the interaction, or of therapy.
3 The plays of Shakespeare were written for performance, and the text we have is one which incorporates the experience of performance – the actors' prompt-book may have been a source for the Quarto version, itself a source for the Folio text on which the present text (Shakespeare 1985) is based. Stage directions are integral to this text, and are therefore to be considered as aspects of the frame as 'managed' by the playwright.
4 This is a recurrent theme for Shakespeare at this particular period, and we may infer his own internal conflict regarding his own sexuality, bearing in mind the known facts about his emotional life: his early marriage, his absence from his wife, the evidence from the Sonnets, etc.
5 Given the capital letter of the word 'Authority', that might well stand for the highest authority in the land (King James I was said to have appalling table manners, and to drool).

References

Bayley, J. (1981) *Shakespeare and Tragedy*. London: Routledge and Kegan Paul.
Bleger, J. (1990) Psycho-analysis of the psycho-analytic frame, in R. Langs (ed.) *Classics in Psycho-analytic Technique*. New York: Jason Aronson.
Cox, M. and Theilgaard, A. (1994) *Shakespeare as Prompter*. London and Bristol, PA: Jessica Kingsley Publishers.
Ignatieff, M. (1990) *The Needs of Strangers*. London: Hogarth.
Milner, M. (1985) The role of illusion in symbol formation, in M. Klein, P. Heimann and R.E. Money-Kyrle (eds) *New Directions in Psycho-analysis*. London: Karnac.
Muir, K. (1972) *Introduction to King Lear*. London: Methuen.
Palaiseul, J. (1973) *Grandmother's Secrets: Her Green Guide to Health from Plants*. Harmondsworth: Penguin.
Shakespeare, W. (1985) *King Lear*. London: Routledge (The Arden Shakespeare).
Smith, D.L. (1995) Free-associations and honey-bee dancers: the unconscious and its place in nature, paper given at the European Society for Communicative Psychotherapy Annual Conference, Regent's College, 12 November.

Part **V**

CONCLUSION

Chapter **13**

Stories, settings and supervision: final thoughts and questions

E. Mary Sullivan

This volume has presented some tentative and imprecise findings, through practice, relating to the communicative theory of psycho-analytic psychotherapy as developed by Robert Langs.

What is striking to many who come into contact with Langs's ideas is how little they have been discussed in the psychoanalytic and psychotherapeutic literature generally, since they seem to offer a more rigorous and 'scientific' basis for research in the field than has existed hitherto. But it is perhaps just this aspect of the approach, together with its focus on the contribution of the therapist rather than of the client within the therapeutic interaction, which is not as attractive to those who prefer to regard the whole psychotherapeutic procedure as more of a subjective and creative interpersonal 'art'. The notion of a manualized and relatively rigorous set of ground rules governing the behaviour and interventions of a therapist does not appear to sit well with this perspective.

However, any new hypothesis in the field of the human sciences must make itself available for the examination and judgement of its peers, and it is in this spirit that this collection of essays is offered. I propose to set out what I see as the important issues and questions requiring further investigation and research which are raised in earlier chapters.

In his introduction to the communicative approach to psychotherapy David Smith sets out the fundamental hypothesis that all of the narrative material presented by the patient in therapeutic session relates to the immediate encounter as an unconscious commentary on the therapist's management of the environment. By abstracting the themes of those stories, therapists can decode this unconscious commentary on their work and access the patient's accurate observations of the interpersonal reality of the interaction. Smith points to this unconscious capacity, common to all of us, as an aspect of the mind evolved to equip us to live within the complex social structures of human society, governed by a set of rules to which we wish to appear to adhere, but on which we routinely default. Smith proposes that our capacity unconsciously to perceive and to communicate our perception of the 'cheating' behaviour of others has evolved as a means of regulating our social interactions in a way which preserves the degree of deception necessary to the continuance of society as we know it.

Without a set of ground rules, says Smith, there is no such thing as psychotherapy. Robert Langs claims that virtually all of us unconsciously seek the same therapeutic 'frame', or set of ground rules, and that any alteration from this 'ideal' frame will constrain and undermine the work of therapy. In communicative psychotherapy, the task of the therapist is confined to, first, setting out the ground rules of the therapeutic interaction, then listening to the patients' narratives for guidance on the management of these rules.

Smith sets out the three types of intervention used by communicative therapists:

1 silence
2 frame management
3 interpretation:

Silence, the basic listening attitude, is appropriate so long as the client has not unconsciously indicated the need for a verbal intervention. Silence is a 'holding' intervention that encourages unconscious communication. Frame management is the handling of the therapeutic environment. It includes both maintaining a secure frame and 'rectifying' deviations: that is, altering the frame in accord with clients' unconscious recommendations. Silence and frame management are probably the most therapeutically powerful interventions. A therapist who remains silent within a well-structured therapeutic environment can do immense good.

Communicative interpretations implicitly acknowledge the validity – or at least the plausibility – of clients' unconscious perspectives.

(see page 11)

After making an intervention, the therapist must await the client's 'validation' of the interpretation, which will take the form of an unconsciously selected, positively-toned story, irrespective of the client's conscious response. Without validation, an interpretation is considered to have missed the mark, to be 'wrong'.

One frequently-heard criticism of communicative psychotherapy is that it pays more attention to the therapist than to the client; in Chapter 2, 'Understanding patients' countertransferences', David Smith uses the 'game theory' of biologists such as Maynard Smith and Axelrod to hypothesize the development of unconscious communication as an adaptive strategy for combating the universal tendency to cheat in social interactions. We unconsciously perceive when someone is attempting to exploit us and communicate that awareness through the stories we tell. The more there is at stake in an interaction, the more vigilant we are to detect, to signal our awareness of and to expose the cheating. What Langs calls the 'deep unconscious wisdom system' is the 'deep psychological structure' which has evolved to meet this need. The context of psychoanalysis and psychotherapy is a relatively simple, two-person social system in which the client has much more at stake than the therapist. This being so, points out Smith, one would expect the therapist to be more inclined to 'cheat' – 'to use the client for the gratification of narcissistic, sexual or aggressive needs' (see page 29). Equally, the client could be expected to be particularly alert to examples of cheating on the part of the therapist. Further, Smith goes on, there would be no point in the development of this adaptive capacity in humans unless the recipient of unconscious messages was able to decipher them and to act upon them, even if they remain consciously unaware of their 'cheating':

> The psychoanalytic situation is such that analysts will, inevitably, be inclined to exploit their patients, and patients will, equally inevitably, be deeply suspicious of their analysts. It is a situation in which patients unconsciously signal their awareness of cheating in almost everything they say and in which analysts are driven by their human nature – their inclination to cheat while remaining unaware of their cheating – to attempt to override these signals.
>
> (see page 31)

Thus, for Smith, the task of the communicative therapist is to understand and respond to clients' unconscious reactions to therapists' contribution to the interaction. Physician, heal thyself!

Carol Holmes discusses the motivation of psychotherapists in general and of communicative therapists in particular: why should individuals choose to engage in this confessional mode?

She sets out communicative practice thus:

Communicative practice hinges upon the therapist's conscientious and scrupulous inspection of their own errors in the consulting room which are considered to be disclosed to them by the patient in their narratives. The therapist is then duly required to confess these mistakes to the patient and to modify them in light of the patient's unconscious suggestions. It should not be difficult to see how this subversive and radical therapeutic position undermines in one fell swoop the very foundations of mainstream psychotherapy, as one of the major tenets of the approach rests on the assumption that a powerful element of cure is derived from the therapist's – rather than the patient's – admission of their interpersonal difficulties or deficiencies.

(see page 40)

Psychoanalysis and psychotherapy have frequently been described as analogous in some aspects to the religious 'confessional'. In this context a 'sinner' utters (in strict confidence) his 'guilty' secrets to a figure imbued with some authority, vested in her either by virtue of her ordination as a priest, or by virtue of some form of election by a (possibly religious) community. This figure uses her authority to 'absolve' the confessee of his guilt. What is startling about Holmes's turning on its head of this notion is that, in the communicative paradigm, the authority is vested in the client, rather than the therapist, and it is this which serves often to affront and scandalize many practitioners of mainstream psychotherapy and psychoanalysis. It may be that some of us are more comfortable with the nebulous association of psychotherapy with religious observation, or with ourselves as a form of secular priesthood, in possession of some form of arcane wisdom denied to our clients, than with a clearly defined set of ground rules for this form of human interaction which expose those parts of our own personality of which we would prefer to remain unaware.

Holmes points to research which seems to indicate that many who seek to work as therapists have suffered various forms of loss or premature separation in early childhood, and/or have found themselves early in life taking responsibility for the emotional well-being of one or other parent. She further speculates that communicative therapists, in their concerns about frame issues, may be attending to their own death anxiety, in the form of a desire for control in light of a fear of incipient chaos: the notion of a secure frame may thus offer a form of exo-skeletal ego structure, offering support for such individuals.

Continuing the focus on therapists' concerns, James Raney discusses the contentious technical issue of questions as an appropriate form of therapist intervention. In this chapter, he shows how helpful it can be in supervision to examine carefully the context of therapists' erroneous questions, which signal conflict in the therapist around his unconscious awareness of the derivative significance of a client's meaning. He makes a strong case for questioning as a defensive procedure on the part of therapists, rather than, as is widely assumed, an integral part of psychotherapeutic technique.

Raney's chapter demonstrates the line-by-line analysis of clinical process notes which takes place in communicative supervision, making an exceptionally well-presented case for the view that questions, as a 'strongly directive therapist intervention', are usually technically incorrect. Questions may contain clues to what the therapist perceives as threatening in the client's material.

Raney clearly exemplifies the utility of the Langsian schema for the close study of the intricate interaction between client and therapist, where therapist interventions trigger client responses, and in turn communications from the client trigger therapist interventions: in their communications clients either validate or refute therapist's interventions in a 'coded' derivative fashion which can be 'read', or decoded, using communicative principles. This is a key aspect of Langs's 'science' of human emotional interaction in a bi-personal field: it is the cornerstone of the controversial claim of communicative therapists to be able to determine what is a 'correct' or 'incorrect' intervention or interpretation on the part of a therapist, based on the client's 'derivative' or encoded communications. This 'scientific' basis for communicative therapeutic practice – exposing, as it does, the 'psychopathology' of the therapist as much as that of her client – may be what therapists find so disturbing about the approach, and may go some way to explain the defensiveness of both those therapists who attempt to put these principles and techniques into practice, and those theorists who fail to address the questions about the practice of psychoanalysis and psychotherapy raised by them. Raney has some observations to offer elsewhere about this curious lack of discussion of Langs's theories (Raney 1984).

Vesna Bonac turns her attention to the concept of transference, which communicative theory so far has largely discarded as unhelpful to this perspective on the psychotherapeutic interaction. Indeed, Smith (1991: 26 ff., 71) has described the superseding of the theory of transference by that of veridical unconscious perception, as proposed by Langs, as a paradigm shift. Bonac, however, advances a new theory of transference, which focuses on the relatively rare moments in therapy when patients suddenly and unexpectedly turn against the therapist and against themselves. She outlines a clinical technique that, she claims, enables the therapist to determine when the

source of acting-out lies within the patient, thus calling for an interpretation of transference. She points to the power of past events to
influence our expectations of the future, based on our veridical
unconscious perceptions, as recorded in our memory, of actual and
specific past events; we are all open to the ravages of our damage
from the past at times when we find ourselves in a situation that
resembles this past (such as for the client in the therapy situation
described in her chapter), and it is for the therapist at these points to
remain solid, to hold to the proper boundaries of her role, in order to
be of help to the client. Thus she relates her revised theory of transference to the communicative concept of secure-frame anxiety.[1]

Another concern which is expressed about the approach refers
to the notion of an 'ideal frame' as either unachievable or 'rigid'. Gae
Oaten's chapter addresses this concern. Working within a general
practice surgery setting, where an ideal frame is perceived as simply
impossible because of resource constraints, Oaten has hypothesized
a 'fixed altered' frame, which has been altered from the 'ideal' in particular aspects, but which remains fixed throughout the duration of
the therapy.

She points out that, in counselling or psychotherapeutic work
within a brief timescale, it is often considered that a 'pure' psychoanalytic approach – emphasizing free association and neutrality and
silent waiting on the part of the therapist – must be abandoned in
favour of a more 'active' therapeutic role, focusing on goals and specific 'problem' areas. Oaten reports that her client responded to her
initially more active therapeutic role by becoming less active, and
more withdrawn, while the material presented from the final session
seems to suggest that particular problem areas in the client's life were
being positively addressed by the end of a therapy in which the
therapist allowed herself to be directed by her client's unconscious
narratives, which drew attention, not only to the deficiencies in the
therapeutic arrangements, but to the therapist's anxieties about
those deficiencies. The therapist was able generally to fulfil the role
of silent waiting, allowing her client to be 'the star' of the therapy.

This account seems to suggest that therapy within a frame
which is altered from the 'ideal' may still be effective, given that,
first, attention is paid to those alterations as the context or trigger for
clients' derivative communications, and, second, the given alteration to the frame is not made the excuse for further modification in
therapeutic technique.

The context of student counselling exerts different pressures
towards modification of the communicative concept of the 'ideal'
frame. Kitty Warburton describes the 'integrated' model of student
counselling that sees the institution rather than the individual

seeking therapeutic help as the therapist's client. But this gives rise, she points out, to ethical and clinical difficulties arising from the lack of privacy and confidentiality, and a sense of confusion, or at least, blurring, of roles.

Like Oaten, Warburton set about establishing a more secure frame within the institutional setting, in order to provide a 'therapeutic hold' (see page 116), finding that she also had to deal, not only with the anxieties of other staff members pertaining to the welfare of the students who came to her as clients, but with her own anxiety to be seen to be doing 'a good job' in her role as counsellor. She highlights the need to 'distinguish between the "administrative voice" [of the institution] (which needs to be able to say "no" on behavioural or academic grounds) and the "psychotherapeutic voice" (which suspends judgement, listens and attempts to understand)' (see page 117). She further suggests that modification of the rule of confidentiality, even when such action seems superficially to be in the student's interests, may offer a 'regressive', or anti-therapeutic experience.

Gabrielle Gunton addresses the difficult issue of serious therapist illness, which disrupts the therapeutic process in ways which therapists very much avoid thinking about, and for which they seldom make adequate provision. While therapists who have suffered serious illness are able eventually to explore the meaning of their illness and its impact on themselves, few have felt able to consider its implications for their work with clients, beyond questions of what and how much information to share with them. Gunton's account does not dwell on the trauma suffered by her client because of the therapist's prolonged absence from therapy; it focuses, rather, on the harmful implications of a too-early return to work after recovery from illness. The therapist had allowed inadequate time for dealing with the emotional residua of her illness: her interaction with her client (and supervision) highlighted areas of unreadiness to resume therapeutic work.

Gunton's chapter, in its admirably candid exposition of a client's unconscious supervision/therapy of her therapist, thus begs the question: how does one truly know when one is fit to return to therapeutic work after serious illness without such help from a client? I wonder whether even one's own therapy can provide a certain answer. Margaret Little's (1951) remark about the mirror held up by the patient to the analyst[2] comes to mind; I doubt whether any other mirror could be as reliable and trustworthy as a client's remarkable unconscious sensitivity to the nuances of her therapist's emotional state of health.

Ivan Thorpe, in his 'deconstruction' of the video demonstration of a therapeutic interaction between Carl Rogers and his client 'Kathy', seeks to show her attempt unconsciously to communicate the impact of the altered frame which encompasses the video cameras and, we must assume, the various technicians who were also present during the recording of the session.

This chapter, in using again the technique of line-by-line analysis of a session in the public domain, seeks to implement the research instrument which Langs, after Abraham, calls the *psychoscope* (Langs 1992: 46). By this he means a method of observing psychoanalytic data, utilizing 'the entire therapeutic dialogue – the unfolding communications between patient and therapist . . . in order to access and define its infrastructure or unconscious elements' (p. 46). Langs points out that this instrument can be used 'only by those who conceptualize a disguised or unconscious layer of meaning in messages, a deeper structure to be accessed and probed' (p. 47). This would exclude Rogers, who, in his client-centred method of psychotherapy, did not work systematically with a notion of unconscious mental processes. This raises the question of whether it is a valid exercise to approach a non-communicative session in this way, but Smith (1991: 237 ff.), following Langs's own research (for example 1988), seeks to show that communicative theory, resting as it does not on theories of cure but on the correlation of observable behaviours with predictable outcomes, should be applicable across different psychotherapeutic paradigms, outside of the domain of communicative technique. I leave the reader to judge.

Thorpe claims to show that although Kathy has agreed to participate in this public demonstration of a therapeutic session, she communicates through her derivative stories that she is unwilling to disclose much that is meaningful to her in this situation, and it is this underlying reality that lies at the heart of another dilemma for communicative therapists. Proponents of the approach are open to the criticism that they are willing to use this method to critique the work of other therapists, but are unwilling to subject their own clinical practice to this kind of exposure; they make the case, instead, that to do so would constitute a severe breach of the ground rule of confidentiality, a breach that clients unconsciously perceive as damaging to their interests.

It is at this point that the needs of clients and the need for wider research into therapeutic interaction are in sharp conflict, but it must also be said that there is conflict for the individual therapist who, after all, wishes to be of help to those who come to her for therapy yet feels herself to be at risk of being exposed, through submission to this searching analysis of her work, to the charge of ineffectiveness or of doing harm to her clients.

Marie-Luise Petersen addresses the use of dreams in communicative psychotherapy, pointing out that no variation in technique is required in order to decode the unconscious guidance of clients regarding important frame issues that stem from the client's current concerns or triggers within the therapeutic interaction, whether working with children or adults. Clients' dreams, she shows, can offer insight into qualities in the therapeutic interaction that are threatening and anxiety-provoking, while therapist's dreams can also be found to throw light on aspects of a therapy which are too disturbing to be noted consciously.

Fiorella Gatti-Doyle's chapter, on the other hand, sets out a distinct variation in communicative technique, that of self-processing through dreams. This new modality formulated by Langs (1993) as an alternative to psychotherapy, is most often taught, as a technique for self-analysis, in the form of small group or individual tutorial sessions. The technique of dream analysis is more fully developed by directing the participant first to expound a dream in as detailed a fashion as possible, and then to develop her associations to each significant element of the dream; further still, from each of these storied associations, a second set of associations is developed. Within this network of associations, triggers will be found which will reveal both the current concerns of the dreamer and the unconscious guidance offered through the disguised narratives relating to the desired resolution or rectification of that current situation.

This offshoot of communicative psychotherapy leads the way into other applications of the decoding of unconscious communication. The simple technique of listening to apparently discontinuous narrative with an awareness of possible triggers to do with boundary issues is being investigated in connection with research into group dynamics, and initial findings seem to show that the bringing to awareness of such unconscious concerns could be a powerful instrument in personal development in this context. A form of peer supervision is being developed which utilizes joint or group free association to uncover concerns which appear to pertain to parallel process issues influencing both therapeutic work with clients and the supervisory interaction itself.

Finally, in exploring the application of communicative theory outside the sphere of psychotherapy, to the field of literature, I claim to perceive a striking similarity of patterns in behaviour between the events and dramatic process which occurs in Shakespeare's *King Lear* and the therapeutic frame which is breached by a therapist's abnegation of responsibility. While literary commentators normally see Lear as the victim of his evil daughters, I claim to find a parallel to the psychoanalytic concept of the frame in Cordelia's emphasis on the contractual 'bond' between parent and child, which Lear, in his abusive demand that his daughters participate in a public contest of declarations of love for him, has broken. Further, I believe that Langs's claims about the universality of unconscious concern for the ground rules of human emotional interaction are presaged in Shakespeare's depiction of the consequences of this breach, and that 'unconscious' representations of the breach are represented in the utterances and behaviours of the various characters in the play. These, together with 'models of rectification' offered to and rejected by Lear, are similar to the model of communication discerned by Langsian theory.

I speculate here – it is difficult to imagine that this could be adequately researched – that similar patterns can be found in many forms of human emotional interaction, but particularly in those where there is perceived to be an imbalance of power, such as parent–child, teacher–student, employer–employee, etc., and that the insights of communicative theory can be useful in uncovering deeper emotional realities in such interactions than we have hitherto been willing to acknowledge.

There are still fundamental questions being asked about the utility and efficacy of psychoanalysis and psychotherapy, and there is general agreement in the field that psychotherapeutic activity should submit itself to evaluative research and audit procedures, despite widespread concerns about the difficulty of describing and measuring 'success', or 'cure'. Theories relating to mental processes described as 'unconscious' are particularly difficult to evaluate in any methodologically rigorous fashion.

This collection of essays is not an attempt to 'prove' anything: it is an exploration of some of the ways in which the writers have utilized in practice the communicative theory of psychoanalytic psychotherapy developed by Robert Langs. I have sought to address some questions and concerns expressed about the approach, but wider application and discussion of the technique is required, along with continuing research, in order to understand more fully its possibilities and limitations.

Communicative theory re-visions the therapeutic encounter; it addresses some of the criticisms which have been levelled at classical psychoanalytic technique. Rather than focusing on the distorted elements of clients' communications, it highlights clients' valid unconscious perceptions of the therapist's management of the therapeutic environment. The hallmark of communicative technique is that it gives precedence to clients' innate capacity to guide the treatment process. Thus the balance of power, which continues to be a thorny issue in psychoanalytic psychotherapy, is consistently addressed.

Notes

1 Smith (p. 10, this volume) discusses the impact of the secure frame on some individuals, both clients and therapists. He claims that death anxiety, the often deep-seated conviction of being trapped and subject to annihilation, is aroused in moments of claustrophobic awareness of the 'limit situation', analogous to death, of the secure frame. This is also more fully discussed in Langs (1997).

2 It is worth reproducing Little's metaphor in full: 'We often hear of the mirror which the analyst holds up to the patient, but the patient holds one up to the analyst too, and there is a whole series of reflections in each, repetitive in kind, and subject to continual modification. The mirror in each case should become progressively clearer as the analysis goes on, for patient and analyst respond in a reverberative kind of way, and increasing clearness in one mirror will bring the need for a corresponding clearing in the other' (p. 148).

References

Langs, R. (1988) *Madness and Cure*. Emerson, NJ: NewConcept Press.

Langs, R. (1992) *Science, Systems and Psychoanalysis*. London: Karnac.

Langs, R. (1993) *Empowered Psychotherapy*. London: Karnac.

Langs, R. (1997) *Death Anxiety and Clinical Practice*. London: Karnac.

Little, M. (1951/1990) Countertransference and the patient's response to it, in R. Langs (ed.) *Classics in Psychoanalytic Technique*. Northvale, NJ: Aronson.

Raney, J.O. (1984) *Listening and Interpreting: The Challenge of the Work of Robert Langs*. New York: Jason Aronson.

Smith, D.L. (1991) *Hidden Conversations: An Introduction to Communicative Psychoanalysis*. London: Routledge.

Index